the organic
GARDENER

the organic
GARDENER

BOB FLOWERDEW

Photography Jerry Harpur

HAMLYN

I dedicate this book to my friends and family and
especially, Bernard and Eliane Condemine of Quincie-en-
Beaujolais, France. During the dozen years I helped
with their grape harvest they showed me the essence of
truly great French meals: good bread, excellent wine
and really fresh fruit and vegetables exquisitely cooked

Art Editor Robin Whitecross
Executive Editor Anna Mumford

Editor Alexa Stace
Production Alison Myer
Plant illustrations Susan Hillier
Garden plan illustration Vicky Emptage
Soil photographs pages 20-21 Mark Williams

First published in Great Britain 1993 by Hamlyn
an imprint of Reed Consumer Books Limited,
Michelin House, 81 Fulham Road, London SW3 6RB
and Auckland, Melbourne, Singapore and Toronto

Produced by Mandarin Offset – printed in China

ISBN 0 600 57461 X

A catalogue record for this book is available at the
British Library

contents

foreword

'Think globally, act locally' is the rallying cry of environmentalists the world over. Because of the cumulative action of each of us going about our daily lives, using up resources and polluting the planet, the Earth is in a mess. If mankind is to survive, we must change the way we live – and co-exist with, rather than dominate, nature. Soil is our planet's most precious asset, so where better to start than in the back garden; by growing plants in the most environmentally-friendly way – organically.

A healthy soil is the key to organic gardening. Not only does it provide plants with the food they need to live, it also confers health and vitality, making them much more able to withstand outbreaks of diseases.

If you are fortunate enough to start off with a fertile soil, all well and good. Most of us, though, are not so lucky. You may have a light, sandy soil which is easy to work and free-draining but, because of this, quickly runs out of nutrients and needs frequent watering. If you garden on clay, the converse is true – you will never suffer from a shortage of plant foods but digging is difficult and you will also have problems with slugs.

Don't despair. The answer to both conditions is to add as much organic matter to the soil as you can get. Years ago, in the days of horse-drawn transport, folk had access to lashings of manure. Nowadays organic gardeners rely on home-made compost, leafmould and a wide range of purpose-sown plants, or 'green manure'. By adding these decayed wastes to the soil you will be nourishing the countless microscopic bacteria and fungi – reckoned to number at least five billion in a teaspoonful of soil alone – that ceaselessly provide the food needed by plants.

By not throwing rubbish in your dustbin, or burning it on a bonfire, you are making a direct contribution to the reduction of global warming. Up to a third of the contents of all domestic dustbins is waste, comprising garden rubbish and kitchen scraps, that can be composted. This normally ends up in a council-run incinerator, or dumped in a disused quarry where it steadily decays over several decades releasing quantities of

Brassicas continue through the winter in the raised vegetable beds providing a nourishing food source as well as aesthetic interest

methane, one of the most polluting of greenhouse gases, into the atmosphere.

No matter how big or small your garden, you should make your own compost. Even if you only have a tiny plot, and no garden waste to speak of, you can still make use of your kitchen waste by recycling it through a worm composter. It makes an ideal ingredient in seed and potting mixtures and is excellent as a top dressing for window boxes, hanging baskets and containers.

Organic gardeners are inveterate recyclers and a lot of what might otherwise be thrown away can be marshalled into service in the garden. Much can be used to provide physical defences against pests. Off-cuts of carpet underlay placed around cabbages stop rootflies from laying eggs next to the stem. Plastic liquid bottles with their bottoms cut off, when placed over plants, confound slugs. Computer tape criss-crossed over winter gardens deter pigeons. And, if you're pressed for time, there is no easier way of clearing ground than leaving it fallow for a year under an old Axminster carpet.

Physical barriers such as these are just one method of combating pests and diseases without recourse to pesticides. Others include planting disease-resistant varieties, employing crop rotations so that diseases do not get the opportunity to build up in the soil, and using biological controls – insects that attack insects.

It is tempting to believe, now that DDT and similar compounds, which caused such havoc in the 1960s have been banned, that pesticides are no longer a threat to human health and the environment. Modern testing procedures are so much more rigorous than in the past and, though pesticide residues show up in most food samples, and are present in almost all drinking water supplies, we are assured by the manufacturers that they present no risk. While I agree that, on the whole, pesticide residues are minute – reckoned to be equivalent to an aspirin in a swimming pool – I do not take such a sanguine view.

In homoeopathy, which is assuming increasing importance in the vetinerary treatment of organically reared livestock, the dosages involved are so dilute they are impossible to measure by scientific apparatus, yet they have a beneficial effect. How, then, can we be sure that pesticide residues – substances designed to kill – are harmless, even when only present at microscopic levels?

Better, surely, not to take the risk, especially when so many alternatives exist? Why, for instance, go to the expense and trouble of spraying greenfly when there are ladybirds, hoverflies, lacewings and a host of other predatory and parasitic insects only too willing to despatch them on your behalf. The secret is to nudge the balance of nature your way by providing the right conditions for beneficial widlife to flourish. Most obviously, if you stop spraying, you won't be killing your garden friends, which are usually present alongside the pests. This apart, there are a number of plants you can grow which are excellent at attracting nature's pest controllers. By growing

native species of shrubs and trees and providing nesting and roosting sites, you will be providing a habitat for birds and bats — aerial defenders of the airspace above your garden! Down on the ground, a plentiful supply of surface mulch will encourage beetles and spiders, which make life difficult for pests that live in soil. Dig a pond, and the frogs and toads which will come to live in it will make a handsome living out of any slugs that are unwise enough to frequent your patch.

Of course, these garden friends don't always have it all their own way and you may have to come to terms with a bit more damage than if you had been out there spraying regularly. But think of what you are doing for wildlife and the environment by not using pesticides — frogs and toads have become rarities in most farmed landscapes, for example.

A few years ago, my colleagues and I at the Henry Doubleday Research Association made a series of programmes for Channel 4 television in Great Britain called *All Muck and Magic?* Our aim was to show that organic gardening, combining the wisdom of the past with the latest scientific discoveries, is the only truly sustainable method of growing plants. Contrary to many expectations, it does not involve more time, expense, or a hair-shirt mentality. On the contrary, it encourages thrift, resourcefulness and a sense of humour — qualities that will be much needed in the testing years ahead.

Limnanthes douglasii **are attractive to beneficial insects and make excellent underplanting in the fruit cage**

ALAN GEAR, Chief Executive,
The Henry Doubleday Research Association
National Centre for Organic Gardening
Ryton-on-Dunsmore, Coventry CV8 3LG
United Kingdom

Any enquiries regarding the Henry Doubleday Research Association in Australia please contact:
Mr R. B. McNeil
HDRA, 816 Comleroy Road
Kurrajong, NSW 2758
Australia

1
WHAT IS
organic gardening?

O rganic gardening is more than simply gardening with a new set of rules, and a list of dos and don'ts. It is much more a question of adopting a new approach – an ecologically sound and environmentally friendly approach.

the basic principles

The aim is to create an environment in which healthy plants can be grown successfully, and pests and diseases discouraged, but without damaging or polluting the soil, or destroying the wildlife. Nature has created a system of checks and balances, predators and prey. If you create an environment in which they can all flourish, the predators will do much of the work for you.

This approach has been developed in response to the damage caused by conventional methods. Gardening – like commercial farming – has long been practised as a form of warfare, in which crops are grown by doing battle with pests and diseases and by artificially stimulating the soil. Bad soil management, profligate use of chemicals, and overcropping have resulted in desertification and loss of productive land throughout the world.

life in the soil Guarding and increasing the life in the soil is the first and most important principle. Without healthy soil, civilization as we know it will disappear. We are dependent on our top-soil to feed us: if it becomes overworked it will erode and blow away.

The henhouse is positioned in the orchard which is beneficial to the fruit trees because of the extra fertility, and to the hens which wander freely under the plum, peach and apple trees

The only way to maintain, improve and increase topsoil is by actively encouraging the multitude of micro-organisms in the soil which convert organic material into nutrients available for plant growth. It is their by-products that build up water-retentive, loamy, humus-rich soil – the soil which promotes healthy plants. Chemical fertilizers and overcropping burn off this store of nutrients, and destroy the very organisms that could create more, in return for very short-term gains.

Organic gardening has a policy of feeding the soil, not the plants, using organic material instead of soluble chemicals. The burgeoning life in the soil uses this organic material, minerals and the greater amounts of retained water to produce more life – the plants then feed on the by-products, taking what they need to make their own growth.

The effect of adding organic material is cumulative: as more is introduced it further encourages increased populations of soil flora and fauna. These larger populations then support yet more life forms living off them. So the variety and quantity of by-products increases, raising the fertility of the soil. The plants living off this balanced diet are much more healthy and resistant to pests and diseases than those living in denatured soil pumped up with cocktails of chemical fertilizers, and kept going with poisonous sprays.

In order to protect this life in the soil organic gardeners use no poisonous substances that can harm them – except for 'natural' ones as a last resort. These are deemed to be safer because they are less wide-ranging in their toxicity and break down rapidly and naturally after use. However, it is not their 'naturalness' but their effect on soil life that is important. For example nicotine, a plant product, is not allowed as it is too harmful to many forms of life, while Bordeaux mixture containing copper sulphate and lime is allowed. This 'chemical' is relatively safe to soil life and is an effective fungicide, so it is acceptable – but only if needed and when other measures have failed. Similarly basic slag, an 'unnatural'

phosphatic by-product from blast furnaces, is allowed because it aids soil life; but the entirely natural guano (seagull droppings) is not permitted as it can burn off humus and damage soil life.

The increasing life in an organic soil then goes on to support more and larger forms of life in the garden and surrounding environment. After all, if you want blackbirds then you have to have worms. Again, the effects are cumulative. As more and larger forms of life come to the table of your soil they bring in minerals and nutrients, further enhancing its fertility. For example, birds shed feathers, eggshells, nesting material, copious droppings and eventually their bodies, all of which contribute to the soil's fertility as they are broken down and reabsorbed into the chain of life.

Other creatures, such as frogs, toads and hedgehogs, take part in the same process, and all give off precious carbon dioxide which is rapidly reabsorbed by garden plants. Few people realize how important this gas is for plant growth, or that growing plants can extract all of it from still air in only minutes of bright sunlight. Animal life of any size in or on the soil gives off carbon dioxide and thus maintains growth; commercial greenhouse management now includes supplementation of carbon dioxide levels with bottled gas.

good husbandry: getting plants off to a good start

The second principle of organic gardening is to do the job well. Good methods and conditions set the plants off with a flying start and keep them growing without check or hindrance. Plants that are once checked or slowed down in their growth never do as well as those that grow consistently: their tissues harden and further growth is restrained.

The aim of the organic gardener is to give plants the best conditions possible, and to prevent them from ever coming under stress. Protection is needed from extremes of heat and cold and, most important, from water stress. The latter is most effectively achieved by increasing the organic matter and thus the humus content of the soil, which then acts like a sponge, retaining moisture.

Birds contribute to the natural fertility of a garden by providing feathers, eggshell, nesting material and manure which break down and become reabsorbed in the chain of life

In many ways growing plants is a bit like looking after babies. It is critical to get them through the earliest stages, but later on they are tough enough to endure less careful treatment with little risk of permanent damage. So organic gardeners ensure freedom from early stress, and also keep down the competition from weeds and other plants. This treatment produces healthy, robust plants that grow well in spite of any attacks from pests and diseases, in much the same way as humans shrug off colds and scratches.

natural methods of pest & disease control
The third principle is derived to some extent from the first two. We want to guard and foster the life in the soil, and also to give plants the best conditions possible, which means controlling pests and diseases – but without using pesticides, which may harm the life in the soil or even the plants themselves. Many, if not most, pesticides actually damage the plants they are applied to

directly, as well as destroying their support systems. One commercial cucumber grower found his yields increased by a quarter when he stopped using insecticides!

Organic gardeners aim to prevent pests and diseases from reaching the point where even an organically approved pesticide might be needed. They do this by building up a wide variety of plants, by creating ecosystems that are stable, and by encouraging predators and parasites, which then control the pests. Growing a more varied selection of plants is beneficial in many ways: it helps to prevent diseases and their spread, and encourages pollinators and recyclers which further add to the fertility and health of the garden.

The most important skill in this area is using wit and cunning to out-manoeuvre pests and diseases. Simple traps, sticky bands, careful timing and mechanical barriers defeat many pests, and good gardening methods such as hygiene and rotation of crops prevent pests and diseases building up. But these follow the

Vegetables and herbs at the edge of the raised beds are left to flower for the benefit of insects. The yellow flowerheads are dill, the lilac-coloured flowers are onion and the white flowers in the foreground are carrot and chervil

13

A cluster of sempervivums flower in front of golden feverfew, flowering parsley and rosemary. Herbs are often decorative enough to work well with ornamentals in mixed plantings

primary task of growing healthy plants that resist attacks in the first place.

minimizing ecological damage

The fourth principle is to minimize any bad effects on the environment – after all, everything we do uses resources and creates waste. Even gardening is not exempt, as left to itself the soil would produce much more plant growth, though not in a form suited to our requirements. Given a season or two of neglect, bare soil soon disappears under a tangle of weeds and brambles, and in time tree and shrub seedlings will turn it into dense woodland. All this growth increases the soil underneath while it fixes sunlight and extracts more carbon dioxide from the air.

In imitation of this, organic methods aim to increase plant cover as much as practicable, by interplanting between crops and green manuring before and after planting. These methods produce a soil cover as natural as possible, at the same time ensuring soil stability, preventing wind and water erosion while building up the soil annually. The increased mixture and variety of plants not only aids pest and disease control, but also improves the local ecology, providing a mini conservation area from which beneficial wildlife can move out to recolonize the local countryside.

The organic system further benefits the environment because it is far more self-sustaining, requiring less input. Home-grown fertility from green manures and compost replaces bought-in chemical fertilizers, and with subtler pest and disease control there is no need for direct intervention with ecologically damaging agrochemical pesticides.

Similarly, organic gardeners prefer not to buy plants robbed from the wild, or bedding plants that need replacing annually and which require excessive peat, heat, light, fertilizer and sprays in their production.

the practice

So much for the basic principles but how can one apply these so that they work in a garden on a long-term basis? Follow these eight steps – it's much easier than you think.

starting from scratch

1 Most important of all, recycle all garden and household wastes for compost and reuse. A household and garden that puts valuable material into the dustbin or sewer is throwing away its hard-won fertility. Anything that has ever lived can be reconverted into fertility with a compost heap.

Although some people may be squeamish, it is sensible to recycle urine (where local regulations do not forbid it). This is not a health hazard in temperate climates, and it is wasteful to use a couple of gallons of water to flush such a rich source of fertility down to the sea. Saved in a bucket it makes a superb compost activator; alternatively, each day's quota can be diluted down about 20:1 and watered on last thing at night to feed grass sward and increase the cuttings for use elsewhere. It gives an emerald lawn the envy of your neighbours, but it is best to keep mum about your methods!

2 Maximize the natural system of checks and balances by growing a wider variety of plants, especially more trees and shrubs. This helps create more habitats for birds and animals, especially if water is supplied with ponds and pools. Make nest boxes and nest sites – simple piles of rubble, or rotting logs hidden under evergreen shrubs or in the bottom of hedges will soon be colonized by many forms of wildlife.

3 Stop using all herbicides. Instead, use the recommended methods of weed control (see pages 56-69). These usually entail no more work, and are much more pleasant and safer.

4 Stop using most insecticides. They are rarely absolutely necessary, though a few of the least harmful ones are permitted as a last resort (see pages 54-5).

5 Stop using most fungicides, except those described in Chapter 3 (see pages 54-5). (To dispose of unwanted chemical pesticides contact your local council for advice. Do not pour them down the drain.)

6 Stop using soluble fertilizers. Although not allowed under most organic standards, they can be used up diluted down to a very weak solution, as used for houseplants, and then watered on to grass during the spring when they will be taken up rapidly with little danger of run-off.

7 Stop using peat from unrenewable sites, unecological plants such as imported wild bulbs and bedding plants, and plastic products wherever natural or longer-lasting alternatives are available.

8 Use wit and cunning and companion planting to outmanoeuvre pests and disease problems (see pages 44-54).

A small, natural looking pond makes a lovely addition to even the smallest garden and is particularly important in an organic garden because it provides habitats for many forms of wildlife

compost & composting

Composting is the accelerated rotting-down of once living things. It converts waste into a brown soil-like mass that is pleasant to smell and use. This mass is almost pure plant food, and is in a form readily available to plant roots with no risk of the overfeeding or imbalance that can be caused by chemical fertilizers. Moreover, the vast number of different micro-organisms that have broken down the compost go on to colonize the soil once the compost is added, further aiding fertility.

All manures and other organic materials for use in the garden are better composted before use, except clean commercial mulching materials and clean straw. Fresh manures contain soluble nutrients which can be too strong for healthy growth but if they are stacked and turned they compost. Once composted, their fertility is less easily lost and they become safer for plant roots. This is why it is always recommended to apply well-rotted farmyard manure. Because of the variety of materials going into a compost heap, garden compost contains a greater spread of nutrients and more varied microlife than well-rotted manure, so it is used in preference.

As the composting process converts most of the nutrients into an insoluble form there is little danger of their washing out into the water table with a heavy rain. However, they do leach out slowly, so compost heaps and rotting manures should always be covered.

The composting process will rapidly break down almost all natural materials, including old clothes made of natural fibres, and wetted newspaper. Large lumps of wood, bone or fat will decay too slowly and should be broken up or buried. Dry, twiggy material will compost if chopped up and mixed with some nitrogenous material such as fresh manure. Thorny material is better burnt, material containing seeds is best put in the middle of a heap, or burned, and live weeds of a pernicious nature can be killed first by wilting them on a path or sheet of plastic before mixing them in. Diseased material may be composted, but only if you are confident that your heap will 'cook' well – otherwise it is safer to burn it.

top Geese and hens peck at the waste material and start to process it before it is loaded into the compost bins
above A handful of natural fertility: home-produced garden compost

There are many different ways of composting, but they all come back to one principle. In general, composting proceeds best when there are many, varied materials well divided, moistened, and thoroughly mixed together with plentiful air. It helps to have roughly equal amounts of dry material and fresh green material as too much of either will cause poor composting. Adding water when mixing is usually necessary as many materials are too dry on their own. An activator is not essential, but speeds things up if added during the mixing. Rather than chemical additives it is better to use urine or poultry manure. Seaweed or blood, fish and bone meal will do instead. Sievings from previous compost heaps are the best activator of all and if you are starting your first heap ever scrounge some from an old hand to mix in.

Perhaps the biggest drawback to effective composting is the problem of accumulating enough material to make an effective heap – the bigger the mass the more heat is retained and the better it composts. Rather than store material until enough is available, I spread mine on the ground for the hens to rummage through, and their feet pack it down. Later I scrape it up and put it in the bins to break down. If you don't have hens it is probably best kept in plastic bags until ready to be combined, but most people just put it in layers in a bin and dig it out and mix it when enough has built up. A heap will always make better compost if it is remade after a week, and the inside exchanged for the outside. Doing this again after another week will be of further benefit. Each turning mixes the ingredients and stirs in air which then speeds up the process. Do not pack a heap down as this has the opposite effect. There are commercial rotary composters which speed up the process, but these are better suited to warmer climates.

containers Various compost containers are sold, but most are on the small side and thus do not heat up enough to make really good compost unless given extra insulation. Simple constructions of wood, wire netting or brick, about one metre (3ft) in height, width and depth are sufficient, and considerably cheaper. I prefer four old pallets tied at the corners. These are very easily obtained. Do not paint wood with creosote as this will slow the process. A lid will keep out the rain, but an old carpet and a plastic sheet will be better for retaining the heat and will prevent a flush of weeds from growing on top.

I plunge a crowbar down into the centre of my heap once it is going. It has little effect, but I love to pull it out and watch it steam, showing me the heap is cooking well. If it fails then I merely remake it. Once it has been turned and cooked at least twice it is then left to mature for six months or so, when it is in the best condition for use. (If I leave it longer, the worms mineralize it, increasing its richness but decreasing the quantity.) Like this it makes excellent potting compost, if a bit full of weed seeds. (It always is: do not believe anyone who claims to produce clean compost unless they are microwaving it!)

The most common problems are too wet a heap, remedied by remaking with extra straw or dry material, and too dry a heap, remedied by adding water, fresh wet manure or grass clippings. The presence of a white coating on the material indicates too dry a heap with insufficient nitrogenous material: add water mixed with urine.

Fresh compost, even when immature, can be mixed into the soil when you are planting trees and shrubs, but if it is to be used as a top dressing or with small plants, such as when planting out cabbages, it is best matured and sieved. This takes extra effort but produces a finer material, and the residue can then be used to start the next heap. In any case, compost or well-rotted manure is best applied to growing crops in early spring, so that the nutrients are taken up rather than leaching out over winter.

Where there is very little material available at any time, there are alternatives to the conventional heap. Cooperation with several neighbours can allow each to make a heap in turn or to share in yours. Another method is pit composting. Dig a hole and put the compost material in, covering each layer with a thin layer of soil. Once the hole is full and proud start another and use the first for growing really hungry feeders on, such as marrows, courgettes, runner beans or potatoes, for a year or two. The pit can then be dug out and the rotted material used as compost. A trench can be used in the same way and, because of its shape, will probably fit into the vegetable bed more easily.

As recycling your own material may not be enough, always be ready to acquire any wastes you can pick up from other gardeners, greengrocers, local stables, zoos and so on. This is good for you and for the environment.

worm compost Making worm compost is more akin to keeping pets. The waste has to be chopped up finely and added a little at a time to a large container containing red brandling worms. (Do not buy these – unearth them from a manure or compost heap, or from under a plank or carpet laid on the ground.) Put the worms in a layer of moist peat or leaf mould in the bottom of the container and keep in the warm, say in the garage. The container should have air holes in the top, and drainage holes and a drip tray to catch any liquids that ooze out. This liquid makes a good feed when diluted down. The worms convert the vegetable waste to a very rich material that is best mixed in when planting hungry feeders or added to potting composts. The worms will die if dug out with the material and put in the soil, so gently sift them out and return them. (They can be sold as fishing bait if you have an excess.) The worms are reluctant to deal with a large quantity of matter at a time, so they are better for the smaller household, or for use in conjunction with a conventional compost heap.

Making worm compost is an ideal way of using up household waste during the winter months, when material rots down very slowly on the compost heap because of the cold.

Courgettes are among the hungry feeders of the vegetable world and they respond particularly well to well-rotted, sieved compost which should be dug in when planting

2 UNDERSTANDING
your organic garden

There are three key components that work with plants to make up an organic garden: the soil, the microclimate and animal life. These all interact, affecting the way our gardens look and yield, and their activities can be modified to our advantage with a little understanding.

The fragrant, thornless rose Zéphirine Drouhin climbs up the telegraph pole to meet the vine canopy which trails elegantly from the top, creating a delightful shady area

your soil, & how to improve it

Few people get the opportunity to choose the site or the soil for their gardens, and most of us have to make the best of what we've got. Many gardens are on old sites, and may well be exhausted and pest-ridden. Some gardens are likely to be polluted and out of balance, especially if many chemicals have been used, while others may have been better treated. Abandoned or derelict sites, full of rampant weeds, will (unlikely as it seems) probably have good soil.

In general, most soils will produce flowers, shrubs or tree fruit without much improvement, but will need more attention if you want to grow vegetables and soft fruit. Problem soils tend to be common to a particular locality, and it is always a good idea to see how your neighbours cope. Almost all soils can be easily improved, but it may be worthwhile putting on extra topsoil as well if it is very poor or very polluted.

Most types of soil need basically the same treatment to improve them, that is, the addition of copious quantities of organic material. Anything else is almost inconsequential by comparison.

However, although most soils can be improved and thus made acceptable to a wider range of plants, there is a difference between improvement and change. It is very hard to change the basic soil type, which determines what you can grow well, and it will make life easier if you accept what you've got rather than trying to modify it drastically. For example, trying to make a lime soil suitable for rhododendrons is futile; far better to grow philadelphus, fuchsias, cotoneasters and other lime-lovers.

composition All soil types contain the same materials: stones, silt, sands, clays, organic matter. It is their proportions that vary. What affects plants most is not the nutrient levels of the soil but its physical texture, aeration and moisture retention. All (except peaty soils) are improved considerably by adding more organic material, especially when combined with a mulch.

Adding organic material contributes to the nutrient level directly (except for leaf mould and bark chippings, which are very slow to rot down). This organic material helps to increase another component of healthy soil: micro-organisms. These micro-organisms, mainly fungi, bacteria and other microbes, break down the organic material to release further nutrients. Some also release nutrients from mineral particles. These resources are then made available to the plants. There is sufficient in most soils of almost every element to last for millions of years of heavy cropping, provided the micro-organisms have the materials and conditions which enable them to thrive.

Most of all they need water: this is the most important factor for encouraging all life. Air is the next most important component of garden soil. Almost all microlife and plant roots need oxygen and give off carbon dioxide. Much of the carbon dioxide is reabsorbed by the soil, but fresh air is needed to restore the oxygen content. Organic particles of varied shape and size and in various stages of decomposition keep soils open and allow aeration. This is greatly enhanced by earthworm burrows, which at their best can descend for several metres.

heavy clay soils are hard to dig, stick to everything, drain poorly and pool with water in heavy rain. They are, however, the richest soils, rarely suffering mineral deficiencies, and resist drought well, though they will eventually become like concrete. Never allow to compact while wet and add coarse organic material and sharp sand or grit. They benefit from liming and fixed-bed gardening. Heavy soils encourage slugs but produce fine cauliflowers.

light sandy soils are a joy to dig, wash off tools and shoes and they never pool with water even in downpours. They need much more organic material, rock dusts (especially ground rock potash) and organic fertilizers than other soils as their wonderful aeration burns off humus quickly and nutrients wash out easily. They warm up early but dry out badly. If not too stony they will produce superb carrots.

silt soils are halfway between sandy soils and clays, but do not retain water and are fairly easy to work. Often built up on old river beds they benefit from ground rock dusts. They are good for most crops if well nourished, but tend to splash and cap badly in the wet.

peaty soils are not always advantageous: though very high in organic material they can be short of nutrients; they also dry out and are not stable enough for large trees. They will grow good salads and soft fruits though, and will be naturally suited to lime-haters like rhododendrons, azaleas and heathers. With the addition of lime many other plants can be grown, and weeds thrive.

Soil composition also varies with depth. Only the top few centimetres throb with life and it is this layer that constitutes the most active and productive part of the soil. Keep it at its best by adding an organic mulch to keep soil warm, fed and moist. At depths of more than 30cm (1ft) the subsoil contains mainly worms and plant roots. The working depth of 'living' soil can most efficiently be maintained by their action alone: it is rarely practical to dig to their depths. Digging may sometimes be necessary, but it does disrupt the soil layers and should never bring up the sterile subsoil.

analysis This is unnecessary for most gardens: you will get better value from a bag of seaweed meal. It is difficult to get accurate readings from the patchy soils in gardens, which can contain all sorts of detritus from dead cats to car batteries. Do not worry about this sort of fine tuning. If you aim to incorporate some broad-spectrum organic fertilizers and as much organic material as possible, most soils will balance themselves.

A far more useful guide is to look at surrounding plants which are growing well. For example, if the neighbourhood is full of flourishing rhododendrons, azaleas, camellias and heather gardens, then grow them, because the soil is obviously suitable whether or not the analysis says it is acid. Good gardeners grow what does well, superbly, rather than coax unsuitable plants to grow in the wrong places.

acidity/alkalinity (pH) The acidity/alkalinity or lime content of the soil is worth testing, but not with cheap meters which are inaccurate. Simple chemical test kits with an accurate colour chart are available in most garden shops. The basic pH may vary at ground level and deeper if the soil layers have built up a rich surface mould, so take samples from a typical worked soil. The pH may change as the soil is enriched, particularly as more organic material is added. This tends to make soils more acid.

Liming the soil every few years will be of benefit, especially for vegetables and grassed areas. (Check if it is needed – over-liming can cause problems.) Lime can be chalk, or better

wet soils tend to be sour or acid. They may need lime and draining, especially if low-lying, but be careful not to overdo it – it is only waterlogging that is a problem. Adding copious amounts of organic material will improve drainage and water dispersion.

loamy soil is produced when old meadow or grass sward is dug up. It can also be achieved by rotting down grass turves or by enriching most soils with organic material. This is the best soil for most plants and comes from clay soil more easily than sandy. The rich 'brown sugar' texture found in the best loams, made up mostly of earthworm droppings, produces masses of fine root hairs.

lime, or worse, *chalky* soil causes chlorosis in lime-hating plants by locking up iron and other nutrients causing yellowing leaves and green veins. Lime soils suit most plants though (especially brassicas if the soil is also rich and moist). Good for many trees, figs and grapes these soils need feeding and mulching. Raised beds will improve them.

stony soils tend to be freer draining. The stones are of little consequence to most plants, but frustrate cultivation, especially hoeing. They are better used for permanent plantings with mulches rather than for growing annuals and vegetables, though the latter can thrive on cleaned beds. Putting down a thin layer of sharp sand will help create a workable tilth and make weeding easier.

dolomitic lime, which contains more magnesium and other nutrients, or best of all calcified seaweed, which contains all the trace elements as well as being lime, though it is rather slow-acting. Never mix lime with manures or compost; apply it before rain on top of the soil or grass, and rake, brush or allow to leach in. Late winter is generally the best time. In a vegetable rotation it is probably best applied before peas, before brassicas, but not before potatoes.

If, on the other hand, your soil has a lot of lime, it may be lacking in available trace elements. To improve the soil you will need to use a raised bed system (see pages 115-16) and dig in plenty of manure or compost.

drainage

Waterlogging kills by driving out air. It is more of a problem on heavy soils, as their finer particles hold much more water than the coarse grains of sand or silt. Obviously installing drainage will be needed in the very worst cases, but often breaking up compacted soil, encouraging earthworms with mulches, applying organic material and using raised beds will help the soil absorb the water, rather than just allowing it to drain away. If drainage is needed then ditches may work, or you may need to lay herringbones of drainage pipes leading to a soakaway.

Clay soils retain more water than sandy, chalky or stony ones, which all need much more watering in dry regions. It is the humus part of the soil which soaks up water, and so the higher the organic content the more water can be retained. Keep the soil moist, hoe the surface or mulch and trap evaporation with layer upon layer of plants.

adding improvers

Various materials are offered as soil improvers. Some flocculating agents based on lime or gypsum do help clay form lighter textures, but most soils will benefit more from extra organic material, though sharp sand and grit will also help open up a heavy soil.

encouraging worms

Worms are probably the most important creatures in our gardens. Their production of casts provides

the best texture improver and fertilizer your soil can have. Worm casts are water stable and have a granular texture that promotes plant root growth. Their burrows act as aeration and drainage channels, and when abandoned are followed down by plant roots for their rich lining. Their digestive process reduces mineral particles in size, making them more accessible to micro-organisms.

Encourage worms by keeping the soil moist and covered with a mulch. I feed all bare soil and most mulched areas with a handful of grass clippings every month or so as they need 'greens' as well as organic material such as compost or well-rotted manure. Ground seaweed, blood, fish and bone meal and hoof and horn meal will also feed them. It is better not to rotavate the soil as this kills worms.

dig or non-dig

There has been much controversy over non-dig versus digging methods. I think both sides are partly right. Most of any garden is no-dig anyway, and it is only the vegetable plot that gets dug regularly.

Certainly, digging a new plot is a good idea, if only to unearth and remove rubbish and roots; but as an annual event it appears to be unproductive. The effort would seem better spent on turning the compost heap or weeding, as any increase in yield from digging is less than that obtained from one good watering at the right time for most crops.

Digging annually breaks up the natural soil layers, the network of earthworm tunnels and decaying root systems. It aerates the soil, causing excessive humus breakdown with a short-

A view over the raised vegetable bed in late autumn. Raised beds are particularly well suited to the no-dig method, partly because the soil does not become compacted by being trodden on

term increase in fertility which may leach out if the digging precedes the crop by long. The need to produce a good seedbed does not justify digging unless the soil has been badly compacted; mulching and surface cultivation will make just as good a tilth. However, most soils show benefit from a thorough digging once every five to ten years. If nothing else, this does destroy mole runs and ants' nests and so on, but many gardens are run successfully without ever being dug.

If digging is deemed necessary then pace yourself. Never work for too long, never dig sodden soil, and never move too large a spit. Break each lump and mix in sharp sand and well-rotted manure as you go. Heavy soils should be dug in the drier autumn weather, while lighter ones are better left till late winter to avoid nutrients leaching out. Digging benefits heavy soils more as frost may then help break them down into a good crumb structure, but if badly dug it can just make clods and airgaps. Light soil, which is easy to dig, needs it least.

No-dig methods mostly include permanent paths and fixed or raised beds so that the soil is not compacted by traffic. These are discussed more fully in Chapter 7. I strongly suggest you use fixed beds and dig rarely.

breaking new ground
At some time most of us want to make a new bed where none was before. The methods for doing this are discussed in Chapter 4 on weed control (see pages 60-9) as it is getting the established weeds eliminated first that is most important. Before embarking on the actual task it is a good idea to check that there are no pipes or wires under the ground and dig carefully, as they may not be buried deep enough!

Without any doubt the easiest way to start a new bed is to put the whole area down to closely cut grass for a year or two and then just cut the bed out of the sward. Thus it helps to be patient and plan ahead.

soil fertility
In general, if you regularly feed your soil with well-rotted manure and compost, it will remain fertile. In addition, the

rotation of crops on the vegetable plot leaves root and leaf residues, and this will be increased if green manures are grown between crops, and then hoed or dug in. Regular feeding of the plants as such does not take place in an organic system, but the soil is fed with these plant residues plus compost or well-rotted farmyard manure mixed in whenever a heavy feeder or perennial is planted.

Mulches of organic material break down and are incorporated, and rock dusts, especially potash, can be added with benefit at any time, but take seasons to act. Ground rock dusts provide additional raw materials of the most needed elements in a finely distributed form and benefit most soils, especially lighter ones. For poor soils in the first few years some supplementary feeding may be undertaken with organic fertilizers of a faster-acting nature. These are crutches, and should be discarded as the soil becomes enriched. Far more important for fertility is ensuring the life in the soil is active; mulching and keeping the soil moist helps most.

organic fertilizers
Conventional fertilizers are ranked according to their nitrogen, phosphorus and potassium ratio and content. These are regarded as direct plant foods, replacing the elements taken away with the crop. Nitrogen is considered to stimulate growth and leaves, phosphorus the roots and potassium fruiting and disease resistance. While it is true these same elements exist naturally in the soil, it is not natural to have them in very high concentrations, as occurs when they are applied as soluble fertilizers.

Organically, we guard the soil micro-organisms by avoiding substances that can damage them, and by applying fertilizers that are effectively insoluble so they cannot become too concentrated in the soil solution. These need to be broken down and incorporated by micro-organisms before they can increase the nutrient supply in the soil and become available to plants. Thus they do not leach out as

A carpet mulch gets to work on breaking in new ground.
top after ten days;
middle after three weeks;
bottom after several months

organic fertilizers from the top: seaweed meal; bone meal; calcified seaweed; rock phosphate

readily and remain beneficial for longer.

Organic fertilizers may therefore be considered more as soil stimulators than as plant fertilizers as they promote increases in soil life, and the by-products from this increased population then feed the plants. Because they are stimulators or catalysts they do not need to be applied heavily. A handful per square metre (yard) every other year is sufficient.

seaweed meal contains a wide spread of trace elements and about 2-3 per cent each of nitrogen and potassium, but only a sixth as much phosphate. The most widely acceptable nitrogenous fertilizer and soil stimulator, it is also a very good compost activator. This is pleasanter and more acceptable ecologically than blood, fish and bone meal for a general purpose feed. Expensive but long-lasting, it is better balanced with bone meal or ground rock phosphate, but is effective enough on its own for most plants, raked in during spring.

blood, fish and bone meal is the traditional, organically based fertilizer, very effective and fast-acting. It should be used in moderation, raked in immediately before planting hungry feeders or mixed in with the planting soil. Beware of cheap brands which are frequently adulterated with chemical fertilizers and sand.

bone meal is an excellent source of phosphates. The finer the soil, the faster it will act. It is expensive, but good for incorporating when planting, particularly woody plants and strawberries.

hoof and horn is very expensive, but an effective slow-release source of nitrogen for hungry and woody plants. These last three fertilizers are all likely to be pinched by animals or birds unless mixed in well with the soil; keep the bags in a safe place.

calcified seaweed is more of a lime than a fertilizer, but because of its high level of trace elements may act like one by stimulating soil life. It is considerably cheaper than seaweed and thus may be used as a general purpose fertilizer where the lime is no disadvantage. It is especially beneficial for turf, brassicas, legumes and stone fruits.

ground rock potash is just that, a ground rock dust with a very slow release. Mix it in

composts or into the soil at any time every other year or so, especially on light soils and in wet areas. It is especially good for gooseberries and culinary apples and for promoting disease resistance.

ground rock phosphate is another rock dust useful for restoring healthy life to abused or over-acid soils and in wet areas. Mix it in composts or the soil at any time. It is especially good for strawberries.

ground rock basalt/granite may also be added to any soil. This finely ground rock dust contains a spread of minerals to encourage micro-organisms and is claimed to revitalize worn-out soils.

wood ashes are a very rich source of potash but in a soluble form which leaches out, so apply to growing crops, especially fruit and onions, for ripening and disease protection. Sprinkle on the surface and rake in or else mix with the compost.

commercial balanced fertilizers are usually even more expensive. Most are based on animal wastes which have been composted or worm composted. They may be contaminated, so only those with the Soil Association symbol can be recommended.

sewage sludge is also likely to be contaminated, so is only recommended for ornamental plantings where it is a slow-release source of phosphate.

liquid feeds Plants confined in containers are restricted and cannot reach further afield for nutrients after they have used up those around the rootball. They need feeding a little and often with a liquid feed diluted down in their water. These liquid feeds may smell unpleasant but this disappears when they are absorbed into the soil. All these feeds are for plants with restricted root runs though they may be used in moderation on hungry plants in the open such as sweetcorn, and for bringing on spring greens in cold years.

comfrey liquid Comfrey leaves are collected, packed into a container (such as a water butt) activated with a little urine and covered in water. They rot down in 4-5 weeks to form a solution like black tea. It smells horrible, but watered down to a pale straw colour is a perfectly balanced feed for tomatoes and other plants. Another method is to stack the leaves in a covered container with a hole in the base, and leave them to rot down without added liquid. After a few weeks a liquid concentrate will start to drip out. This again can be diluted and used as a liquid feed. The concentrate can also be used as the fertility constituent in potting mixes.

nettle tea is made and used in the same way as comfrey liquid and as well as being a good balanced feed is claimed to make plants more resistant to disease and pests. Similarly, bags of manure can be hung in sacks in water butts and the resulting solution used in the same way as nettle tea.

seaweed solution can be diluted down and used as a beneficial liquid feed. It carries the benefits of a wider range of trace elements but is expensive to use for general watering and should be saved for use as a foliar feed. The effect on plants is rapid and marked. They take on a darker, healthier colour and resist pests and diseases better.

fish emulsion is a very rich source of nutrients and is especially effective mixed with seaweed solution as a liquid feed.

animal manures

Manure is probably the best soil improver of all, but you have to take what you can get. All animal manures make a contribution to soil fertility, but they should always be well composted before use as they may be contaminated with hormones, pesticides and other chemicals, and the straw or wood shavings they come in may also be polluted. Stack the manure in a heap, cover to protect it from the rain, and leave for a year, if possible. As a general rule, allow one barrowload of manure for every 10 square metres (12 sq yds).

In order of preference: horse, sheep and goat are all sweet to handle; cow manure is less pleasant; pig is vile and often contains unacceptable contaminants. Rabbit and pet droppings can be added to the compost heap, but cat and dog tray litter is best buried deep under trees. Poultry manures are very strong, highly nitrogenous and a good source of potash. They make a compost heap cook!

Never put raw poultry droppings on plants; always compost them first. Litter from intensive rearing units may contain unacceptable residues.

green manures

These are any plants grown as temporary ground cover and for their use in fertilizing the soil when dug in, though the tops may be cut and composted for use elsewhere. Predominantly grown when the soil is vacant over winter, they may be grown in between crops and incorporated as seedlings after only a week or two. Green manures prevent soil erosion and leaching, and convert otherwise wasted winter sunlight into useful organic plant matter.

Any plants that grow over winter will do, but those easiest to incorporate or creating most bulk are best. Leguminous plants that fix nitrogen are frequently used, as this nutrient is always in short supply. The manures are usually sown as soon as the ground is bare until the first frosts start. Those surviving over winter are then killed off by impenetrable mulches or are dug in before the crops need the soil. Several weeks of breakdown are necessary for some of the more fibrous ones such as grazing rye; less time is needed for younger and more succulent growth. Never let green manures flower and seed or the goodness is lost. It is better to grow two or three short crops than one long-lasting one.

alfalfa (lucerne) is best used for leys and longer periods of manuring as it is slow-growing. To ensure nitrogen fixing, the soil has to be inoculated with Rhizobium bacteria, which is sold with the seed. It is very deep rooting, pulling up minerals from 6 metres (20ft), so it is a rich source of nutrients when dug in.

beans and peas Any variety may be used, but only hardy ones will over-winter. These are pulled up minus their roots before they form pods, leaving nitrogen-rich nodules in the soil. Do not use them in the vegetable plot without considering rotational requirements. Banner is a hardy variety of field bean often grown as a green manure.

One of the most convenient green fertilizers because it is constantly available throughout the summer months, grass clippings provide a moisture-retentive and nutritious mulch for potatoes and other deserving plants

Buckwheat is an excellent,
fast-growing green manure

buckwheat is a summer crop growing quickly in late spring/early summer. It can be left to flower as it is good for beneficial insects. It is deeply rooted and will choke out most weeds. Remove or dig in before it sets seed. It is not nitrogen-fixing.

clovers These are a very rich source of nitrogen, but need a year or so to show full benefit and are inclined to regrow. Good for bees if allowed to flower. Alsike is the best for poor, wet or acid soils, white is better on lighter and limier soils. Essex red is considered the best for green manuring though not as hardy and does better on loamy soils.

chicory A long-term green manure, chicory is best used in grass and clover leys as it has deep tap roots that take time to form, and kill.

fenugreek A quick-growing manure that is leguminous and can come after early crops, or between others. It is unrelated to vegetables and so is no problem in rotations. It can be sown late spring to late summer and is killed by the first frosts.

fodder radish is a not very hardy, deep-rooting radish that is killed by hard frosts leaving considerable bulk which can be easily incorporated in the spring. Unfortunately it is related to brassicas, so has to be used sparingly in rotations containing them.

hungarian grazing rye Sown from late summer to mid autumn, this provides quick ground cover for overwintering. It must be well dug in a month or so before the crop to give it time to rot. It is not nitrogen-fixing.

lupins Ordinary lupins may be used, but agricultural ones are better and are sown in the spring to incorporate in the autumn. They are deep-rooting, help improve sour acid land and are leguminous, fixing nitrogen.

mustard One of the fastest growing manures and if incorporated as seedlings can reduce many infestations of the soil, but will not stand hard winters. Grown between crops or up until the frosts and allowed to incorporate in situ it is excellent. However, it is in the brassica family and must be grown with care in rotations – ideally only to the seedling stage. It is not nitrogen-fixing.

phacelia (*P. tanacetifolia*) is very expensive seed but beloved by bees and hoverflies so should be grown for them anyway. Sow early spring to early autumn and it may overwinter. It is easy to remove from the soil or to incorporate in it. Save your own seed for the next time. It is not nitrogen-fixing.

trefoil Similar to clover and related to alfalfa this is another nitrogen-fixing legume. It prefers a limey soil and is shade tolerant so can be used under taller crops. It is sown early spring to late autumn to overwinter.

winter tares can be sown from early spring to late autumn for overwintering. They are excellent for producing bulk, fixing nitrogen and suppressing weeds.

mineral accumulators
Some garden plants and many weeds are particularly good at accumulating very large amounts of minerals and trace elements. This occurs even if the soil is deficient in whichever mineral they accumulate. In fact, these plants often abound on deficient soils just because they are the most successful at grabbing scarce resources.

Although they extract most of any available nutrient, more will be dissolved into the soil solution from otherwise insoluble mineral sources and thus the mineral accumulators go on taking in the nutrient from very dilute solutions. Growing these plants as green manures removes scarce minerals, but once they are composted the concentrated material can be put back to boost the soil. Remember that only annual weeds should be used as green manure as perennial weeds such as dandelions are hard to eradicate (see pages 56-69 for more details on weeds).

nitrogen is taken from the air, not the soil. It is best accumulated with leguminous plants and by digging in any succulent seedlings in their first flushes of growth.

phosphorus is concentrated by fat hen, corn marigold, purslane, vetches and the weed *Datura stramonium* or thornapple.

potassium is accumulated by a number of plants including chickweed, chicory, fat hen, goosegrass, plantain, purslane, thornapple, sweet tobaccos and vetches.

calcium is concentrated by buckwheat, corn chamomile, corn marigold, dandelion, fat hen, goosegrass, melons, purslane, shepherd's purse.

silica imparts disease resistance and is made active by plantains, couchgrass, stinging nettles and the perfidious weed horsetail.

sulphur is excellent for the promotion of disease resistance and accumulates in the alliums or onion family, brassicas, fat hen and purslane.

your climate & microclimate

In addition to the soil several other factors affect the growth of your plants: air, light, rain and wind all have positive and negative effects. It is possible to modify these to a certain extent, thus increasing your garden's potential range of plants or increasing their season.

light Although all plants need light not all need full sunlight. Many ornamentals, especially golden varieties, need partial shade or they get leaf burn. Similarly, plants may 'cook' under glass in very hot weather, hence the need for good ventilation, or even glass shading or

The evening sun streams into the area shaded by the vine canopy. Shade during the hot midday sun and then warmth later in the day is the perfect combination of conditions for this attractive area with the summerhouse and garden seat

top A Conference pear grown as an espalier enjoys the warmth which is trapped by the red brick wall

above A Siegerrebe grape vine is trained against black felt for the extra warmth that this wall covering provides

blinds. To prevent overheating under cover, automatic vents are indispensible. Generally, though, the problem is insufficient light, especially from overhanging trees and buildings. Pruning may allow more light in and dark places can be brightened with white paint. Under cover, electric light can supplement weak winter sunlight and may be used for early sowings and valuable plants. Ordinary incandescent bulbs are counter-productive as they give the wrong spectrum; use special fluorescent tubes and discharge lamps made for the purpose. All glass and plastic should be kept scrupulously clean in order to prevent further light loss.

warmth This interacts with light and shelter – the more light reaching the garden the more warmth. Warmth is blown away by winds, so shelter not only protects from buffeting but also keeps the garden warm. In fact, a good hedge extracts heat from the wind: as the wind is filtered through the hedge, it is slowed and this slowing gives off the energy of the wind as heat. Thus a good hedge can raise the temperature of a garden by several degrees. So establish hedges as windbreaks rather than using fences and walls, though the latter can be improved by mounting trellis or climbers on top.

Warmth can also be harnessed by including brick walls, paths and other features which soak up heat and then radiate it. Brick rubble, dark stones and gravel all throw up heat and can be used to help ripen fruit sooner. Similarly, bare soil will give off warmth to ripen fruit or protect flowers from frosts better than grass or a mulch.

access It is no good having a lovely garden if you can't get round it in the wet, or if obstacles make it difficult. Ease of access is important, because anywhere hard to reach will be neglected.

patios From a few humble slabs by the garden door to a full terrace, patios are the viewing-points as well as the access for most gardens. Make sure these areas are tidy, as junk and litter not only spoil the appearance but make access difficult and dangerous. Loggias and overhead timberwork combined with the patio help blend an unsympathetic building into a garden and cast a pleasing dappled shade, but they may drip in the wet. A patio makes a microclimate, hot and dry above combined with a cool, moist root-run below, though it may be drier if sheltered by the house from prevailing wind and rain. This makes beds within patios ideal for climbers such as clematis, grapes or roses, though the flowers will thrive better climbing around posts rather than on hot walls, which are best reserved for grapes, pears or other fruit.

paths and drives can create microclimates as well as providing access. The hard standing again creates a cool, moist root-run and water run-off. It throws off heat day and night, making it warmer nearby while the openness allows a better airflow. This makes plants grown near paths and drives bigger and healthier than those further away, and is beneficial to the less hardy shrubs.

grass paths soon wear badly where traffic is heavy, but can be cheaply improved by setting in stepping stones. A slab path set on sand is probably the best as it can be moved, yet is low maintenance and very durable. Gravel, done properly with board edging and hardcore underneath, makes a very attractive path and if the gravel is deep enough can be kept tidy and weed-free with raking. However, if mud and soil are frequently dropped or weeds seed nearby, it will become difficult to keep looking good as plants germinate so readily in gravel.

brick paths, crazy paving and badly laid cobbles with many gaps have a similar problem. Point gaps well and fill all potential niches with creeping thymes or chamomile before they become a weed problem. Concrete paths are fine but can be expensive or arduous to make, are rather permanent and give a somewhat utilitarian appearance. Shredded bark or pine needle paths are good if they are laid over hardcore where traffic is heavy, otherwise they can be churned to mud. Bark and pine needles look best as paths in woodland or shrub settings. They are also useful in vegetable areas to help repel slugs, but avoid using them near the house as they carry in on feet.

ventilation
Although we need to prevent excessive winds, all plants need fresh air. Stagnant air encourages pests and diseases, especially mildews and botrytis. Good spacing and open pruning is required, allowing the plants to breathe. The carbon dioxide content can be increased by encouraging more animal life of all kinds, big and small, in the garden and by allowing winds filtered through hedges to change the air.

Under cover, always give as much ventilation as possible without chilling your plants. As it is difficult to ventilate adequately in cold springs, fortify the air under glass or plastic with bottles of fermenting wine or beer which give off carbon dioxide, replacing that which is used up by the plants in photosynthesis.

watering
This is crucial to success. More plants do badly through over- or under-watering than from almost all other causes together. In times of strong growth it is almost impossible to over-water plants in the open ground. Indoors, in pots in winter it is difficult to under-water. Between these two extremes is where the difficulty lies. In the open ground try to conserve winter rains with mulches and except during droughts restrict watering to: before sowing; newly emergent seedlings; new transplants; and crops at a critical stage (usually when their flowers are setting). In times of drought, water the most valued plants with one long soak rather than giving everything little and often, as much of this will just evapo-

above Mounds of thyme enjoy their position by the path, which provides warmth at ground level combined with a cool root run

left Grass paths are suitable for parts of the garden which have little traffic. This one works well with the dense leylandii hedge and acid green feverfew border to create an enticing alleyway

rate. Above all, keep down weed competition and mulch well.

Do not try to wet large areas of soil around each plant as this mostly evaporates. Instead, try to soak water down to the roots. A hole, half-buried pot, or a trench beside plants that need copious watering speeds up the task. A neat idea is to take clear plastic bottles with the bottom cut off to use as mini-cloches. Invert and push in beside each plant; a litre or two can then be poured rapidly into the funnel to trickle in slowly. A pair of watering cans with sawn-off spouts carry easily and pour faster than through roses or long narrow spouts (but always use a rose when watering directly on to the soil surface), and a water butt by each greenhouse door or in the middle of a plot cuts down carrying time.

Obviously, the more rainwater that can be stored the better. Every effort should be made to save every drop. Excess is better run into soakaways than down the drain, so it can benefit trees and deep rooters. Similarly, provided local regulations do not forbid it, water from sinks, showers and baths can be diverted from the drains and run directly out or siphoned down a hose in times of drought (water from washing machines may carry too

many chemicals for safety). When hosepipe watering is not restricted because of drought, organize a system whereby all parts of the garden can be watered from a short length of hose connected to one of several hidden points. This saves dragging long lengths around, decapitating plants. The permanent pipe layout can be made from ordinary hose buried in the ground or run along fences and hedges. If it is easy to water a plant with only a short length of hose and a couple of quick connections, then it is much more likely to be done.

In pots and containers keeping the soil or potting compost moist but not waterlogged is difficult, and more so with the new peat substitute composts. Daily checking with a thumb is essential and more often in very hot dry weather. In winter err on the side of caution: water rarely but thoroughly and drain well. In summer water frequently but still drain well. For large numbers of pots on benches it is worth standing them on capillary matting fed from a simple reservoir.

Under cover in pots or borders and outdoors against dry walls and in corners air moisture is also important. Too much encourages moulds and botrytis, too little encourages mildew and red spider mite. In general, during the growing season it is better to err on the side of too moist, so spray the walls, plants and floor with a fine jet in the morning so it can dry before nightfall. It will save time to arrange an overhead sprinkling system for plants under cover. Sprinklers are inexpensive and will soon repay their cost, but for only a little more you can have seep hoses and trickle feeders which use water more efficiently by applying it directly to the roots. If you are willing to make a larger investment a microchip-operated system can be installed in a greenhouse. This will accurately maintain soil and air moisture levels as well as the heating and ventilation. There are less expensive systems can be run with timers or moisture sensors.

shelter Apart from hedges and walls, shelter can also be provided on a smaller scale with tough evergreen plants, sticks and

below A cunning water butt made from a recycled deep freeze, which has been painted matt black.
bottom With forty raised vegetable beds at the opposite end of the garden to the ornamental area, an efficient watering system is essential. In the foreground, you can see the permanent hosepipe layout designed for easy watering

twigs, netting or cloches. All of these help nurse tender and establishing plants through cold weather.

fences have the advantage that they are quick to erect and take up little depth. They need some maintenance and rarely last longer than a decade or two. Panel fences which stop the wind tend to fail before open fences and trellis, but they do allow borders in front and fruit or climbers can be quite easily trained against them. Unfortunately weeds come underneath very easily unless deep gravel boards are fitted. Open fences only act as boundary markers and look better covered with climbers.

walls are much more expensive but last for centuries. They exclude weeds with their deep foundations, retain warmth and block wind. They are harder to train plants against as the fixings take more work, but are excellent for ripening fruit. Remember that it may be too hot and dry at the base of a sunny wall for some plants, especially roses. Red brick is the best material as it retains warmth, and dry stone walls are good as they provide excellent niches for many forms of plant and animal life.

hedges are generally the best choice for most gardens other than the very tiny as they are the cheapest of all, though they take longer to be effective. They establish much more quickly given a temporary fence of windbreak material. Their own wind filtering provides warmth, and they are a superb habitat for many forms of wildlife as well as adding to the variety of plants in the garden. It is a good idea to have a path rather than a border right next to a hedge as the soil will be impoverished – and it will make the trimming easier. See page 93 for varieties of hedge.

cloches & coldframes These can be as simple as a jam jar, or large constructions of brick and glass. They keep off the worst weather, provide a longer season of growth, and keep off pest attacks. Glass ones are most expensive but last longer, and keep warmer than plastic which always degrades and becomes brittle. Larger ones are expensive and more difficult to move than smaller, and none are cheap.

clear plastic bottles with the bottoms cut off make excellent mini-cloches for bedding plants, salad plants and transplants such as brassicas and sweetcorn. Larger containers can be used to cover bigger plants such as pelargoniums, marrows or tomatoes.

When using cloches make sure they do not form a wind-tunnel – block the ends off and pay extra attention to watering. Secure them well in windy weather and harden off the plants first before removing them. The low hoops covered with plastic film are least costly, but they use ecologically expensive plastic sheets which do not last long. If you have the space it is probably better to get a longer lasting walk-in polytunnel instead.

tunnels & houses One of the most useful if time-consuming accessories to a garden is walk-in cover. This is much better than using cloches or coldframes for shelter and warmth as the extra capacity gives a more stable environment and it allows the gardener to work in comfort.

A greenhouse or a polytunnel can be used for sowing, giving most plants an early start and protection from pests and weather. They can also be used for winter salads or flowers, for plants a little too tender for outside, and for forcing or protecting fruit trees. A greenhouse is lighter and warmer and the frame can be easily used to attach staging, potting benches or plant support. This makes a greenhouse more suitable for plants in pots or perennial fruit growing. Wooden-framed ones are more aesthetically pleasing and warmer than metal-framed ones, but need more maintenance.

polytunnel A polytunnel is cheaper but colder. It may be very humid and tends to be unsightly. The plastic cover needs replacing every few years which makes it poor value ecologically, but it does give the opportunity,

top A young peach is protected by an ingenious black tyre shelter – the black rubber feeds back extra warmth to the tree and also gathers small pools of water which beneficial insects enjoy
above Mini cloches are made from recycled plastic bottles; they are ideal for sheltering sweetcorn seedlings in their early life

top The polytunnel in summer
with French beans,
sweetcorn, tomato plants and
summer herbs
above The external
appearance of the polytunnel
is much improved by
growing climbers and lush
herbs immediately outside

where space allows, of moving the whole thing, making a rotation possible. As the frame is also unsuitable for fixing benches or staging tunnels are mostly used for growing annual or short-lived plants directly in the soil.

With either a polytunnel or greenhouse get the biggest you can afford, as the larger they are the better value, and the more stable the environment produced. Site them with their longest axis east-west to maximize sunlight and do not put them in heavy shade. Make sure they are securely built and have adequate ground fixings against strong wind. Money spent fitting automatic ventilation and watering systems will be recouped in time and better plant growth thus doubling their value.

organic greenhouse management

While a cloche isolates a plant to an extent, it is still in the soil and only temporary. Growing under walk-in cover is more artificial and requires more intervention as the natural sys-tems cannot control pests and diseases, the temperature may rise too high and the rain does not fall. So pest and disease control requires special consideration under cover.

There are two approaches. With the 'sterile environment' approach the greenhouse or tunnel is cleansed thoroughly – a high-pressure water or steam jet can be used – and the plants treated only if they are subject to any attack with the methods described in Chapter 3. This resembles the conventional approach. The alternative is to try and build up semi-natural systems concentrating more on predators for pest control. Water in saucers, nests of straw-filled pots and ground-cover plants can be included under staging and in shady corners for beetles, frogs and toads. Ladybirds, spiders and bought-in predators can be introduced and encouraged with rolled up cardboard nests tied in dry nooks and crannies. With this approach even organic pesticides must not be used or these natural predators may suffer, but companion plants can be used as suggested in Chapter 7.

your lodgers

Although humans may recognize legal boundaries, nature as a whole does not. Unless we glass our gardens over we cannot decide which forms of wildlife – animals, birds, insects and micro-organisms – are going to live there.

the chain of life We can encourage wildlife though; and the more we can gather into our garden the more vitality it will have and the more it will produce, as the plants feast on the waste, by-products and eventually bodies of the wildlife. This is contrary to the conventional view, in which almost every creature is regarded as a threat and needs instant and complete annihilation.

The variety of inhabitants in a healthy garden is enormous, from the larger creatures down to countless species of bacteria, fungi and other micro-organisms. We can categorize these creatures as pests, parasites, predators, pollinators and recyclers, but in practice they are all links in nature's continuous chain of life, and each creature plays many parts, interacting with other creatures and with the plants.

For example, butterflies which serve as pollinators were once caterpillars eating leaves. A blackbird may be a pest when it is scratching mulch on to the lawn or eating fruit, but it is a predator when it eats wireworms or leatherjackets. It may not be much of a pollinator but it is constantly recycling living and dead creatures, and it converts berries into concentrated fertility as droppings, with the seeds of the next plant generation inside ready to take advantage of it. The feathers, the failed young, their eggshells, the nest, all become fertility enhancers shortly after they hit the soil; and in the end the blackbird will make of itself its final contribution.

The value of all that fertility is easily the equivalent of many handfuls of organic fertilizer: but it is distributed unseen and unnoticed in a healthy garden, where material is quickly incorporated by the soil life. Our aim as organic gardeners is to get as many such chains of life going as possible, attracting wildlife of all forms to our garden for the hidden contribution to fertility that they make,

Plants that attract
BENEFICIAL INSECTS & WILDLIFE

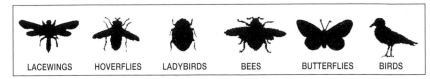

| LACEWINGS | HOVERFLIES | LADYBIRDS | BEES | BUTTERFLIES | BIRDS |

| Honesty *Lunaria biennis* |
| Mint *Mentha* |
| Cherry pie *Heliotropum x hybridium* |
| Ice plant *Sedum spectabile* |
| Candytuft *Iberis matronalis* |
| Soapwort *Saponaria officinalis* |
| Scabious *Scabiosa atropurpurea* |
| Valerian *Centranthus ruber* |
| Meadowsweet *Filipendula ulmaria* |
| Borage *Borago officinalis* |
| Teasel *Dipsacus fullonum* |
| Cranesbill *Geranium* |
| Chives *Allium schoenaprasum* |
| Balm *Melissa officinalis* |
| Marjoram *Origanum vulgare* |
| Wallflowers *Cheiranthus cheiri* |
| Alyssum *Lobularia maritima* |
| Alkanet *Anchusa azurea* |
| Mignonette *Reseda odorata* |
| Mallow *Lavatera rosea* |
| Honeysuckle *Lonicera* |
| Thyme *Thymus* |
| Sweet cicely *Myrrhis odorata* |

33

top The aphids on this foxglove appear to be doing no harm and are distracted from plants which they might really damage. The foxglove in this instance acts as a 'scapegoat plant'

opposite Unused artichokes never go to waste because their flowerheads attract beneficial insects into the garden

and for the pest and disease control that comes from building up natural populations with their inbuilt checks and balances.

pests Pests are pests only when they eat our chosen plants – if they didn't we would perceive them as wildlife, as recyclers and as pollinators. Yet pests are an essential part of the ecology and a resource for others. In nature, plants and pests reach a balance; it is when we grow monocultures or eliminate the natural controls that pests run rampant.

However, pests seldom do much harm to healthy plants that are growing well. The pests we have to take note of are few, and mostly attack vegetables and fruits. They can be readily controlled by the methods suggested in Chapter 3; and it is control, not elimination, that the organic gardener is after. We need a background level of pests or there is nothing to keep the predators alive, and without them any new pest would escalate into a problem. If there were no snails there might be no songbirds; there would certainly be fewer.

predators The predators and parasites in a stable system need pests to live on. Left to themselves they control pest numbers very effectively, in a complicated web where they prey not only on the pests but also on each other. This is particularly true of the larger predators such as hedgehogs and birds, which will eat almost anything regardless of whether it is a friend or foe to us. Ladybirds are well known predators and almost all beetles are predatory, accounting for slugs and other small pests. Spiders, which number many millions in a large healthy garden, are all predatory. Hoverflies, lacewings and wasps all help in controlling aphids, caterpillars and other pests. Similarly, there are numerous parasitic wasps and other creatures that live on pests.

But predators tend to be fewer than their prey and breed more slowly. When a pesticide is used and predators are killed along with the pests, the next generation of pests surges

out of control. It can take many years to rebuild a complex self-regulating system if it has been badly disrupted; so organic gardeners try to avoid all pesticides, even those that are less indiscriminately toxic and are organically approved.

By growing a wide variety of plants, especially scapegoat plants that can have pests on them to little detriment, such as honeysuckles, sweet cherries, nettles and lupins (for aphids), we can breed up a background level of predators to control the pests on plants throughout the rest of the garden. Groundcover plants are particularly important for the crawling predators such as beetles, and even strips of rough grass will increase their numbers. We can provide nectar to attract flying insect predators into the garden where in addition to working for us we can also enjoy having them around (see the charts on pages 33, 35, 37 for plants that attract beneficial insects and wildlife).

pollinators Bees are the best known pollinators, but of course hoverflies, flies, butterflies and wasps all visit flowers and pollinate them, as well as being predators. Bumble bees are more important to early flowerers than honey bees, which fly only in warmer weather; some can even be bought commercially in cardboard 'huts' to hang in greenhouses. Beetles are good pollinators in cold, wet conditions when other creatures cannot fly; and many flowers can be pollinated by pests feeding.

Bees and the other pollinators not only pollinate the flowers but also recycle pollen and nectar by generating more bees and pollinators. These then live and die, adding their droppings and bodies to improve soil fertility. This is not an insignificant contribution: a colony of bees has from 30,000 to 100,000 bees in it at any one time and most of these live for only six to eight weeks in summer. Thus a colony loses about 10,000 bees a week to natural death and predators.

recyclers In a sense we are all recyclers: everything living depends on absorbing bits from other now dead things in order to live. Plants build up their materials from air, light, water and the breakdown products of everything else, while everything else breaks down plant materials. The faster the rate of turnover and the more forms of life we can encourage, the more our garden will produce and supply the means of support.

Most of nature's recyclers (such as beetles, snails, and so on) live on or in the soil surface where most things fall at the end of their life. Without them the world would long ago have filled up with nasty, smelly little corpses! These recyclers convert dead and diseased material back into life and plant food. The once living tissues are rapidly broken down into smaller pieces, eaten and digested to become droppings or converted into other forms of life. These processes go on most rapidly in aerated, warm, moist conditions as found under groundcover plants, leaves or mulches. By duplicating these conditions we aid the recyclers with their habitat, and if we supply organic material as a mulch they will rapidly convert it to fertility.

However, the predators are just as keen to eat recyclers as they are to eat pests, so refuges for recyclers are needed. Small piles of rotting logs, rocks or even bricks can be hidden under hedges and evergreens to provide shelters where they can build up numbers. Some recyclers, such as snails, are often regarded more as pests, so these refuges can also act as traps where they can be found and dispatched.

Plants that attract
BENEFICIAL INSECTS & WILDLIFE

LACEWINGS	HOVERFLIES	LADYBIRDS	BEES	BUTTERFLIES	BIRDS

Lovage *Ligusticum levisticum*	
Dill *Anethum graveolens*	
Comfrey *Symphytum officinale*	
Borage *Borago officinalis*	
Poached egg plant *Limnanthes douglasii*	
Foxglove *Digitalis*	
Firethorn *Pyracantha*	
Flowering currant *Ribes*	
Bugle *Ajuga reptans*	
Baby's breath *Gypsophila*	
Catnip *Nepeta*	
Poppy *Papaver orientale*	
Delphinium	
Sunflower *Helianthus*	
Phacelia tanacetifolia	
Tickweed *Coreopsis grandiflora*	
Sea holly *Eryngium*	
Yellow loosestrife *Lysimachia punctata*	
Shasta daisy *Chrysanthemum*	
Marigold *Tagetes*	
Gypsophilia *Gypsophilia paniculata*	
Bergamot *Monarda didyma*	
Alyssum	

above Buddleia is worth growing for the beautiful Peacock butterflies it attracts
below Foxgloves and an old rotting log in front of the wood pile provide shelter for wildlife and an attractive wild corner

creating habitats In order to maximize the number and variety of forms of life in the garden we need to provide for their needs. Creatures exist in their natural habitats: if the niche exists then they will move into it. It is up to us to provide as varied and dense a planting as we can without choking the plants and under and within this to provide shelter and refuges for the creatures to escape from our tidying or to overwinter.

Within each garden create damp corners, warm dry spots, and shady overgrown areas. Avoid over-cleanliness and uniform tidiness. Even a strip of long grass beside a hedge is a surprisingly good habitat and will be found to be full of beetles, spiders and other predators. Nests of dry twiggy material for small creatures can be hidden in every evergreen. Making nest boxes for birds and hedgehogs is very effective in increasing their numbers as in our tidied world natural holes are few.

Extra food is supplied to the recycling system with the organic material and fertilizers we add to the soil; a wide variety of flowers gives nectar over a long period for the pollinators; berries, and in hard winter weather food scraps, provide help for the birds, who are useful allies. All of these need water; make it accessible in many places in ponds, pools and just plastic cups. Especially useful are teasel plants, which have cupped stem/leaf joints that trap a little pool of water.

planting for wildlife Especially good is the butterfly bush *Buddleia davidii*. *Sedum spectabile* is equally well known; goldenrod, lavenders and valerian are nearly as good. Honeysuckles, lilac, marjoram, violas and many other flowers are visited by butterflies, especially flowers with yellow, orange or red colouring. Evening-scented flowers are appealing to moths, which can smell them from further afield in the still moist air.

Bees do not use their sense of smell much and tend to go for blue or white flowers. Amongst the best bee plants are: alliums, arabis, campanulas, clovers, cotoneasters, delphinium, echinops, hyssop, lavenders, lemon balm, *Limnanthes douglasii* (poached egg flower), mints, myosotis, nepeta, papaver, rosemary, salvias and thyme. Brassicas gone to seed, raspberries and lime trees are also loved by bees. Bumble bees like much the same flowers but go especially for deadnettle, comfrey, flowering currants, fuchsias, globe artichokes, jasmine, knapweeds, mallows, Michaelmas daisies, thistles and wallflowers.

Without any doubt, if you want to attract birds grow fruit: redcurrants and cherries disappear fastest, but hardly any fruit ever makes it to the new year. Berries of any sort are similarly appreciated, though yellow ones confuse them for a short time before disappearing rapidly. Seeding plants, especially sunflowers and wheat, will attract and feed them and some heads can be saved for winter. All dense growing hedges, evergreens and climbers favour birds by providing lots of useful nooks and crannies for nest building and shelter.

plants, their types, natures & needs

Plants are the most important forms of life on the planet: without them nothing much else would be able to survive. They are equally the most important part of a garden.

annuals and perennials

annuals live, flower and die in a short period, usually from spring to autumn. They are some of the prettiest flowers and their rapid growth makes them useful for filling gaps. Generally annuals are best sown in situ. They resent root disturbance and can normally be propagated only from seed. Many vegetables, such as tomatoes, sweetcorn, peas and beans, are the fruits or seeds of annuals. In practice, many perennial flowers are treated as annuals – discarded or killed by the frosts and replaced with fresh ones the following year.

biennials live longer, they grow one year to flower the next. Many vegetables, including root crops and onions, are in fact biennials that are eaten before they complete their cycle. Some of the most attractive flowers are biennials – long spikes such as foxgloves and hollyhocks and sweet-scented flowers such as wallflowers and stocks. Some biennial plants may live for another season or two before dying but it is usual to replace them with freshly sown stock. They can easily be moved when they are dormant.

perennials can live for many years, though some are quite short-lived. Those that spread with creeping roots continually form new plants, so may perhaps be said to be immortal. Apart from those it is the trees that tend to live longest. Perennials are semi-permanent, do not need annual replacement, and their established root systems help them to endure poor conditions. Most can be moved when they are young, but increasingly resent it as they grow older and larger. Often it is easier to propagate and plant a new one than move an old one. Perennials can be divided into those with soft growth that dies back in winter, and those with shrubby or woody growth that endures the winter and regrows each year.

soft perennials put out new growth from the roots and are mostly propagated by root division. Herbaceous plants form larger clumps each year but do not grow taller. They need no pruning – only a tidy-up in the autumn.

woody and shrubby perennials grow larger each year and may need pruning in order to control their size. They are mostly propa-

Plants that attract
BENEFICIAL INSECTS & WILDLIFE

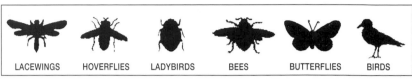

LACEWINGS HOVERFLIES LADYBIRDS BEES BUTTERFLIES BIRDS

	LACEWINGS	HOVERFLIES	LADYBIRDS	BEES	BUTTERFLIES	BIRDS
Arabis				✶		
Campanula				✶		
Clover *Trifolium*				✶		
Forget-me-not *Myosotis*		✶				
Dead-nettle *Lamium album*				✶		
Rosemary *Rosemarinus*				✶		
Yarrow *Achillea millefolium*	✶	✶	✶	✶		
Fennel *Foeniculum vulgare*	✶	✶	✶			
Angelica	✶					
Anthemis	✶					
Bergenia				✶		
Buddleia davidii		✶			✶	
Marigold *Calendula*		✶	✶			
Centaurea				✶		
Convolvulus tricolor		✶	✶			
Cosmos	✶	✶	✶			
Echinops ritro				✶		
Eschscholzia		✶				
Hyssop				✶		
Lavender *Lavandula*				✶		
Grape hyacinth *Muscari*		✶				
Rudbeckia				✶		
Goldenrod *Solidago*	✶	✶	✶			

The mixed border in midsummer shows shasta daisies, bergamot and phlox in bloom while trees and other perennials provide structure during the winter months

gated from cuttings or layering, though some need grafting onto suitable rootstocks. Shrubby perennials grown from seed may be variable and slow to flower or fruit.

deciduous/evergreen While herbaceous plants overwinter protected by the soil, most woody plants drop their leaves in autumn and go partially dormant, which protects them from hard weather. This is generally a good time to prune or move them, as they recover much better than when moved in leaf. Although they appear totally dormant some processes continue, and unless the soil is frozen they start rooting immediately.

Evergreens drop their leaves a few at a time and suffer badly in hard weather from drying winds and frozen soil. Moisture is sucked out of their leaves and cannot be replaced, leaving scorched foliage which is sometimes fatal. They have evolved waxy coatings which prevents water loss from the leaves and this is partly why these are slow

to break down. The dense cover they provide makes excellent winter shelter for ladybirds and other predators large and small, so include some evergreens in different parts of the garden as refuges. Most evergreens are best moved in early spring once the soil has warmed enough for them to regrow their root system quickly: they are never dormant.

tender/hardy Plants that can stand in the open and survive some degrees of frost are considered hardy. Hardy annuals are a large group of flowers, grown from seed each year, which do not need protection and can be sown in situ once the soil warms up in spring. Most can also be sown in the autumn and overwintered to provide an earlier display.

Most garden perennials are effectively very hardy and in favourable positions survive many years unless there is an extremely harsh winter. Given a very good position against a wall some surprising plants, such as Opuntia prickly pear cacti, passion flowers and palms, can be grown successfully, especially if the roots are protected in the worst frosts. Similarly, other less hardy plants such as fuchsias and lemon verbena can be brought through bad weather by mulching the roots thickly with straw or loose, airy material; the tops die back but the roots can shoot in spring.

Plants that have been grown hard, with strong but not too vigorous growth, tend to stand frost and temperature change better than plants grown soft or lushly. Never feed plants heavily in late summer or autumn as this promotes soft growth that does not ripen well and is then prone to disease as well as frost damage. Most plants are more frost-resistant if they are not wet at the roots: well-drained soil and a warmth-retaining mulch protects roots against many degrees of frost.

Often frost is not the killer when it damages plants: it is the warm, damp period that follows it that encourages rotting and finishes them off. This is one reason why dry spots, as at the base of a wall, shelter plants so well. For silver- and hairy-leaved plants, rotting is the main problem. They survive almost any weather if the rain is kept off with a cloche or just a sheet of glass on two bricks.

Plants suffer shock and their growth is set back by changes of temperature, which should be kept as gradual as possible. Plants that are to be moved to a colder position can be hardened off by putting them outside in the day and bringing them in at night for a few days. Similarly, do not move plants from outside to a hot room in one go: allow them to adapt gradually.

half-hardy is a term usually applied to bedding plants which need to be sown in warmth and hardened off before being planted out after the last frosts in spring. Tender plants die with the least touch of frost and do badly if at all cold. Stovehouse plants require real heat. They were popular with the Victorians, but most are now considered unsuitable except as houseplants or for well-heated conservatories.

establishing plants

Watering is the most important part of establishing plants, especially for the slower-growing ones. Fast-growing annuals sown in situ with enough soil moisture initially fend for themselves. At the other extreme, for a large, newly transplanted, woody plant, watering may be essential right through the first season of growth, while it builds up a root system in the soil. Herbaceous plants fall between these extremes. Provided they are moved when they are dormant they can usually look after themselves. Even so, they will benefit from watering during early dry periods.

Generally, unless you live in a wet or waterlogged area, it is better to water all woody transplants during their first season of growth, to water herbaceous plants during any dry period early in their first season, and to water seedlings well before and after they are planted out. Mulches help immensely. They retain moisture, suppress weeds, and aid quick establishment: but they must be put on early to retain winter moisture.

transplanting and planting

Transplanting is used to describe the process of moving plants growing in the soil from one place to another. Planting usually means putting into the soil plants that have arrived with bare roots from a nursery or that have been grown in pots. Usually, only vegetables and bedding plants are transplanted while

Given the right position, some surprisingly tender plants do well in a temperate climate. This pair of *Cordelyne australis* are protected in winter

they are still growing strongly (see page 132). Most other plants are better moved while they are dormant.

In either case, the bigger the rootball and associated soil that can be transferred undisturbed the better – undisturbed, that is, unless the plant is rootbound. Plants become rootbound by being confined too long in too small a container – their roots then encircle themselves, preventing effective outgrowth. In such cases, tease out the roots and plant them spread out in the soil as for bare-rooted plants.

If plants have been out of the soil for a long time, or have dried out, the roots need a good soak for a few hours before planting; always keep them covered to prevent sun-scorch and drying, especially in strong winds. If they have been under cover or in a protected environment they need to be hardened off. Check them over and remove any badly damaged roots or shoots. Some gardeners cut back woody plants very hard when planting them, to encourage strong regrowth. I find it is better for most plants to let them establish themselves for a year first, and to prune them back once they have developed good roots.

To establish a plant the soil needs to be firmed around each root: roots need a good grip to force their tips into the surrounding soil. Too wet is as bad as too dry or frosted: the soil must be friable and moist. Water a planting hole well beforehand, but always let the water drain away before planting. If it drains slowly, help the drainage under the plant by breaking up the subsoil in the bottom of the hole. Always try to dig a generous hole to give the roots a free run. It will also break up existing root systems and aerate the soil, stimulating the microlife. This encourages the plant to reroot quickly, but the microlife needs raw materials to convert, so mix compost and rock dusts in with the planting soil. Then add a mulch to keep the soil weed-free, moist, warm and alive while the plant reroots and establishes.

propagation
The best, most vigorous plants are produced from seed, especially when they are sown in situ and so never disturbed. But to do this is often inconvenient, especially if they are slow-growing, so most plants are started off in pots or in a nursery bed and planted out when they are large enough to survive in their final position. Vegetables are the plants most commonly sown (see page 117).

Growing from seed has one major drawback: the best varieties of perennial plants cannot normally be propagated in that way. To come true, they have to be vegatatively propagated – from cuttings, layers, grafts, buds or root division. These are slow processes but quicker to produce results than from seed.

hardwood cuttings
For many woody plants the simplest way to propagate is with cuttings taken in the autumn. These have the summer's energy stored away, and cleanly cut 15-25cm (6-10in) young shoots root easily. Cuttings from the nodes in a stem are usually the ones best able to heal and root. Cut them close below a node at the bottom. A few plants, such as clematis, are best cut between nodes. Remove lower buds unless, as for blackcurrants, you want many shoots from the ground to form a 'stool'. Firm the cuttings in a slit trench with sharp sand in the bottom, keep them moist, shelter them from the worst of the weather, and they will be ready for planting out the next autumn.

Cuttings of some less hardy plants, such as rosemary and lavender, will not stand hard winter storage as cuttings, but can be rooted succesfully if taken in mid spring. 'Lazy cuttings' are best for this – small shoots pulled off with a tiny heel of old wood.

softwood cuttings
'Soft' cuttings are taken in summer from the fresh young growth and would wither before rooting unless given the special conditions which a propagator can provide. They need warmth underneath, moist air, and shading (with a sheet of paper) to prevent them from being scorched in strong sunlight.

Soft cuttings are shoots of current growth.

It is usual to leave a pair of leaves and to remove two or three pairs to give a short, bare stem to firm into a sterile medium. Sharp sand in pots is excellent as it is well aerated and the grittiness helps rooting, but the cuttings must be potted into potting compost to continue to grow. The cuttings form smaller plants than autumn cuttings but take more readily. In spring they can be planted out into a nursery bed or potted up.

layering Layering is used for plants that do not take easily from either sort of cuttings. Simply bury the shoot in the soil while it is still attached to the parent and it will root. Better still, damage the bark, and peg down the shoot in moist soil with added sharp sand until it roots. Once it has taken (usually by the following autumn) you can detach and plant it.

root division This is used to propagate most herbaceous plants. These plants grow into large clumps which become poor in the middle. The technique with these is to dig them up, divide the vigorous perimeter into chunks for replanting, and discard the impoverished centre. If you want a large number of new plants, every segment of root with a bud, replanted in fresh ground, will form a new plant. Often the clumps merely need to be split into two.

pruning This is better left undone than done badly. For most woody plants, the less pruning the better, although for some, especially trained fruit trees, some careful pruning is absolutely essential (*see page 151 for fruit trees*). Apart from the special method for fruit trees, prune out only diseased, unhealthy, rubbing or ingrowing shoots, and shoots that are getting in the way or stealing light. Remember that growth is soon replaced, so tends to grow back just where it was. The ideal is to take out buds that point in the wrong direction long before they become shoots.

When pruning, leave one healthy bud or shoot to draw the sap or cut off the growth flush where it springs from: never leave a

snag of wood with no bud. A snag will die back and give somewhere for rot to take hold, so cut as close above a bud as possible.

Most plants can cope with being pruned lightly at any time that you spot a problem; they can lose up to a quarter of their leaf area before they suffer greatly. Do not wait until the right time – cut out problems before they grow larger. Heavy pruning, where a quarter of the old growth or more is removed, is best done when the plant is dormant. However, stone fruits and ornamentals related to plums are best pruned only in spring and summer to avoid silver leaf disease. Most soft fruit should be hard pruned after midsummer to promote fruiting.

Younger plants recover far better from heavy pruning than old, and young growths better than old. Never cut into old growths that have no new buds as, like snags, they rarely resprout. There are a few exceptions, such as privet, yew and quickthorn, which often grow again from mere stumps. Before pruning a plant which is making poor growth, stimulate it for a year with watering, compost and a mulch to give it vigorous roots.

Spring growth from well pruned raspberry canes promise an excellent crop

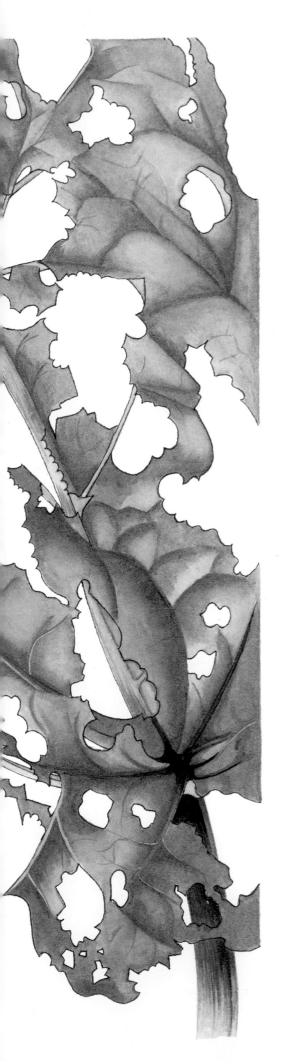

3 PESTS & DISEASES
in an organic garden

The conventional solution to the problem of pests and diseases relies heavily on the routine use of sprays which drench plants and soil with chemical poisons. But organic gardeners have a very different approach. They try to help plants to resist attacks in the first place, by manipulating the natural system of checks and balances in their favour. Pesticides, even organic ones, are used only as a last resort. We should expect to have pests in our gardens – and some are needed to feed the predators which the organic system encourages. The aim of the organic gardener is *control*, not elimination, using wit and cunning to make life difficult for pests and diseases, so that plants and crops thrive in spite of spite them. Healthy plants should be able to endure minor infestations in much the same way that healthy human beings can shrug off a cold. Commercial pesticides are used mainly to protect the appearance of crops, not to protect the actual yields. When growing produce for home consumption minor blemishes are acceptable to most people.

In addition to building up self-regulating systems you will occasionally need to take direct action – and the earlier it is taken the more effective it will be. All gardeners should make a regular inspection of their plants, trees and bushes so that small infestations can be spotted and dealt with before they have spread.

It is a good idea to keep things in proportion, and not become a plant hypochondriac. The prime cause of loss in the garden is bad weather.

Slugs and snails feed on a wide range of plants. Seedlings are destroyed completely and leaves shredded. Watch out for tell-tale slime trail in warm, wet weather. To minimize damage, try some of the following techniques. Cover plants with plastic bottle cloches or surround with dry sawdust or ashes. Trap in slug pubs (see page 51). Encourage birds and frogs which eat them. Lay out old lettuce leaves as bait and pick them off at night, using a torch

43

Bad practice, such as overcrowding and poor weed control, comes a close second. Pests come third in the ranking, with birds worst of all – they eat seeds, seedlings, leaves, fruits and buds. In some areas two-legged pests are the next greatest source of damage and loss, followed by slugs and snails. Most other pests and diseases are far less common or troublesome than these!

What must also be considered is the economics, in time, cash and labour, of any measure in relation to the increase in yield returned. For example, flea beetles make shot holes in radish and brassica seedlings: maintaining moist conditions reduces their damage and is worthwhile, but spraying with derris may cost more than a radish crop is worth. Similarly, pheromone traps for codling moths are expensive. With one tree the extra fruit saved may not be worth it; with four or five trees near each other it may be worthwhile. In an orchard of twenty trees where four traps would be required the extra clean fruit may not be needed.

control measures

There are many different approaches to reducing pests and diseases: few problems are solved with just one measure, but by a combination of several. They are presented here in order of minimum intervention: passive methods first and the least ecologically acceptable left until last.

good husbandry Using good methods is 95 per cent of organic gardening. Plants want to grow, and will if we give them the right conditions. So organic gardeners should choose plants that are suited to their local conditions, and avoid those that present obvious problems. For example, it is pretty daft to try to grow watermelons in a temperate climate such as the UK (I know, I keep trying), or to grow rhododendrons on chalk, or cauliflowers in hot, dry, sandy soil. Grow plants suited to your soil and climate and they will have a good chance of success.

Healthy plants overcome minor problems – and for health they require steady, continuous growth rather than stop-go conditions. Never check the growth of your plants by allowing them to become potbound, crowded, dried out, cooked, frozen or choked. Any check to their growth reduces yield, and may lead to disease. Crops grown in season always do better than early or late sowings. It is also daft to try to grow fruit out of season, such as strawberries in winter (another of my follies).

Of all the checks to growth, water imbalance is probably the most common. Dessicated plants will die, but if they even reach wilt point they will be severely checked. Waterlogging can be equally serious, especially in cold, low-light conditions. Plants in containers are as often sickened by overwatering in winter and spring as they are by drought in summer. Dry roots and damp or stagnant air inevitably lead to mildews and botrytis rots, especially for roses and climbers on walls.

Air and light are also very important factors in preventing infection: each plant must be given sufficient space. Never crowd plants – grow a few well rather than many poorly. Vigorous and woody plants need pruning or tying, not only to allow in air and light, but also to allow access to useful predators.

hygiene Regular inspection of all parts of the garden, followed by prompt action to remove infected material will significantly reduce further pest and disease attacks. For example, the removal of any infested tips controls aphid attacks on broad beans. Similarly, coral spot is a common disease of woody plants; prompt removal of infected branches prevents its spread. All diseased and infested material should be immediately burnt or deeply buried. Secateurs, saws and knives should be sterilized with surgical spirit to prevent cross-infection.

Take care not to introduce any problems with bought-in plants, manures or dirty tools. It is always a good idea to keep new plants in isolation for a week or two before putting them with others, just to see if any problems develop. Never buy soil-grown brassica plants because of the danger of clubroot. There is no need to become over-fastidious though: a small level of pest infestation is necessary to maintain predator populations. With manures, always make sure that it is well composted before use. This will help to get rid of some chemical contaminants. Avoid manures from farms that use intensive rearing methods as there will be contaminants from the feed or from drugs or hormones administered to the animals – pig and poultry manure from intensive farms should be particularly avoided. Mushroom compost should also be avoided as it is likely to be contaminated with persistent chemicals.

variety

Organic gardeners believe that growing a wide variety of plants creates a diverse ecosystem which prevents the build-up of pests and diseases. Where there is only one crop any problems are easily spread. Where plants are mixed and intercropped it is harder for an initial infection to occur, and much harder for it to spread. Having a wide variety within a particular crop also helps, as the varieties will mature at different times, and may be more or less susceptible to different pests and diseases in any season. This greatly reduces the risk of total loss and also spreads the workload at harvest.

resistant varieties

In many ways the plants we grow have been selected because they are inherently trouble-free, but few cultivars are immune to all pests and diseases. The more important crops are grown most frequently, and thus have acquired the most pests and diseases to bother them. For these important crops much research has been done to find varieties resistant to the most common ailments. Most success has been against diseases. For example, there are blackspot-resistant roses, scab-resistant apples and canker-resistant parsnips. Pests are harder to discourage, but there are lettuces resistant to root aphids, and blackcurrants resistant to leaf midge. However, choosing resistant varieties may entail some loss of flavour or quality in comparison with other varieties.

cultivation methods

Rotation is the most important of these methods – move

PESTS & DISEASES
recognition & direct action

Some pests and diseases attack any plant, whether it is fruit, vegetable or ornamental, while others only attack specific types of plant, such as fruit bushes. Many pests can be controlled by companion planting, and by attracting natural predators, while an increasing number can now be controlled by biological methods. Growing healthy plants will help combat diseases, and there are also organic sprays for some, if all else fails.

the plant each season, and pests and diseases overwintering in the soil emerge to find their target has gone. The same applies to replant disease: never replace a dead shrubby plant with another of the same. Rotation also changes and modifies the conditions in the soil, ensuring that fewer pests or disease spores survive until the crop returns.

timing can also be important. As mentioned above, plants grown in season are the healthiest and survive most diseases, but there can be an advantage in early or late sowing if the crop thus misses the worst attacks. In most years, early potatoes are out of the ground before blight becomes a problem.

FIREBLIGHT: Bacterial disease that affects various trees and shrubs. Cankers appear at base of dead shoots and red-brown discoloration appears inside. Causes dieback or browning of leaves. ACTION: cut out diseased wood to a point 60cm (2ft) below affected tissues. Disinfect pruning tools after use.

45

CELERY FLY: *The larvae tunnel through leaves, and the holes dry up to give a scorched look. A bad attack can stunt growth and make celery tough. Flies emerge in spring to lay eggs on leaves – there are 3 generations a year.* **ACTION**: *Grow plants under protective netting or fine fleece. Pick off infested leaves or squash larvae.*

Overwintered broad beans are usually too tough early in the season for black aphids to bother them. Early sown carrots miss the root fly especially if harvested early, late sown ones may also do so.

Indoor or under-cover propagation can help to give plants a better early or late start and thus escape attacks, but can also prevent them entirely by isolating the crop during its more vulnerable stage. Beetroot sown in the open can be razed to the ground by birds, but survive if planted out when they are bigger. Accurate sowing and indoor propagation also avoid the need for thinning, which can attract pests by spreading the plants' scent, as happens with carrot root fly or onion fly.

summer pruning of shrubby plants is beneficial because it controls growth and so encourages flowering and fruiting. It can simultaneously remove a developing pest population, especially aphids, as these cluster on tips.

rake aside heavy mulches put down in the autumn during the winter months. This will disturb many pests which may be hibernating – they are either killed directly or through exposure to the birds. This is especially useful against gooseberry sawfly and raspberry beetle. A heavy mulch applied before regrowth in

CATERPILLARS *(cabbage moth): Large plump caterpillars feed on leaves and bore into the hearts of cabbages and lettuce. Watch out when you see the white butterflies which lay eggs on the underside of leaves.* **ACTION**: *pick off caterpillars by hand. Grow plants under fine netting or fleece. Spray with bacteria Bacillus thuringiensis which kills caterpillars but is harmless to humans.*

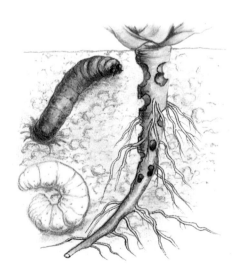

CUTWORMS: *Moth caterpillars which live in the soil. They feed at night on the soil surface, eating young plants at soil level and also attacking stems and roots of vegetables and strawberries.* **ACTION**: *protect individual plants with collars. Regular hoeing and winter digging will expose them to birds. Can be picked by hand at night, using a torch.*

ONION FLY: *Looks like a small house fly. Attacks onions, shallots and leeks. Lays eggs near base of seedlings – maggots bore into young bulbs, causing foliage to turn yellow.* **ACTION**: *remove infected plants to reduce spread; dig infected land over winter to destroy larvae. Grow seedlings under fine net or fleece.*

WIREWORMS: *Larvae of the click beetle which lays eggs in grass or weedy soil. Attack stems and tubers of many vegetables, including onions, potatoes, carrots, peas, beans. More of a problem on old pasture land.* **ACTION**: *keep land cultivated, to expose them to birds. Catch them on small pieces of carrot or potato spiked on sticks and buried. Renew regularly.*

spring seals spores and infective material beneath it. This is recommended for most plants, and is particularly effective against blackspot on roses.

seaweed sprays are applied to boost growth and are also very good for reducing pest and disease problems. They do not act directly as pesticides but aid the plants to make resilient, vigorous growth that throws off attacks. The smell of seaweed may also help by confusing pests.

hide-and-seek companion plants

As mentioned above, mixtures of plants are less bothered by pests than mono-cultures, but we can also use companions such as the aromatic herbs deliberately to camouflage or disguise the scent of the crop. French marigolds are particularly effective – they not only hide other plants but actually discourage and poison pests. They discourage whitefly from coming into the greenhouse and they kill nematodes. Similarly, in the USA nightshades are grown with potatoes to poison Colorado beetles. I use golden feverfew for its strong scent and cheerful appearance. Most of the daisy family of *Compositae* seem helpful in this way, as well as being pretty. Many gardeners believe that companion plants such as nettles and alliums can help prevent fungal and bacterial attacks to other plants. Chives and garlic are traditionally grown under roses and fruit for this purpose.

sacrificial crops

are plants grown to attract pests away from the main planting. They may be the same plant grown around the perimeter, or a more attractive lure. For example, redcurrants will keep birds off the blackcurrants. In the same way, if you shred surplus leaves or seedlings when transplanting and spread the mixture around the transplants, it will fob off slugs.

Trap plants are similar to sacrificials. For example, sweet tobaccos, especially *Nicotiana sylvestris*, have sticky stems and leaves and are very attractive to whitefly and thrips. Growing these among other plants draws pests which can then be further 'stuck on' with a sugar solution spray and removed with the plant.

APPLE SAWFLY: Cocoons in soil hatch out in spring and adult flies lay eggs in open blossom. Larvae tunnel into fruitlets, feeding on flesh and seeds. Affected fruitlets drop early, while mature fruit has characteristic ribbon scarring. ACTION: spray with derris at petal fall. Pick up and destroy infected fruitlets immediately you see scarring.

PEAR MIDGE: Females lay eggs in unopened flower buds. Larvae hatch out within developing fruitlet. After petal fall fruitlets turn black and drop. Maggots then crawl into soil to pupate. ACTION: collect and compost all fallen fruitlets. Remove affected fruitlets as soon as noticed. Dig over soil near affected trees over winter to expose cocoons for birds.

CODLING MOTH: Affects mainly apples, pears and quinces. Causes traditional maggot in the apple. Adults hatch from cocoons in midsummer to lay eggs in leaves or fruit. Caterpillars tunnel into maturing fruit and feed for several weeks before pupating. ACTION: hang pheromone traps in the trees. The trap contains sticky paper with substance exuded by female which attracts male moths.

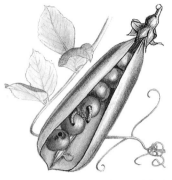

PEA MOTH: Caterpillars live and feed inside pea pods. Moth lays eggs midsummer on pea plants in flower. Caterpillars eat their way into developing pod. ACTION: Sow peas early and late to avoid midsummer flowering when the moths are laying. Dig over infested soil in winter to disturb pupating caterpillars. Protect plants with fine netting or fleece while in flower. Spray with derris after flowering.

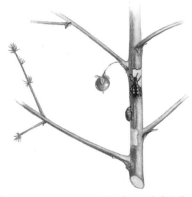

ASPARAGUS BEETLE: Beetles and their larvae feed on foliage and stems from late spring onwards. Persistent attacks may check growth. ACTION: Clear plant debris from bed in autumn as beetles overwinter there. Spray infected plants with liquid derris or dust leaves with derris powder.

CARROT FLY: Larvae feed on roots of carrot and other root vegetables. Seedlings may be killed, older plants have stunted growth. Roots are tunnelled through with white larvae inside. Fly overwinters in soil and in roots left in ground. ACTION: Sow early spring or midsummer to avoid fly. Grow carrots under fine netting or fleece, or erect a barrier of fine netting about 75cm (30in) high around plot. Lift any infested plants at once.

predator & parasite encouragement

Building up self-regulating ecosystems means making good provision for predators – plants for nectar, fruits and pollen; shelter on the large and small scale; sites for nests and hibernation quarters; a water supply; and sacrificial plants to breed up pests on which the predators and parasites can be maintained. Companion plants that encourage predators should ideally keep flowering throughout the whole season and particularly early on. Not all flowers are equally useful though: deep-throated ones intended for moths and butterflies, and double flowers specially bred for their beauty at the cost of nectar are less effective.

hoverflies are probably the most important beneficial insect and are attracted to *Limnanthes douglasii* in particular. This can be grown to advantage as a self-seeding annual under roses, shrubs and fruit. See the charts on pages 33, 35 and 37 for the many other plants that attract hoverflies. Ladybirds, lacewings and predatory wasps are attracted to much the same flowers as hoverflies but also like alliums, anthemis, fennel and yarrow. Aphids can be encouraged on patches of nettles, honeysuckles, sweet cherries, and lupins, which then maintain a background level of predators and parasites.

ground-cover plants encourage ground beetles, slow-worms, lizards, newts, frogs and toads, all of which will eat slugs, snails and other pests. These are further encouraged with water and nest sites. Plastic containers, old flowerpots and similar containers can be part buried in moist, hidden spots under evergreens, hedges or dense shrubs.

birds are most easily increased by the provision of nesting boxes as suitable sites are now rare. It is important to encourage the most useful birds: blue tits, great tits, tree sparrows and other small insectivorous birds need little wooden boxes about 13-15cm (5-6in) all round with a hole at the front of 4cm (1 ½in). Robins, wagtails and flycatchers prefer the box to have a bigger opening, of 5 × 7.5cm (2 × 3in). These resemble natural nesting holes and should be fixed to trees where cats and other predators cannot get at them. Put them where

STEM EELWORM: *Attacks a wide range of fruit, vegetables and ornamentals. On onions and leeks leaves swell and distort and bulbs crack and rot. Eelworm survives in soil for a considerable time.* **ACTION:** *no cure for infected plants which should be burned. Grow only brassicas and lettuce on infested plot for next 2 years and keep weed-free.*

EARWIGS: *These attack fruit trees, especially apples, and also flowers, but they do eat codling moth eggs and woolly aphids.* **ACTION:** *if they are a problem, trap in bamboo canes, or in flower pots filled with straw and propped on canes upside down.*

CUCUMBER MOSAIC VIRUS: *Affects cucurbits, particularly marrows. Diseased plants are stunted and have puckered, distorted leaves with mottled yellow patches.* **ACTION:** *destroy plant immediately to prevent disease spreading. Spread by aphids, so encourage predators by planting marigolds and nasturtiums in the vegetable garden.*

CABBAGE ROOT FLY: *Larvae eat roots, causing stunted, wilting plants. They overwinter as shiny brown cocoons in soil and emerge to lay eggs around plants.* **ACTION:** *Grow plants under fine netting or fleece, or lay 13cm (5in) square mats of carpet underlay around plants, fitting snugly around stems. Intercrop with beans in alternate rows, to confuse pests (plants should be same size when planted out). Dig over soil in winter after infected crop.*

SCALE INSECTS: *Small flat insects that attach themselves to fruit and other trees, vines, and ornamental plants under glass. Suck sap from plants and smear leaves with sticky honeydew which encourages growth of sooty mould.* **ACTION:** *spray with insecticidal soap and purchase the predatory wasp Metaphycus helvolus.*

RASPBERRY CANE MIDGE: *Adults emerge from soil late spring, early summer and lay eggs in cracks and crevices of canes. Larvae feed for a month. Cane blight often invades damaged area, causing canes to die back.* **ACTION:** *Spray base of canes with derris in mid-spring. Hoe around base of canes overwinter to expose pupae to birds.*

you can watch from a window, except those for the robins, which like the boxes to be well hidden away in shrubs or hedges. Many other birds, such as blackbirds and thrushes, find ample nest sites in dense evergreens or thick hedges. Birds are also encouraged by providing water, by feeding them scraps on a bird table, and by fitting berry-carrying shrubs into the garden design.

hedgehogs need somewhere dry where they can hibernate undisturbed. A wooden box about 30-45cm (12-18in) square is ideal, but a cardboard box may do if well insulated and put under the floor of a garden shed or other protected place. You will need to provide an entrance and a bowl of water. Hedgehogs should not be given bread and milk as it is not good for them; cat and dog food or pilchards are much better.

direct action Hand picking is effective against many pests. Gooseberry sawfly or cabbage caterpillars, for example, can be dealt with in this way, and many minor infestations can be squeezed with finger and thumb. Slugs and snails come out on warm, wet evenings. They tend to return to the same site, so they can be spotted with a torch and picked off. Battery-operated vacuum cleaners are excellent for rounding up flying insects such as whitefly or flea beetles which jump when disturbed. Using the jet from a hose pipe, you can knock aphids and other pests off plants; some may return but many will not. This works well in combination with sticky bands .

barriers & traps Many simple mechanical methods can be used to exclude pests and reduce their numbers. These cause little harm to the environment and many can be made from recycled materials.

nets are the best way of protecting fruit. A complete cage is best and makes economic sense, but any pieces of net can be used to protect a branch or two and can be held in place with clothes pegs. The netting bags that fruit and nuts come in are good for individual fruits and bunches; nylon stocking feet do as well. Whole stockings or tights can be pulled over long branches of fruit such as redcurrants.

PEACH LEAF CURL: Leaves become thickened and curl, and red blisters develop, covered with fungus spores. Leaves fall early and tree is weakened. Fungus overwinters in bark or on shoots. ACTION: spray with Bordeaux mixture in late winter/early spring to prevent spores entering buds. Repeat 10-14 days later and again just before leaf fall. On fans or espaliers erect a polythene cover in early spring to keep off rain, which carries spores. This reduces infection considerably.

BOTRYTIS: Common greenhouse problem, affecting grapes, strawberries, cucumbers, tomatoes and lettuce. Affected plants covered with grey-brown velvety fungus. Thrives in cold, damp conditions. ACTION: remove dead leaves and overripe fruits to avoid infection. Ventilate well to reduce humidity – water morning, not night. Be sparing with fertilizers and avoid over-watering.

 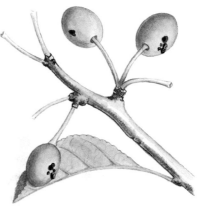

WASPS: These only become a pest in high summer and early autumn, damaging fruit. Worse in hot, dry summers when the numbers increase. ACTION: Fill jam-jars with sugary water, or jam and water and cover with paper, with a hole in the middle. Hang in the trees – wasps crawl in and drown. You can also use a bottle with a pierced foil cap.

PLUM SAWFLY: Similar to apple sawfly. Fly lays eggs in open blossoms and larvae then tunnel into fruitlets, eating fruit and seeds. Unlike apple, attack does not cause distinctive scarring of skin. Damaged fruitlets drop prematurely. ACTION: Collect and compost all fallen fruitlets. Spray trees with derris at petal fall to kill caterpillars. Hoe under trees to expose pupae to birds.

RED SPIDER MITE: Normally a greenhouse pest, but can also attack strawberries, raspberries and currants in hot weather. Undersurfaces of leaves are bronzed, older leaves are withered or crisp. You can see greenish mites with a magnifying glass. ACTION: Cut off all leaves after fruit is harvested. Introduce biological control Phytoseulis persimilis into greenhouse.

RASPBERRY BEETLE: Adults feed on blossom in late spring. Larvae tunnel into ripening fruit – often not noticed until fruit is picked. Overwinter in soil near canes. ACTION: lightly hoe soil near canes during autumn/winter to expose pupae to birds. Spray with derris when fruit turns pink.

MILDEWS, downy and powdery: Pale grey fungus forms on leaves, flowers and young shoots. Affects many ornamentals, including roses. Downy mildew affects vines and vegetables. ACTION: Both thrive in humid, overcrowded conditions. Remove and burn affected leaves. Spray with Bordeaux mixture.

Fine mesh bags can exclude wasps as well as birds, but may encourage mould or botrytis.

Fine netting, woven fleeces and punctured plastic sheets can all be used to keep pests off vegetables as well as fruits and are very effective at preventing carrot root fly attacks. This fly is about the size of a housefly. It has to lay its eggs next to the seedling, so a barrier gives 100 per cent control. The same materials can also be used to protect cabbages from root flies and butterfly caterpillars, and to keep birds off beetroot and salad crops. Carrot root flies can be stopped by a simple barrier or netting. Anything 60-90cm (2-3ft) high around small beds stops the fly, which will go round rather than over.

carpet squares Cabbage root flies need to lay their eggs in the soil next to the stem. A barrier made of 13cm (5in) squares of old carpet, tarred roofing felt or cardboard fitting snugly around the stem, will seal the soil underneath and prevent access.

Carpet can be used to seal larger areas, trapping insect pests underneath when they emerge from hibernation or their pupae. This can considerably reduce infestations of gooseberry sawfly, raspberry beetle and pear midge. Carpet laid on a wet lawn will bring leather-

PLUM RUST: Can also attack apricots, peaches and nectarines. Fungus disease causes yellow spots on upper side of leaves and brown or orange pustules on lower surfaces. ACTION: rake up and burn fallen leaves to reduce infection. Reduce susceptibility of tree by feeding, mulching and watering. In dry weather ensure that soil does not dry out completely.

RUST: Affects a wide range of plants. Leaves and stems develop red, brown or yellow pustules. Leaves may wither and die and whole plant may wilt. ACTION: remove and burn affected leaves. Destroy severely affected plants. Spray plants with sulphur. Under glass improve ventilation to reduce humidity and make sure droplets don't remain on leaves.

BACTERIAL CANKER: Serious disease of plums. Elongated cankers on branches exude gum and leaves have brown, circular spots. Buds fail to open on cankered branches and if leaves do develop they yellow and die as branch dies back. ACTION: affected wood should be cut out and burned. Bacteria live in the leaves, so spray with Bordeaux mixture in midsummer, and again in early and mid-autumn.

CHOCOLATE SPOT: Affects broad beans. Small dark spots and streaks develop on stems and leaves. In wet spring affected plants may blacken and die. ACTION: lime plot to give pH of 7. Spray with copper fungicide at first sign of trouble. Burn diseased plants at end of season to prevent fungus overwintering.

jackets and other soil pests to the surface overnight. They can be swept up or left to the birds in the morning.

bands Cloth bands, carpet bands and corrugated cardboard bands tied round trunks and stems simulate shredding bark and attract many insects. Examine your catch: the beneficial ladybirds can be retained to continue work in the garden while the pests are evicted.

earwig traps Many creatures, especially earwigs, will crawl into hollow bamboo tubes and can then be blown out into a bucket. Earwigs are especially attracted to straw-filled flowerpots on sticks.

sticky bands prevent pests from climbing up tree trunks, which few predators need to do. They are especially effective against the female winter moth (which cannot fly), earwigs and ants. Ants farm aphids, moving them to tender shoots and milking them for honeydew. A sticky band reduces aphid populations as the ants cannot tend and protect them. Sticky bands can be applied to the bark of old trees but on young bark are better on top of a foil strip as the sticky material may soak in.

sticky boards and flypapers are especially good in the greenhouse where they trap many pests, especially whitefly and thrips. Different colours attract different insects: white attracts sawfly; blue attracts thrips; and yellow attracts whitefly. They are even more effective if they are given a pheromone scent. Hung in the trees these are a very good way of reducing codling moth and plum fruit moth attacks.

wasp traps Wasps are beneficial in the early part of the season as they hunt other insects in great numbers: but when they turn their attention to fruit they should be trapped. A bottle half-full of water and jam should be given a foil cap pierced with a small hole that allows the wasps to crawl in but not to fly out. Do not use these traps near flowers or with honey, as bees may also then be lured in.

slug traps Slugs can be stopped by barriers of wood ashes, pine needles or sawdust. They are reluctant to climb over rings 10-13cm (4-5in) high cut from plastic bottles. Slugs can be trapped in slug pubs, saucers or yoghurt pots half-full of fermenting beer, in which they obligingly drown themselves. Friendly ground

PEA/BEAN WEEVIL: Chews a scalloped edge on leaves. No problem on strong plants, but serious if plants are very young. They overwinter in plant debris and larvae emerge as adults in midsummer. ACTION: encourage strong, fast growth. Sow beans under cover and plant out when growing strongly. Dust plants with derris powder.

REVERSION DISEASE: Carried by the big bud mite (page 54) which attacks blackcurrants. Difficult to recognize: leaves are narrower than usual and have fewer than 5 pairs of veins on the main lobe. Flower buds turn bright magenta instead of grey. Bushes lose vigour and crop is less. ACTION: no cure except to dig up and burn affected bushes. Plant certified disease-free bushes on a different site.

LEAF-ROLLING SAWFLY: Small, blackfly-like insect lays eggs on rose leaves, causing them to roll up. Larvae then feed on the rolled leaves which eventually wither and die. ACTION: pick off and burn affected leaves before larval stage is completed. Spray leaves with derris.

VINE WEEVILS: Beetles feed on leaf margins of rhododendrons and azaleas, as well as vines, while the plump white maggots attack roots and tubers of ornamental plants under glass. Roots usually destroyed and plants rarely recover. ACTION: use biological control by introducing parasitic nematode Nemasys.

WHITEFLY: Small winged insects which live on leaves of brassicas and fly up in clouds when disturbed. The young scales remain on plants. ACTION: Dig up winter brassicas as soon as finished cropping and bury in trench or compost heap before planting out new ones. Remove leaves infested with scales before they turn into adults. Suck up adults with mini vacuum cleaner or spray with insecticidal soap.

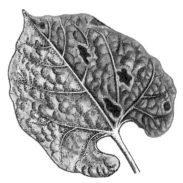

HALO BLIGHT: Seed-borne bacterial disease affecting French, dwarf and runner beans. Angular spots develop on leaves surrounded by lighter-coloured halo. Spots turn brown and white encrustation can develop. ACTION: buy only good-quality seed. All plants likely to be infected – burn at end of season and don't save seed.

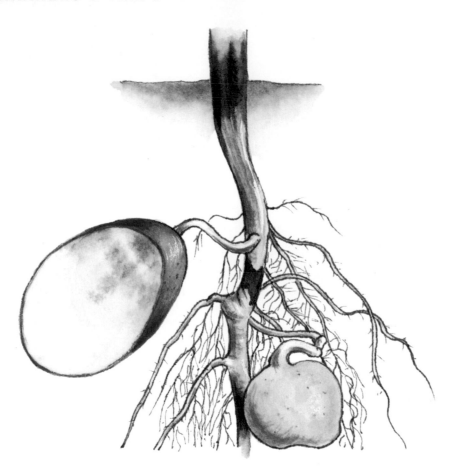

*LEAF SPOT: affects many plants, especially in wet seasons. Leaf surface can become totally brown and shrivelled and plant loses vigour. **ACTION**: Remove and burn diseased leaves. Spray plants with Bordeaux mixture. With brassicas, remove alternate plants to improve ventilation and avoid too much nitrogen fertilizer.*

beetles also drown unless you give them some twigs to climb out on. Slugs and snails also collect under melon or orange shells and upturned saucers.

mousetraps are too well known to need describing. They are needed near peas and beans that have been sown or stored and near crocuses, which mice love. Mole traps are similar. There are humane traps for both mice and moles so that if you catch them you can release them elsewhere.

lures can be made for many pests. Tins or yoghurt cartons buried in the ground with bits of potato or carrot will attract mostly millipedes and woodlice; slugs and snails will come to fruit, and wireworms to bran or germinating grain. Dead-fall traps are the same but without the lure.

isolation trenches of about 25 x 25cm (10 x 10in) around vegetable beds present mice, slugs and other small creatures with a barrier and so exclude them more effectively than the conventional drop of a couple of inches.

child and people proofing Human pests can be the worst of all and their senseless damage is sometimes worse than their thefts. Fences, barriers and locks are sadly now required, especially for succulent fruit. Signs

*BLACKLEG: Bacterial disease of potatoes. Foliage turns yellow and stems blacken and die. Tubers may also be affected, developing a brown slimy rot inside. **ACTION**: Remove and burn affected plants. Lift rest of crop carefully to avoid contact with infected tubers. Do not save any tubers for seed as they will reintroduce infection. Only buy certified seed.*

*SPUR BLIGHT: Troublesome disease of raspberries and loganberries. Fungus attacks new canes in early summer – dark purple blotches which turn silver and studded with black fungus. Buds die or die back in the spring. **ACTION**: cut out and burn diseased canes at first sign of trouble. Remove superfluous canes early. Spray with copper fungicide when buds first open.*

*APPLE CANKER: Destructive disease which also attacks pears and plums. Sunken, discoloured patches on bark and branch becomes swollen. Whites pustules appear in summer and small red fruiting bodies develop in winter. **ACTION**: cut out diseased patches, branches or shoots and burn immediately. Cut back to clean wood. Worse on trees lacking vigour, so feed and mulch.*

*LEATHERJACKETS: Larvae of the cranefly which live in the soil. Mainly a problem on vegetable plots dug from old lawns or old pasture land, or on very weedy plots. They feed on the roots of vegetables, especially brassicas. **ACTION**: keep soil weed-free. Hoe and dig regularly, to expose them to birds.*

52

saying 'Beware of the wasps' nests!' can be singularly more effective than 'Keep out'. Dogs are considered the best guards, but geese are as good and have other benefits.

bird scarers are psychological barriers: they all work for a short time but garden birds rapidly learn not to fear them. Use several and change them daily. Scarecrows, glitterbangs (coffee packaging bags are good), flashing humming tape (video or cassette is cheaper than the bought tapes) are all worth trying. Black cotton gives birds a fright when they touch it; Scaraweb is an artificial spider's web to give them arachnaphobia. Fur-hat cats, hosepipe snakes and paper hawks all worry them, but they will be back.

bought-in predators & parasites

These have been used commercially for some time, and many are now available to gardeners. They are most suitable for greenhouse pests, which are difficult to control because of the absence of natural predators. Of course, once they are introduced virtually all pesticide use has to stop. They are most effective if introduced early in the season – but not before the pest has appeared or they will starve. If pest populations get large before the predators arrive, thin out the numbers with traps, trap plants and safe sprays before introducing them. Full instructions come in the packets.

whitefly parasites *Encarsia formosa* have been used since the 1920s. These are small wasps that rapidly reduce whitefly populations – the white scales turn black once attacked by the wasp. Infestations of aphids or other pests can still be controlled by dipping the tips of the plants where they concentrate in soft soap solution. Yellow sticky traps can be left in the greenhouse once the wasps are introduced so long as they are hung high enough (the wasps tend to fly low).

Red spider mite predators *Phytoseulis persimilis* are tiny, but still bigger than the pests, which cover shoots with a webbing that repels sprays. The leaves then turn yellow and dessicated, with thousands of tiny pinpricks. The red spider mites can be thinned out first with soft soap and discouraged with wet conditions

PARSNIP CANKER: *Disease which causes rotting of the shoulders with red-brown and black marks. In severe cases can rot whole root.* **ACTION:** *Practise rigorous crop rotation and make sure soil is deep and well-fertilized. Add lime if pH is below 6.5-7. Grow resistant varieties such as Avonresister and White Gem.*

SOFT ROT: *Affects swedes and turnips, particularly in wet weather. Flesh rots into an evil-smelling mess and rind remains intact. Most troublesome on heavily manured and badly drained soil.* **ACTION:** *practise crop rotation and make sure drainage is adequate – grow roots on deep beds to improve drainage. Control slugs to save foliage – disease can get in through wounds. Remove and burn affected plants.*

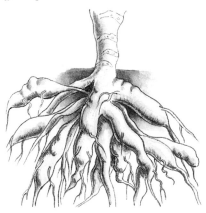

CLUB ROOT: *Disease which mainly affects brassicas, causing wilting, stunted plants. When pulled up roots are swollen and distorted.* **ACTION:** *dig up and burn affected plants. Disease can last in soil for 20 years, so practise good rotation and never grow brassicas in infected plot. Keep soil well limed as disease likes acid conditions. Raise seedlings in pots so they make a healthy start. To prevent disease coming in, never buy in seedlings.*

POTATO BLIGHT: *Causes brown patches on leaves, especially in warm, wet weather. Foliage blackens and dies and tubers may rot. Spreads rapidly in humid conditions.* **ACTION:** *spray with Bordeaux mixture at fortnightly intervals until harvesting. In severe cases cut down and burn foliage. Delay harvesting for 2-3 weeks so tubers are not affected. Grow resistant varieties: Cara, Wilja, Kondor.*

ROSE BLACK SPOT: *Common fungus disease of roses, especially in wet, humid weather. Leaf spots may merge into large dead areas, and leaves wither and die.* **ACTION:** *Prune hard in autumn to kill off overwintering spores and burn prunings immediately. Pick up fallen leaves in autumn and mulch soil well. Plant in sunny, open site and space to ensure good ventilation.*

SCAB: *Disease which affects potatoes, causing ugly ragged scabs on the skin. Most often found in dry, sandy soil lacking organic matter.* **ACTION:** *Dig in plenty of humus such as compost or manure and do not lime soil prior to planting. Water in dry spells. Add a layer of grass clippings to the trenches at planting time for added protection. Grow resistant varieties such as Arran Pilot, Arran Comet, King Edward or Maris Peer.*

53

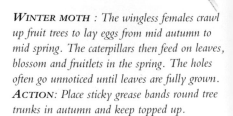

WINTER MOTH *: The wingless females crawl up fruit trees to lay eggs from mid autumn to mid spring. The caterpillars then feed on leaves, blossom and fruitlets in the spring. The holes often go unnoticed until leaves are fully grown.* ***ACTION****: Place sticky grease bands round tree trunks in autumn and keep topped up.*

until the predator is introduced.

aphididoletes aphidimyza is a parasitic midge for controlling aphids.

mealy bug predator *Cryptolaemus montrouzieri* is a ladybird. The white shaggy larvae rapidly control mealybugs but need a temperature of 21°C (70°F).

Vine weevils are very difficult to control with chemicals as they live in the soil, but Nemasys, a parasitic nematode, works.

cabbage white and other similar caterpillars can be easily killed with a disease *Bacillus thuringiensis*. This is sprayed on to the crop and as the caterpillars eat they pick up the spores and soon die. This disease is no danger to humans or to the environment.

trichoderma virides is a predatory fungus used to prevent other fungi attacking pruning wounds. It can also be used to cure silver leaf disease in plums and Dutch elm disease, if these have not progressed too far. Pellets are inserted into holes drilled in the trunk and the predatory fungus then permeates the tree. This is available only to commercial growers.

organic pesticides Organic gardeners prefer not to use poisonous substances unless they are needed to save a valuable crop. However, they are there as a last resort,

FLEA BEETLES*: Attack cabbages and other brassicas, covering leaves with small holes. Hibernate in plant debris and under loose tree bark.* ***ACTION****: cover plants with fine netting or woven fleece. Go along rows with sticky, greased board – beetles jump up when disturbed. Spray with pyrethrum or derris.*

BIG BUD MITE*: Affects blackcurrants. Mites breed inside developing buds, causing them to become round and swollen. Mites carry reversion disease (p51) which causes slow deterioration of bush and poor cropping.* ***ACTION****: remove and burn all swollen buds before spring. In severe cases cut back all growth to ground level and burn cuttings.*

BLACKFLY*: These aphids cluster on growing tips of broad beans in late spring, and can spread to rest of plant, stunting growth and reducing crop. May also spread to other beans, beetroot and chard, and ornamentals.* ***ACTION****: Sow hardy variety in autumn so that plants are tougher and less attractive in spring. Pinch out affected tips. Spray with soft soap or derris.*

WOOLLY APHIDS*: Species which attacks treetrunks, branches and twigs. Covers itself with white, wool-like covering. Attacked wood becomes swollen and may crack, allowing entry to canker and other diseases. Soft, lumpy galls develop on bark.* ***ACTION****: spray with derris, soft soap or insecticidal soap. If this does not work, infestation may have to be cut out.*

54

though you must take great care not to disrupt ecosystems that have slowly built up. Follow the instructions on the packaging as to their uses, application rates and precautions and keep them in a safe place.

soft soap is just that, traditionally used as a spray to kill aphids, red spider mite, whitefly and other pests. Insecticidal soap is even more effective. Safe to use and made from natural products it is the preferred pesticide, but cannot deal with the larger insect pests.

quassia solution is made from a tree bark. It kills aphids but is harmless to bees and other beneficial insects. It is no longer available on its own but is sold combined with derris, which makes them both more effective.

pyrethrum is no longer available in pure form and is commonly supplied with a synthetic synergist. However, it is useful for killing many insect pests, including small caterpillars. It also kills beneficial insects and fish, but is safe for mammals. It is made from the flowerheads of chrysanthemums and breaks down in half a day once it has been exposed to air and light.

derris is a liquid or powder, made from a tropical plant, which kills most insects, friends and foes indiscriminately but is particularly effective against mites. It is also lethal to fish, pigs and tortoises. It breaks down in sunlight and is slower to act than pyrethrum. Wasps' nests can be treated by puffing the dust into the entrance at dusk. Wasps returning to the nest carry it in with them thus exterminating the nest contents. Repeat a week later.

bordeaux mixture is a fungicidal suspension of copper sulphate and slaked lime. Although it is an inorganic chemical it is allowed under organic standards as it is not very harmful to us or to soil life. It is effective against potato blight, peach leaf curl, raspberry cane spot and many other fungal diseases. It is a preventative, not a cure, and must be applied thoroughly and in good time.

sulphur (the pure element) is allowed under organic standards as a control for powdery mildews on fruit, flowers and vegetables, and for preventing rots in overwintering bulbs and tubers. Take care when using it with fruit trees and bushes as a few varieties are allergic to sulphur. Read the label and instructions.

DAMPING OFF: A fungus disease which causes seedlings to collapse at ground level. Troublesome where seedlings are overcrowded or growing in wet, compacted soil. ACTION: sow thinly and use sterilized soil or compost with a good tilth. Over-watering can induce damping off. Use clean tap water, not tank or butt water which may contain infective organisms.

SILVERLEAF: Fruit tree disease, caused by fungus that enters through wounds. Leaves become silvered and then brown. Progressive dieback of affected branches. Small, purple, white or brown fungus fruiting bodies develop on dead wood. ACTION: cut back all dead branches at least 15cm (6in) beyond infection in the summer, when least chance of new infection. Sterilize tools before and after use.

MEALY BUGS: Infest cacti, succulents and many other plants, especially under glass. Pinkish-grey soft-bodied insects suck sap from young stems. In heavy infestations foliage and fruit sticky with honeydew and sooty mould will grow on it. ACTION: spray with derris or pyrethrum. Under glass introduce parasitic beetle Cryptolaemus montrouzieri.

APHIDS: Otherwise known as greenfly and blackfly. They live in fast-growing colonies and feed on plant sap, which weakens and distorts growth. They also transmit viral diseases. ACTION: spray with soft or insecticidal soap. Pick off infected leaves and prune infected shoots. Encourage natural predators, especially hoverflies, by growing suitable flowers and plants (see p33, 35, 37).

AMERICAN GOOSEBERRY MILDEW: Affects blackcurrants too. White powdery coating on leaves, shoots and fruit. Patches become brown and felted. ACTION: avoid overcrowded bushes and weedy soil. Prune regularly to keep bushes open and let air and light in. Cut out and burn diseased shoots. Spray with Bordeaux mixture at flower stage.

FRUIT TREE RED SPIDER MITE: These mites affect apples, pears, plums and damsons, causing speckling and bronzing of leaves. Leaves become dry and fall prematurely. The mites overwinter as eggs which hatch out in early summer. ACTION: pick off infected leaves. Spray with derris if badly infested.

4 WEED CONTROL
in an organic garden

Good weed control is essential for organic gardeners. Self-sown weeds have the advantage over carefully bred plants, and will rapidly out-compete and choke them. They also spoil the appearance of the garden, lock up fertility in seeds and roots, and harbour pests and diseases – and weeding probably takes up most gardening time after grass cutting

Organic gardeners do not use chemical herbicides, which kill not only weeds, but other forms of life as well. However, it is still possible to have good weed control. As with pests, the aim is control, not elimination, as some weeds have their uses as well as drawbacks. The timing and method of control varies with the type of weed, situation and crop, so much effort can be saved by knowing your weeds.

friendly & unfriendly weeds

Weeds are just plants in the wrong place. Many are otherwise valuable garden plants or even crops, for example poppies, feverfew and red valerian. Many weeds are edible: chickweed and dandelion leaves are delicious in salads, fat hen, nettles and ground elder can be cooked like spinach, while the roots of dandelion, horseradish and vetch are all edible. In some gardens, weeds may be the last remnants of the original flora and so help preserve insect and wildlife populations. A stand of weeds not only fixes and stabilizes the soil, but can act as a miniature hedge and windbreak, sheltering emerging seedlings, though it will

The field bindweed is one of the prettiest weeds but do not underestimate its tenacity

need eradication before it competes too much.

Remember too before you get rid of all weeds that some are attractive to bees, butterflies and insects. They should not be allowed to compete with other plants, but if you have a patch of ground at the end of the garden where they will do no harm, it is worth allowing some to survive. Weeds that attract beneficial insects include the following: nettles, poppies, groundsel, herb robert and dandelion.

Most of all, weeds are a useful source of fertility, admirably well suited to their conditions by self-selection. They produce a wealth of green manure at times when other plants cannot use the soil, and act as valuable ground cover over the winter. They are also superb mineral accumulators, making these accessible to crops after they have been dug in or mulched. Clovers and vetches fix nitrogen, comfrey is well known for accumulating potassium, as do nettles and thistles, while phosphorus is collected by fat hen, sorrel, yarrow and thornapple. Stubborn-rooted perennials such as comfrey and nettles will have to be mulched, rather than dug in, if used as green manure – and you will need to dig up the roots later, unless you want an annual crop.

what weeds indicate Any piece of ground left untended rapidly becomes covered with weeds. As the weeds slowly build up the fertility of the soil it becomes suitable for nettles, brambles and tree seedlings. A profusion of these weeds, especially nettles, can indicate a potentially rich site. Deep-rooted weeds like dock and thistle are also good for the soil as they bring up nutrients, making them available for future crops. The types of weed will always be those most suited to the conditions, so if they consist of acid-lovers such as daisies, small nettles and sorrels, then the topsoil is probably acid. Lime soils are similarly indicated by cat's ears, cowslips, knapweed and silverweed, while

damp conditions encourage nettles, buttercups, bugle and rushes. Lots of docks means that horses or their manure have been on the land as the seeds pass through unchecked. Similarly, lots of tomato seedlings could mean sewage sludge has been used. Beware of any land that grows few weeds!

types of weed What is needed for efficient and effective control is recognition that weeds come in two types, annuals and perennials, and that once the latter have been totally eliminated then the former are easy to control with very little time or effort.

annual weeds Annual weed seeds germinate as soon as soil is exposed to the light, warmth and wet, but they can be prevented from doing so by mulching or deep burial. As seedlings, these weeds are relatively easy to kill, but they rapidly become tougher. Some can even set seed lying on the ground if they have reached the flowering stage. From the point of view of weed control it doesn't matter if the seedling weed is actually a biennial or annual; it is small and easily killed if it is not long established. These are the best weeds to use as green manure or winter ground cover, as they are not deep-rooting and are easy to eradicate.

perennial weeds Established perennial weeds are much more difficult. They survive from year to year by means of underground roots and bulbs, and the worst creep, spread and regrow from pieces of root. Most of them also produce seeds. Weeds such as docks, horseradish and dandelions have long tap roots which store food for the plants, bringing up water and nutrients from deep in the soil. Destroying the leaves once is no good, for the root will simply produce new ones. And if you cut off the root, leaving even a small piece in the soil, it will grow again, though dock can be killed by taking out the top 10cm (4in) of root. Creepers such as couch grass, nettles and ground elder develop a mass of stems just below ground. These have to be dug up, with every small piece of stem removed, for again even a small section of stem left behind will develop new plants.

If you have taken over a new garden or

identifying PERNICIOUS WEEDS

The following pages show the most pernicious weeds: annuals that should not be allowed to increase and the most persistent perennial weeds:

Winter heliotrope

Japanese knotweed

WEED TEST

A good experiment is to put your garden soil in a pot and water it. Place the pot on a windowsill where you will see it every day and watch what comes up. You can remove anything as soon as you recognize it - these are your common annual weeds. Once you know them you can spot the rare finds such as tree and shrub seedlings.

allotment, or are simply breaking in a new piece of ground, it is essential to clear each and every bit of these weeds. Clearing them methodically reduces later weed control effort to the seedling annuals, which can be easily hoed or mulched. Never plant up beds or borders without first removing or killing all perennial weeds – if they are allowed to interpenetrate plant roots weeding becomes far more difficult.

Once all the perennial weeds have been cleared from an area there are almost certainly going to be thick flushes of weed seedlings for a year or two, but after some seasons of regular weeding there will be fewer seedlings. If you want to use weeds to give good winter cover, digging or deep raking will bring up more seeds. Also, selected weeds or other favoured plants can be allowed to seed on vegetable beds and other areas needing cover and the added benefit of green manuring.

Where the weeds are being mulched, dug, or hoed in, their goodness is retained. They can also be put on the compost heap, and their fertility thus used for more important crops. All weeds can be composted, but those with pernicious roots should be withered on a path for some days first. Seeding and diseased weeds are best burnt.

weeding methods

There are many ways to kill weeds but some methods are impractical in small gardens. Some, like digging up, are better used initially to break new ground, and then other methods such as hoeing or flame-gunning can be used to maintain control. Mulching is probably most important, as it not only prevents weed seeds germinating, but conserves the fertility and moisture of the soil.

Hygiene precautions are valuable for preventing undesirable new weeds being brought in – dirty manures, uncomposted mulches and especially bought-in plants in pots can smuggle in seeds and even whole live specimens. Protect sensitive areas such as flowerbeds,

gravel paths and drives by never letting anything set seed nearby or upwind. Rotation is as useful in weed control as in pest and disease control. By moving the crop and changing the conditions no weed species is favoured and allowed to become established.

digging is best for starting a new bed or border where the ground has been under turf or grass for a while. Regular grass-cutting will have reduced weed populations, leaving grasses and rosette weeds such as daisies. From early autumn to late winter the turf can be skimmed off and stacked for loam, used elsewhere or dug in. Tap-rooted weeds can be dug up as they are uncovered and wilted for compost. But if there are many creeping weeds such as couch grass, then digging up becomes exceedingly laborious; completely excluding light with a black plastic mulch is then easier.

Dig in overwintering, ground-cover weeds in the early spring, so that they have time to decay before anything is planted. Dig and chop small spits methodically rather than labour with larger pieces. Alternatively, the surface can be lifted and inverted in shallow slices and the weeds prevented from re-rooting by later hoeing.

rotavating is really chopping up the weeds and is not at all like digging. Moreover, it kills earthworms, damages some soil textures and is noisy, dangerous work. It is not really suitable for breaking in ground badly infested with perennial weeds as most rotavators have insufficient power, and if they succeed they chop each weed root into many pieces which then regrow. But rotavators are useful for incorporating green manures and overwintered annual weeds which are less likely to regrow. They can also be used for regular weed control, provided the plot is laid out in long, straight, wide-spaced rows. They are most definitely for the larger not the smaller garden because of their awkwardness in confined spaces. To break in a large plot, which is not compacted and is down to clean turf or light cover, rotavate two or three times during the spring, about a fortnight apart, to incorporate the cover as well as any regrowth as it occurs.

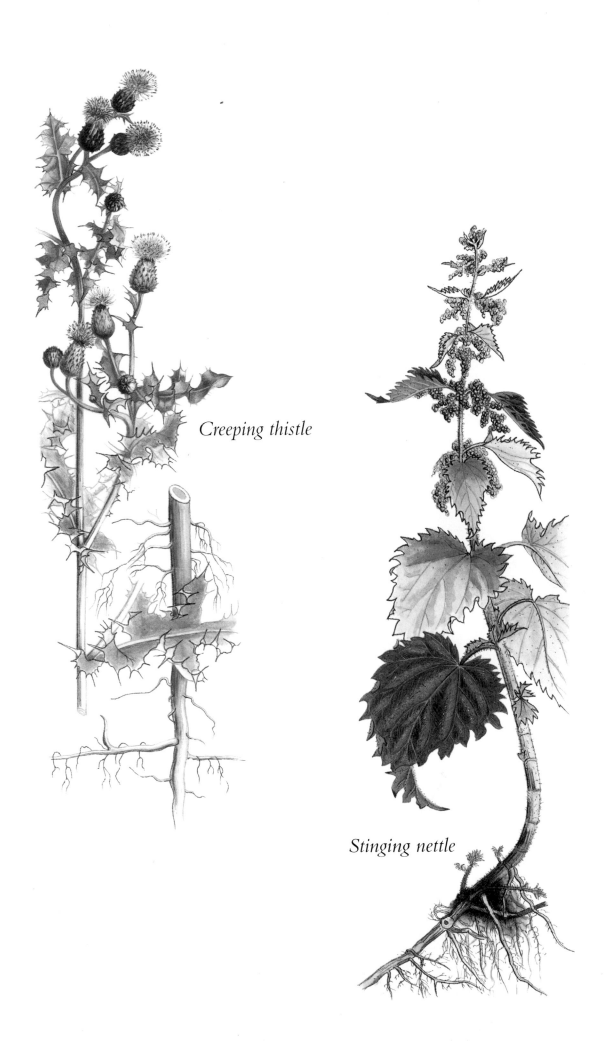

Creeping thistle

Stinging nettle

handweeding is usually needed to remove weeds from among other plants. Gloves make handweeding more pleasant and I prefer the fabric 'brickies' gloves, covered with plastic mesh, which are sold in hardware shops. Kneeling pads as used by skateboarders protect the knees and a sharp knife helps cut stubborn roots rather than pulling them up with a large clod. Use an old washing-up bowl or bucket to collect the weeds and transfer them to a barrow or heap when it's full to save getting up and down too often. Remove the weeds close by the plants first then the larger ones between. Small seedling weeds may then be killed with the edge of the knife, a hand rake, onion hoe or scuffler rather than by pulling up. Although it is laborious, you can convert perennial weeds into fertility if every new leaf is pulled off each week until the root system expires. Some much-feared weeds such as ground elder or bindweed can be eliminated in a season if every leaf and shoot is removed weekly; any lapse though, and they may recover from just one little piece.

hoeing is the usual method of maintaining weed control. Severing the top growth just below ground level is most effective, but the hoe must be sharp. I always sharpen mine on a wheel and then keen it up every 10 minutes or so with a whetstone. In heavy, sticky or stony ground it may pay to put a hoeing mulch of sharp sand or sieved compost on top of the soil to make the going easier. It is said to be better to work backwards so you do not firm in the weeds, but I go forwards and look where I'm going.

There are two basic hoe patterns: the swan-necked or draw hoe, and the Dutch hoe (see page 68). The draw hoe, which is used with a chopping action, is good for incorporating weed seedlings and young green manures but makes hard work. It is also good for earthing-up potatoes and making drills. The Dutch hoe is pushed to and fro through the soil just below the surface, which is easier work. It does not incorporate seedlings so well, but deals with big weeds more effectively than a draw hoe. Weeds are further damaged by the Dutch hoe's rolling action, which also makes a good dust mulch. It is hard to draw up soil or make a drill with the Dutch hoe.

Hoeing is excellent for maintaining clean soil in beds and borders. If there are only annual weeds, then they need hoeing fortnightly from early spring to late summer, but little thereafter. Hoeing every fortnight takes very little time, but if left longer the weeds become established and it then takes more effort and time. Hoeing is also effective against perennial weeds so long as it is done weekly, so that the top growth is continually hoed off. The roots become exhausted using up their reserves to make new growth, and will die.

flame-gunning is is not as frightening as it sounds. A gas- or paraffin-powered blowtorch gives an intense blue flame about the size of a wine bottle that will splay out over 30cm (1ft) square or so. This is passed over the weeds at a walking pace and will cook but not char the leaves, leaving them to further weaken the root system as they wither. It only warms the soil, but is very effective against young weed seedlings. However, if the weeds are well established some may recover from the roots and need a second treatment a week or so later. It is possible to kill perennial weeds with repeated weekly flame-gunning, though it is probably more ecological simply to dig them up and compost them.

Timing a flame-gunning just before a crop emerges can be very useful; it removes the weed competition without disturbing the crop or soil and bringing up more weed seeds. For example, carrots take 12-18 days to germinate so if these are sown into a weeded seedbed then all new weeds emerging in the next 10 days can be removed in perfect safety with a treatment on day 11. The carrots then emerge deterring further weeds germinating.

Annual meadow grass

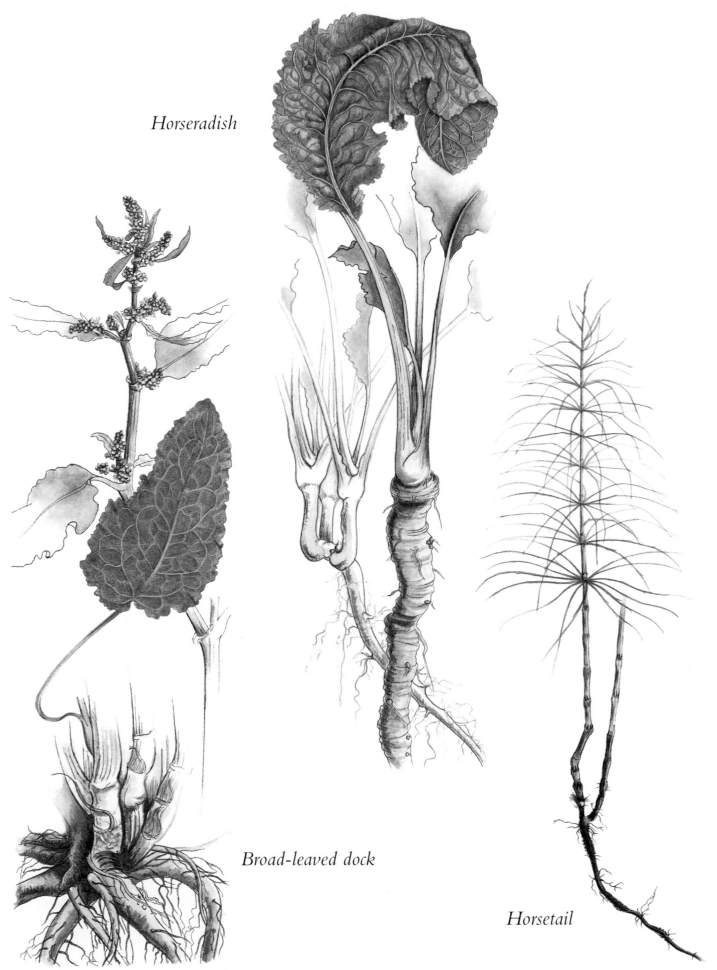

Horseradish

Broad-leaved dock

Horsetail

Flame-gunning is most useful for weeding large areas such as seedbeds, gravel drives and so on, but should obviously be kept away from cars, buildings and inflammable materials. It is possible to use flame-guns under and up to trees, because of their thermal mass and the insulation of their bark. You can even flame-gun around tough-stemmed plants like mature Brussels sprouts, but conifers, evergreens, dead leaves and hedges catch fire easily. Herbaceous plants can also be flame-gunned while dormant to kill winter weeds if the crowns are covered with sand – asparagus beds especially. Small blowtorches are superb for weeding rockeries, and can also be used on weeds growing in the cracks and crannies of paths and patios.

Shepherd's purse

mulching This is probably the most important yet under-used method of weed control. Mulching materials can be expensive to buy, but can save much time and effort by suppressing weeds. They all help moisture conservation, and improve soil temperature stability, encouraging growth. Organic mulches, when applied regularly, add fertility and improve the soil texture.

Mulches do have a few drawbacks other than the cost though; they may encourage pests underneath, such as voles, moles and slugs, and loose ones tend to be scattered on to lawns by birds. There is also a danger of rotting crowns or bark in excessively damp conditions, and grafts may take root if the union is covered by a mulch. Mulches can also seal in the soil warmth, with the result that growth above becomes more prone to frost than it would over bare soil – important for strawberries, bush peaches in flower and potatoes.

However, mulches are still

the easiest way of breaking in new ground, as well as a good way of keeping weeds down later. Providing the top growth is not woody and has at least been cut with a rotary mower, then an area can be turned into weed-free clean soil in six months with little effort or preparation. All weeds are killed by completely excluding light with impenetrable mulches. The tougher perennial weeds are only stopped by thick opaque plastic or fabric such as old carpet, but the majority of weeds can be killed off with a thick mulch of straw, hay or grass clippings on top of cardboard and newspaper. Avoid using opaque black plastic on areas larger than 1 metre (3ft) as lack of air and moisture can cause problems with the soil; on these large areas it is better to use perforated black plastic or old carpet. It helps if an isolation trench 30cm (1ft) deep and wide is dug round the perimeter first and the mulch continued over the edge.

Mulching new ground works best if an impenetrable mulch is put down just as the weeds have started into growth, flattening them underneath – usually in early spring when the soil is also full of water; later than mid-spring is far less effective. The weeds turn yellow through lack of light and rapidly rot, followed by their root systems, feeding soil life and increasing fertility. After a month or so the sheet of mulch can be rolled back early in the morning to expose any creatures for the birds. Worms and beneficial insects move quickly and escape, but pests such as slugs are slower and do not.

If an area is mulched like this in early spring, then it can be cropped from late spring. The weeds may recover if the mulch is simply removed, but some vegetables can be planted out through holes in the mulch where they will grow wonderfully in the moist enriched soil underneath. Tomatoes, courgettes, marrows, ridge cucumbers, melons under cloches and sweetcorn will all do well. The brassicas also thrive but most occupy the land through the winter so do not fit in if the area is needed for the autumn.

In the autumn after any crop has been removed the mulch can be removed and the area dug over if thought necessary. Almost all

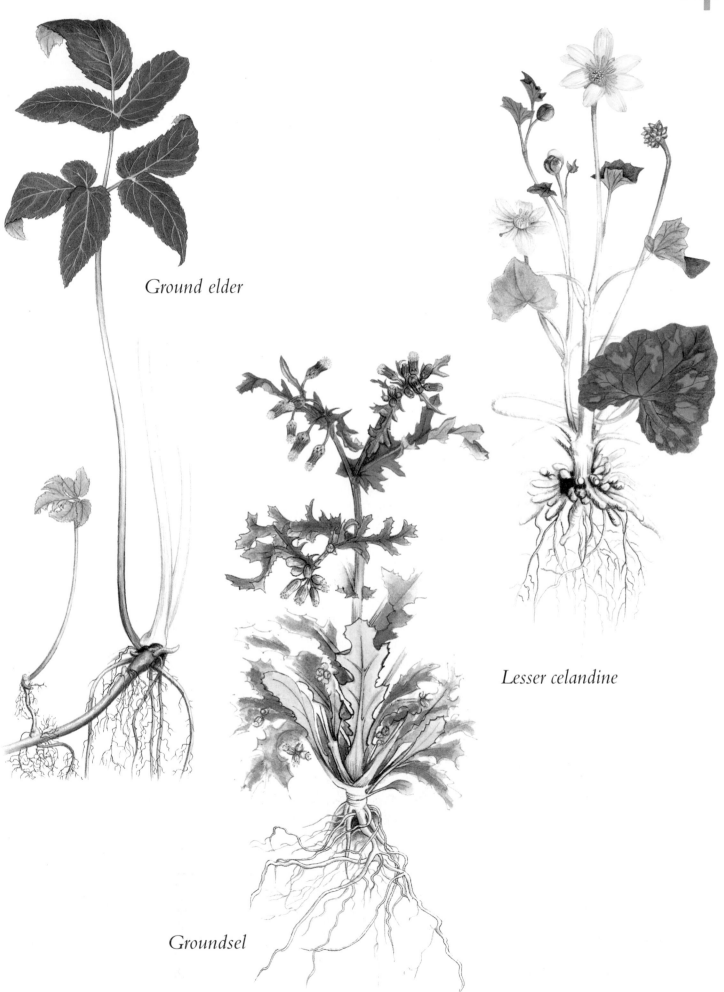

Ground elder

Lesser celandine

Groundsel

the weeds and roots will have rotted and disappeared, leaving a rich texture and natural stratification that may be better left undisturbed. Winter crops can be planted through the mulch, or the plot can be overwintered under a green manure, which has the advantage of restoring the pH of the soil (which tends to drop under mulches).

In exactly the same way, green manures and overwintered weeds can be mulched in early spring with sheets of plastic or fabric, or even grass clippings in quantity. Again, crops can then be planted through the mulch into the enriched soil in late spring. Compost can be added as well before mulching, for optimum results when growing hungry feeders.

Impenetrable or loose mulches can be applied on to bare soil or annual weeds in the vegetable plot during autumn. These hibernate the bed, protecting the soil from erosion and encouraging soil life, especially earthworms, so that when the mulch is removed or planted through in spring the soil will have excellent texture and fertility. Autumn mulching can benefit herbaceous and less hardy plants by protecting them from frost, though plants subject to rot in damp conditions should only be mulched with light airy materials like loose straw or bracken to avoid worsening the problem.

All mulches can be applied at any time but are most beneficial applied in spring – when the soil is warming up but before the winter rain has evaporated. Mulches applied too early will keep the soil cold and slow down growth. If there is a long dry period then it is a good idea to rake or roll aside mulches when it rains and replace them afterwards, to prevent the mulch soaking up all the water.

plastic sheets are a great aid to weed control, but they are unsightly, costly, and environmentally undesirable. They can be used in a variety of ways. Clear plastic similar to that used for polytunnels can be pinned to the ground to warm up the soil in spring and encourage flushes of weeds. Black or opaque plastic sheet thick enough to exclude all light warms the soil and kills weeds, even perennials. It can be laid permanently and then covered with a loose mulch of wood chippings to improve the appearance so that it is suitable for shrub borders, soft fruit and other permanent plantings. In the same way it can be laid under gravel paths and drives. Use perforated plastic on large areas to prevent water problems, and lack of aeration to the soil. Black and white plastic sheets are useful: after the black surface has warmed the soil and killed weeds it can be reversed to the white side to reflect light onto the plants and confuse pests.

Squares of plastic, with a slit for access and the edges buried in soil, make a superb mulch for young trees, keeping them weed-free and preventing evaporation for a year or two. Long strips a metre or so wide are excellent for starting hedges; cuttings of easy rooters such as quickthorn can even be pushed through them. Strips of plastic can also be used for strawberries, vegetables and particularly lettuce, which then get less dirty, though slugs may become more of a problem. All plastic sheets have to be very well anchored with earth or stones, otherwise in high winds there is a danger of them and the plants blowing away or becoming damaged.

woven materials are similar to plastic but are heavier, and more resistant to weeds growing through. Their porosity allows much better aeration of the soil and less water run-off than with impermeable plastic. These are too expensive for use where plain plastic will do, but are better for growing valuable crops like strawberries, where their wear resistance will also be useful. Bed-sized pieces on the vegetable plot will kill and incorporate green manures for many years, and are tough enough to have flaps cut for planting through. Carpet is the best woven material: heavy, weed resistant and not unattractive laid upside

Hairy bittercress

Couch grass

Dandelion

Buttercup

My most valuable tools: a
swan-necked hoe flanked by
two draw hoes

mulch they kill weeds almost as well as plastic or fabric materials, but rapidly rot. Using them under a loose mulch stops birds mixing weed-seed-infested soil into the mulch material. They also improve the effectiveness of thin plastic sheet which otherwise lets some light through. Wet them first so that they lie flat.

peat, bark and coir are very much more attractive to look at as a backdrop than any other mulches. Peat is now considered eco-logically undesirable, and is gradually being replaced by bark by-products, coir and other wastes. They are very expensive compared to other mulches, but they are generally weed-seed free, of good texture and beneficial to most plants. Because of their cost these mate-rials are best used for important ornamental areas. They can be made to go further if used on top of newspaper, cardboard or plastic mulches. On their own these mulches must be at least 5-7.5cm (2-3in) deep, and this will need topping up every year – thin layers just disappear. Hold down fine grade material with a coarse top layer to prevent the wind blow-ing it away. Do not put these mulches down unaided on top of weeds as they will just grow through.

compost and manures These are applied more for their fertility than just as mulches. Sieving beforehand makes them more attrac-tive but is laborious and inevitably they are full of weed seeds. These mulches are of most use on the vegetable bed and around trees and shrubs. In thick layers they suppress many weeds, but not creeping or vigorous ones. These mulches disappear quickly and so need continual topping up.

straw and hay These makes a good mulch under trees and in the fruit cage, as well as for strawberries. There tend to be quite a lot of annual grass seeds in these mulches so be prepared to keep mulching once you start. They are best on top of a layer of newspa-pers; a 7.5cm (3in) thick slab will then last for two years or more and look quite attractive as the colour mellows. Loose straw and hay are good for protecting less hardy plants in severe weather but best of all are bracken fronds. Take care with bracken and with mouldy hay or straw as the dust can be dangerous.

down – and often available free. This is the material for breaking new ground; even a bramble can't push through a bit of heavy car-pet. Pure synthetic carpets last for ever and make good paths, especially in the fruitcage and polytunnel. The brighter ones look much better covered in a skim of loose mulch. Organic wool or cotton carpets rot after a year or two and so are perfect for establishing trees and shrubs. Mixed fibre carpets partly rot, leaving a stringy mass to dispose of.

paper and cardboard are no good on their own except in the greenhouse or poly-tunnel where they are safe from the wind and useful for keeping lettuce and salad stuff clean. Outside, they blow away unless used with another mulch on top. Used under any loose

above A selection of mulches. From the top: woven materials; paper and cardboard; straw and hay; grass clippings

right Primroses beneath flowering currant bushes provide attractive ground cover in spring

grass clippings are usually freely available home-grown. Laid in a heap they make a wet smelly mess, but put in thin layers which are then topped up regularly they make one of the very best mulches. They feed the soil and encourage worms, and thus benefit almost every area of the garden. Thicker layers are good for earthing up potatoes and under soft fruit bushes and trees. Grass clippings 'glue' down the edge of plastic sheets and can help disguise them, allowing a more attractive finish, when added as a skim on top. They can be made more effective and longer-lasting if put down over newspaper.

sand and gravel These materials are not usually thought of for mulching, but they do have many advantages for weed control, even though they do not add any fertility. They can be very attractive and are cheap and sterile. They retain the moisture in the soil but do not get wet themselves, which makes them good for winter protection of less hardy plants. They provide one of the best mulches for ornamental areas, and for fruit where they reflect heat and light to help ripening. Sand is excellent for asparagus, but should be darkened with soot or it will not warm up quickly enough. Be warned – anything seeding into gravel germinates, so practise good preventive hygiene nearby. It is a good idea to put gravel over perforated plastic, confining the worms and soil underneath.

weed control in non-soil areas
Paths, drives and patios are often a problem as windblown seeds lodge in every niche. Prevention is better than cure, so either point up holes and cracks with cement or mastic (after cleaning them all out by hand with a knife and a pressure hose) or grow plants you want there. A mixture of potting compost and thyme and chamomile seeds worked in will soon establish and prevent other plants getting in. Flame-guns are best where they can safely be used, knives remove weeds from cracks, and I use a strimmer to flay them, though the occasional stone has done for a window or two. A carpet or plastic sheet laid on top for a few weeks will kill off many weeds. It can also be laid permanently and covered with fresh gravel.

ground cover
Under shrubs and over large areas mulching becomes expensive in materials and time as there will always be some weeds that arrive on the wind. It then becomes more effective to go over to ground-cover plants, especially grass which is so simply maintained (see *pages 88-90*). In shady areas, ivy will be better and is easily weeded by strimming anything that grows up out of it. Planting out bulbs, primroses, violets and other naturalizing plants can further improve appearances and the wildlife habitat without upsetting weed control: a strimmer can be used up to and around the chosen plants. The most vigorous and beneficial ground cover wherever height allows are the mints; these suppress most weeds and are loved by insects when they flower. They can be kept within bounds by a mown grass path.

5 PLANNING
an organic garden

Although most of us would prefer a larger garden given the choice, it is surprising what can be done even with tiny ones. In a small garden you can produce quantities of fruit, vegetables and flowers with the same amount of time and effort that in a larger plot would be spent just cutting the grass. Moreover, in a small area any money spent is much more effective: you can buy slow-growing evergreen shrubs, or low-maintenance features such as paved areas, whereas in a larger garden far more investment is needed.

One advantage of a larger garden is the extra privacy, especially if you have room for an informal hedge and windbreak. An extra benefit for the organic gardener is the isolation that comes with a well-hedged garden: spray drift, pests and disease spores from other gardens are less likely to arrive on your plants. Also with more space for plants and habitats more forms of beneficial wildlife can be encouraged and retained, aiding pest control. A large garden also contributes plenty of prunings, grass clippings and leaves to compost for use in the vegetable beds and elsewhere. With more land the vegetable plot can be less intensively cropped, and longer rotations and green manure leys will give better crops, less prone to disease. There is also room for livestock which can convert your waste to eggs or meat, and provide a source of high-value fertilizer – though there is no reason, byelaws allowing, why even the smallest garden should not have a chicken or two in an ark.

A drawing of the author's one-acre organic garden which includes forty raised vegetable beds surrounded by trained fruit trees (*foreground*); a triangular fruit cage (*centre*); ornamental and herb beds (*left*); an apiary and orchard (*top*); and specialist fruit and vegetable beds (*right*). For further details see the plan on pages 78-9

making a decision

The forty raised vegetable beds are at the centre of the food production area with the fruit cage, vine canopy and outhouses nearby

Before planning your garden it is important to consider what you want from it. Is it to add value to your property, give you an interest in life, impress your friends – or is it just for the exercise? Do you need to provide a play area for children? If you want to grow fruit and vegetables, which ones do you want, and when? After all, if you always go on holiday in late summer then there is not much point planting early apples. Similarly, do you want to grow flowers for cutting or for outdoor beauty? All gardens need somewhere to sit but is it to be an outdoor room or a vista from a window? If you want privacy then effective screening may be more important than saving money or maximizing self-sufficiency. Once you know what the parameters are then it is much easier to plan around them. Consider and plan a garden in the same way you would buy a new car or refit the kitchen – and be similarly prepared to spend a realistic amount of money.

planning on paper

It will help to make a scale map showing the boundaries, walls, pipelines, immovable objects (such as fuel tanks), solid paths, trees, major shrubs and so on, which are very difficult to alter. Given time and money anything is possible in garden design, but it is much easier to work around the more permanent features rather than alter them. On the other hand, areas of grass, vegetable plot, beds and borders can be moved around or altered at will. Choose the areas you want for food production first, as these need the best sites, then add other areas as space allows.

Looking at the map will help you to see the garden as a whole, so you can organize it more rationally. Try to get the maximum use out of each item. For example, place a store shed so that it shelters a bed and so that the largest blank wall faces the sun: you can then train a fruit bush against it. Put hedgehog nests underneath the floor and bird boxes under the eaves. The overflow from the water butts can be fed to a pool.

garden features There are many different features that can be added to a garden, in much the same way as doing a house conversion: greenhouse, pond, fruitcage, hen run, etc. You do not have to have conventional front and back gardens – you can have your garden any way you like, with vegetables in the front and flowers at the back, or even made into an enormous fruitcage, or just a woodland area full of naturalized bulbs and a pond. I've always thought how much more interesting, ecological, and greener in summer, a pond would be in the front garden instead of an unused and expensively maintained emerald sward.

herb bed Herbs are useful, easy to grow, and attractive to beneficial insects. Every garden should have one, especially as herbs do not need very much space or attention. See pages 166-79 for details of individual herbs and their requirements.

patio area One of the most essential areas in any garden is somewhere to sit and relax outside – after all, this is one of the most important aspects of gardening! There are also plenty of chores such as shelling peas that need a seat and a table for comfort. Hard standing, slabs or even gravel are more practical than grass and take far less upkeep. A patio must be easily accessible from the house, ideally extending out from a conservatory or kitchen, or it will rarely be used.

Patios in sunny positions soak up heat, and give early ripening crops of fruit planted around them, especially grapes, which can be wound round posts or over wires. Varieties of creeping thyme and chamomile will grow happily in holes or between slabs and give an exquisite scent when walked on. The patio can be edged with scented plants and aromatic herbs to add more sweet smells and help discourage flies and mosquitoes. Bird boxes fixed to the wall and under the eaves can give extra interest and pest control; a bird table and birdbath will attract even more.

water in any form will give a lot of pleasure and is almost essential in an organic garden: even a tiny pond adds to the atmosphere and is also wonderfully attractive to wildlife. Birds, insects and animals all need water and will come to your garden if you supply it; once there, they help with pest control. Frogs and toads will eat lots of slugs and snails. Also, if water is more accessible, birds might eat a bit less fruit. A birdbath can be fitted into every garden – ideally where it can be seen from a window and is safe from cats. A fountain or cascade, however humble, is a delight and can be combined with a pond (though water-lilies like still water). Ponds do not have to be very large to attract wildlife, provided they never dry up. Even an old bath set in the ground will do very well. All water needs a sloping edge to let creatures in and out, and secure fencing if young children are around.

With larger gardens several ponds can be provided in different areas. Large ponds create microclimates that can shelter tender plants nearby, and they reflect sunlight on to surrounding plants as well as providing an emergency source of water.

When making a pond, line it with newspaper and old carpet first to prevent the liner being punctured on stones. Similarly lay old carpet upside down over the edges to protect the liner from light and wear, so that it lasts longer. Butyl rubber is the best value as it lasts longer, but the cheaper alternatives are just as good if well protected. Fill the pond and let it stand for a week to warm up and lose chlorine before stocking it (see page 109 for details of suitable aquatic plants). Take a bucket to a 'natural' pond and scoop up some mud and water for an instant ecosystem.

salad bed After fresh herbs, salad vegetables are the most valuable crop. Every garden should be able to find space for a small intensive bed for salads: with larger gardens this becomes part of the vegetable plot. See pages 110-39 for growing vegetables.

fruitcage & trained fruit As soon as any space is available, especially on walls, fill it with fruit trees, bushes and vines. Tree fruit

A pond provides valuable habitats for wildlife as well as being attractive in its own right. It is pictured here in midsummer with water-lilies and flag irises in bloom and comfrey flowering in the background

can be fitted into every garden, trained as espaliers or cordons alongside paths and drives. In small gardens have a fruitcage rather than a vegetable patch as the rewards are much greater. Designed well, it can provide a pleasant vista for most of the year as well as being productive of food. With a larger garden a big fruitcage is still better value than a vegetable plot as it takes less maintenance. See pages 140-65 for growing fruit.

greenhouse This is a great boon for raising plants and extending the season. Greenhouses come in sizes to suit most pockets and gardens and are worthwhile as an aid to gardening but can take up a lot of time and money if you fill them with tender plants in pots. The smaller the garden the more valuable greenhouse space will be, as it enables you to start off plants for later planting and intercropping as beds becomes vacant.

A greenhouse needs to be near the house for access and services but is also difficult to site attractively as screening may rob it of light. In many ways a conservatory may be a more practical solution and saves siting a greenhouse within view of the house. Water nearby is essential, and electric light and power allows evening work and the use of thermostatic propagation, further increasing the value of the greenhouse. Wooden greenhouses are slightly easier on the eye than metal-framed ones and tend to be warmer. Extra plastic insulation is a mixed blessing – although it keeps greenhouses warmer it reduces the light too much. Ventilation must be adequate for hot weather and automatic, unless you are at home all day.

polytunnels are less visually appealing than greenhouses but they are ideal for the larger garden as they give a lot of space for the money and are easy to move. They need to be well ventilated, as they are prone to high humidity which can cause fungal diseases. The cover needs replacing every four years

Ventilation in hot weather is essential for all greenhouses. The large plant in the doorway is the shoo-fly plant (*Nicandra physaloides*) which discourages whitefly from attacking valuable food crops

or so when the tunnel can be moved to a different piece of ground: on the vegetable bed is convenient as it can then be incorporated into the crop rotation.

bog garden Although many attractive plants will thrive there and it is a wonderful source of predators, a naturally boggy area is undesirable as it indicates low-lying, frost-prone and badly drained ground unsuitable for productive gardening. However, an artificial bog garden laid over plastic next to a pond or pool will be very beneficial, encouraging many forms of life.

vegetable plot Most people probably think of the vegetable plot when referring to organic gardening and it is certainly very important in gardens of all sizes. But for those with little spare time it may be better to think about growing fewer vegetables and more fruit (*see Chapter 8*). See Chapter 7 for advice on the siting and layout of vegetable plots and how they are most suited to different gardens.

livestock These add a lot of interest and value to a garden, as well as building up fertility and helping with pest control. Everyone should try and fit at least bees and a couple of chickens into their garden.

bees Bees are an asset to any garden and are ideally suited for the town dweller Although the picture book WBC hive is still made there are cheaper models which are as good, and the entire set-up with a couple of colonies costs less than a new petrol lawnmower. Bees are no problem except when you steal their honey; left alone they look after themselves. They can become upset though if you get in front of their entrance or disturb them, so site the hive in a quiet corner. Best of all put it on a flat roof such as a garage. Here it will be safer and drier than on the ground and the bees can fly unimpeded.

hens Keeping hens is easier than looking after a cat or dog. As the legal cage size for a battery hen is less than an LP album cover, anything you can supply will be an improvement. All they need is a dark box to nest in, a covered perch, food including greens, water and a little grit and oyster shell. A couple of hens (a rooster is not needed) can survive mainly on the average family's scraps and garden waste, with just a little grain, and they will lay hundreds of eggs a year. They can be moved around in an ark to crop grass or clean the ground between crops and are the finest pre-processors for compost material, adding their own powerful activator. Manure from the hen house should be added to the compost heap and never placed on a plot as it is very strong and concentrated. If you let them run free hens will destroy the garden, but they are safe enough confined in a fruit cage or orchard. The fruit will be safe if it is out of reach – hens flap but rarely fly and 1 metre (39in) high netting is usually enough to keep them in. Bantams are the best value but are harder to confine.

ducks do less damage to the garden than chickens and are as good if not better pest controllers. They lay similar eggs and need the same conditions but seem to produce more droppings. They eat more grass than hens so are cheaper to feed. They don't need a pool, but certainly appreciate one.

geese make a lot of noise and are good watchdogs. Like ducks, they live mostly on grass, but they will debark young fruit trees and eat your carrots, so they need to be confined. They are ideal for a large orchard where they will maintain the grass and return fertility, giving eggs as well. They need a pool more than ducks and live for many decades.

rabbits are best kept in hutches or mobile arks to crop the grass. As pets they are easy but timid, for meat they are unbeatable as they quickly reach an edible size. They are suitable for any size garden.

goats are very risky: they will convert almost anything into compost more efficiently than a shredder, including most of your treasured plants if they ever once escape. They give milk but require more attention than smaller livestock. Only suitable if kept in a well-fenced section of a larger garden.

orchard With dwarf rootstocks you can have a small orchard in any garden. In larger gardens they are the most productive area for time and money, taking little maintenance for enormous returns. See pages 140-65 for all the fruit-growing possibilities. Orchards

can be easily combined with lawns, livestock, wild flower meadows and play areas.

vineyard Grapes are amazingly prolific and very attractive: they should be planted in every garden. A vineyard is most feasible for the larger garden, but well-tended grapevines would do well in a town and can give 6.4kg per square metre (14lb per square yard) equivalent to two bottles of juice. There may well be some who decide to make the whole garden into their own château. Vines can easily be trained up posts, over wires and on most walls, but for serious production they really need to be netted or in a cage. A vineyard is really no more than a specialized fruitcage. See pages 162-3 for cultivation and varieties of grape.

wildflower lawn or meadow This can be any size and can even replace the front lawn but be prepared for a lack of understanding from the neighbours! Most grassed areas are too fertile to make good wildflower areas, and if just sown and left the grasses overwhelm everything else. Reduce the fertility by removing the turf. Stack it for loam or lay it elsewhere, and then plant out pot-grown wildflower plants. Keep the grasses and weeds down by hoeing until the flowers have established and set seed for a year or two,

above Geese and hens rarely cause problems in a well-established orchard and are worth keeping for the valuable fertility which is returned to the soil – and, of course, for the eggs

below Bee hives work well in a semi-wild area which is slightly apart from the rest of the garden. It provides quiet habitats for a whole range of creatures including the bees

then allow the grass back in. Cut the grass back after midsummer once the wildflowers have set and dropped their seed. Grow late flowering wildflowers in a section that is cut in early winter instead.

Bulbs are less demanding and can be planted under turf as they outcompete grass fairly successfully. They look best if planted at random, but are neater out of season if they are concentrated at the base of trees and hedges, or round the perimeter of the lawn. The grass must not be cut until after the bulb leaves have started to wither. Areas treated like this can be under trees, in an orchard or coppice and make great play areas for children as well as making a habitat for wildlife.

coppice If the land is available woodland looks beautiful extending from the garden and will provide a home for all kinds of wildlife. It will also be highly productive in fuel and free-range livestock combined. Something most of us can only dream about!

paddock With spare ground many people make a paddock for a pony, thus exchanging a little grass cutting for a lot of horse care, but the by-product is great stuff for fertilizing.

play area Something I have noticed missing from most gardening books is any reference to children. It is more pleasant, and effective, to lure them to safer spots than to try and exclude them from others. Swings and ropes, large trees and water in any (safe) form will concentrate their attention to suitable grassed areas leaving more precious areas of the garden untrampled.

small town gardens
Gardens in dense urban areas often enjoy wonderful shelter and warmth, compared with those in more open country. Brickwork, tiles and pavements store heat, while buildings reduce low-level wind. Heat is also produced by people, buildings and cars, and enhanced with their carbon dioxide. All this warmth means that the growing season begins several weeks earlier. The last frost of spring always comes much later in pretty little valleys than it does in the city nearby.

Size does not so much limit the kind of garden, as the number of internal subdivi-

sions. You cannot sensibly fit a fruit cage, a rose border, a vegetable plot, lawn *and* a water feature into a 3 x 3 metre (10 x 10ft) plot. However, you could make a very beautiful and productive combination from a couple of these features. So concentrate on one or two of the options rather than trying to squeeze in as many as you can.

Even the tiniest plot has room for herbs, in pots and containers if not a whole bed of them, and where there is space a salad bed gives valuable returns. A patio area is much better value in all weather conditions than a small piece of grass. With scented plants, and a small pond, you can create a tranquil little retreat from the hurly-burly of life. Fruit can be grown trained on walls and as screens, or even in large pots or containers. There may be room for a small vegetable patch or an ornamental area with productive plants.

There is always room for a compost bin and for bees! Beekeeping is ideal for town gardeners – bees add life and interest to the garden, are very productive, and thrive on the longer, milder seasons and myriad urban plants. They are more productive with increased attention, so are ideal if you have a small garden and plenty of spare time. Nest boxes and food for birds and hedgehogs can also be squeezed into the tiniest plots.

larger suburban garden
For most people the typical garden is divided up into several areas, often with a more formal front garden, and enough space to produce significant amounts of fruit and vegetables if well planned. This is perhaps the optimum size for most gardeners without much spare time, as the entire area can be kept attractive and productive without extra help. The larger garden does need careful planning and good routines, as otherwise too many chores can eat up the time. However, I maintained gardens for a living for many years, and nearly all were managed in a few hours per week. I had the benefit of practice and professional tools, but what made the difference was the regularity of the work throughout the year.

There should certainly be room for a fruitcage, greenhouse, vegetable plot and fruit trees, which are best placed furthest away from the house. Ornamental areas with lawns, patio, pool and the herb garden should be as near as possible to the house for convenience.

When deciding on other features, it is probably better to concentrate on a few, rather than trying to cram them all in. That way, each can have sufficient space to be worthwhile. For example, it may be preferable to have a vineyard or an asparagus bed but not both.

small country garden
With up to 4000 square metres (1 acre), what and how you grow is mainly limited by time and money. The choice widens, but then the garden either needs rigorous planning and/or ruthless maintenance or hired labour. I have squeezed more and more into my country garden, but it does take up the equivalent of every weekend throughout the year to stay on top of it. This is the optimum size for a very keen gardener – any larger and it needs to be simplified in many areas, or you have to acquire help.

Intensive methods are better replaced with extensive – half-standard trees in a grassed orchard rather than trained cordons ; vegetables on the flat instead of in raised beds; fewer, bigger, more shrubby borders with sweeping curves and less edging. Grass-cutting is effective for maintaining large areas neatly, but is one of the most time-consuming chores: it may prove a good idea to hire labour for this rather than for the more enjoyable work. Ease of access, good pathways and locating the least visited areas furthest away are vitally important – a lot of time can be wasted going backwards and forwards to fetch tools. The space available allows for a wide range of wildlife habitats, as well as a hen run and a small pond. A garden this size should be self-sufficient in fertility.

large country garden
With one hectare (2.5 acres) or more almost any garden imaginable can be created. You could certainly become self-sufficient in fruit and vegetables, and would be able to keep whatever livestock you have time for. In order to keep the labour down large areas need to be simplified, grassed and cut or strimmed regularly – enabling you to feed the rest of the garden with clippings as mulch and fertility. Machinery and hired labour becomes a necessity for many more of the tasks though four-legged lawnmowers can replace this to a great extent. Gardening as such becomes landscaping around the house and effectively then a very large garden becomes more of a larger suburban garden with a couple of acres of paddock or private woodland extending out from it. Without careful planning, too much space could prove more of a curse than a blessing!

Creating interesting views is essential to the success of any garden. Here, a rampant honeysuckle creates a natural arch over a path bordered by daphne and ferns. The combined effect is to entice any wandering explorer to creep through towards the lion's head at the end

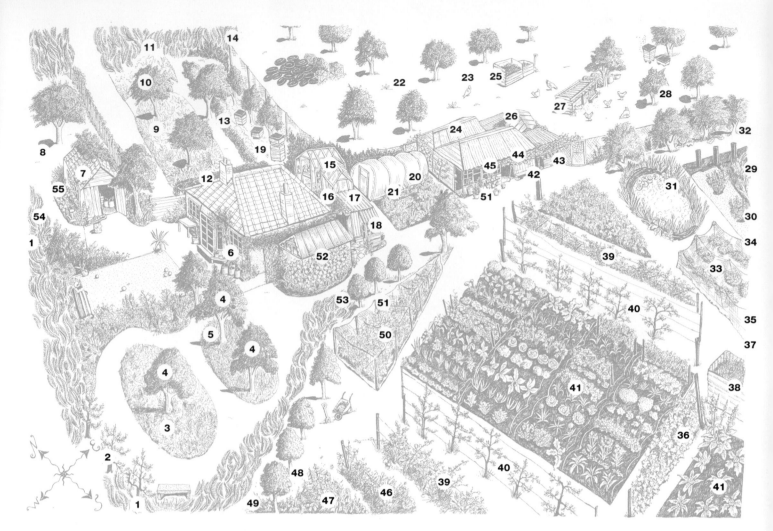

my garden plan

My garden was planned to provide as wide a range of fruit, vegetables and flowers as possible, organically and for my own use. Labour had to be kept to a minimum with nearly an acre to look after in my spare time. So every plant began with a really good start. Sufficient space, light and moisture, freedom from competition and good shelter enabled them to grow strongly and resist disease. I also planned to maximize the natural checks and balances so that pest control could be achieved with little direct intervention.

Initially, my plot was mostly overgrown with just half a dozen old trees, so I put the whole lot down to grass while I tackled one area at a time. Regular grass cutting improved the fertility and also eliminated most of the weeds. Athough initially onerous, I have reduced grass cutting to one hour per week; all that is left are grass paths with large patches of unbroken lawn. I now use the clippings as mulches all over the garden so no time is wasted taking them to a central point for disposal.

Trees were planted the first autumn with soft fruit and perennial vegetables following close behind. The vegetable bed was completed by the third year and the last of the three long rotation beds by the fourth. The ornamental areas and herb and companion plantings had to wait until the perennials were established before they were allowed to grow underneath to prevent them competing too fiercely. Of course these plantings now continue on a constant renewal basis.

Fertility is mostly home-grown and supplemented by dilute seaweed extract and any organiç materials I can scavenge. Weed control is mainly with a sharp hoe at fortnightly intervals and by mulching wherever possible. Watering (even here in the driest village in the UK) is restricted to plants in pots, under cover or when sowing and transplanting. Time is saved with this chore thanks to a permanent system of hoses radiating from the cottage. Pest and disease control is totally organic but little direct action is required except for introducing predators to the greenhouses and polytunnel and soft-soaping aphids on the roses.

Note The author's garden is located in Norfolk, England and hence all compass directions are appropriate for the northern hemisphere.

1 Leylandii hedge 2.4m (8ft) giving shelter and predator nest sites.

2 Pear espaliers, utilizing the heat from a sunny brick wall, look excellent as a backdrop all year round.

3 Flower garden designed for a long season of scented plants which aid predators and pollinators as well as giving pleasure to humans.

4 Mulberry, apple, pear and old plum trees in the flower garden.

5 Herb bed near to the kitchen for easy access.

6 Cottage walls used for tender and climbing plants

7 Cider press and 'cellar' in a converted garage.

8 Dappled shade garden for hot days with mainly foliage plants.

9 Front garden full of scented plants for pleasure and to provide a long season of flowers for predators and pollinators.

10 Sweet cherries planted here where noisy neighbours and road traffic reduce bird damage to only 90% losses. They also hang over the drive which would otherwise be wasted space and the roots do little harm.

11 Silver border with good protection from the north and east for tender plants.

12 Pergola with climbing scented plants filtering noise and view.

13 Hunza apricot hedge grown from seed with hope of fruit yet to come.

14 Mixed hedge, initially cut back and now grown to 2.4m (8ft) for shelter.

15 Greenhouse located near to the house for easy access; this ensures provision of water, electricity and regular inspections.

16 Fan apricot using best cottage wall for extra warmth.

17 Wood and fuel store near house for easy access in inclement weather.

18 Fruit and root store close to the house for access. Fruit and roots are stored in old deep freezers.

19 Apiary set in sheltered area so bees fly up and away.

20 Polytunnel and seed/salad bed near to greenhouse to reduce transport and near to house for water and electricity.

21 Polytunnel aligned to allow maximum sun and the seed/salad bed raised about 15° to increase the effects of the sun for an earlier start. The seed/salad bed is effectively in a small walled garden but is open to the south, though sheltered by the fruitcage.

22 Orchard with apples (some original); new plantings did badly so now being replaced by peaches. Large old trees provide shelter for others on southern side.

23 Under the trees run ducks, geese and hens for eggs, manure and pest control. These are allowed in other areas during winter, under supervision!

24 Storage shed complex for all the junk. By aligning this with the cottage, store and polytunnel and with the henhouse down the middle, it continues the belt of shelter but shades only the roots of the orchard trees. At the same time it makes a far warmer microclimate on the southern side. Most importantly it is at the centre of the garden with paths radiating from it so there is less time wasted going to and fro.

25 Compost bins near henhouse, the hens peck at and start to process the waste material before it gets loaded into the bins.

26 Henhouse and compost near plums which can use the extra fertility, the plums also shelter the other trees on their south side.

27 Hen dust bath with ashes; hens use this to rid themselves of parasites and the ashes are then usefully spread around. Roof also functions as an onion drier.

28 Pears, peaches and other smaller top fruit benefit from the shelter made by the plums, apples and storage sheds and have full sun.

29 Asparagus bed, well away from house as rarely needs attention.

30 New vineyard under construction for even more juice and wine.

31 Pond, only dug four years ago, has brought in a tremendous number of newts, dragonflies and even a grass snake. The overflow feeds a comfrey bed and the peach trees which benefit from reflected light. Around the pond is a wildlife log fence grown through with beneficial plants. The predators can walk from this wild area to the vegetable beds but pests like slugs are less mobile

and rarely cause problems.

32 Old mixed hedge initially cut back hard and now cut at 2.4m (8ft).

33 Massive strawberry bed. This rotates with a potato bed and a globe artichoke bed, each being on one bed for three to four years. Although it is not considered a good idea for potatoes to be planted in the same place for more than one year I find this is offset if, after their four years, they do not return for seven or eight years. All three crops like rich conditions and have few common pests or diseases.

34 New blackcurrant bed may be eradicated as the bought-in plants appear to be less healthy than the old ones I wanted to replace!

35 Southern avenue shaded by neighbours' hedge but suitable for apple trees for juice and cider and grass survives where little else can.

36 Grapevine wall kept to 1.8m (6ft) to prevent shade on vegetable beds, the roots encouraged by mound and trench to go under path rather than bed. This wall filters the wind like a hedge so warms and shelters the vegetable beds on the south side helping to create the walled garden effect without the expense.

37 Walnut planted where it can grow over grass as it will hinder other plants underneath as it gets bigger with shade and from the substance it exudes.

38 Bonfire area. The bonfire is surrounded by corrugated iron and raised to keep out hedgehogs and other little beneficial garden helpers as much as possible.

39 Rows of brambles 2.4m (8ft) high on wires with grass paths on either side and a grass bank for predators underneath. These provide excellent shelter for the fruit espaliers and vegetable bed.

40 Fruit espaliers, encouraged to root under paths with trench and mound, provide shelter for the vegetable bed. Underplanted with various strong aromatic herbs as companion plants for these and for the vegetables. The espaliers are supported with both stakes and wires and also by an overhead wire supported by four corner posts of out-of-use telegraph poles which likewise support the grape wall and grape bower.

41 Forty raised vegetable beds, aligned north/south for maximum sun saturation and each raised at the north end to counteract the slightly north-facing slope. Narrow access paths run north/south; wide paths for wheelbarrow east/west. A card index allows me to keep track of rotations.

42 Grape bower utilizes shelter of shed complex to give central dappled garden area.

43 Summer/kiwi house made from posts and recycled window frames.

44 Tool and potting shed, central for ease of access.

45 Old corrugated iron chicken shed converted to vinehouse with plastic sheets for roof and recycled window frames for front.

46 Blackcurrants now getting old and poor but stlll cropping well. Rows run north/south for equal sun and these require little attention so are fine in this isolated corner.

47 Raspberries enjoy semi-woodland at edge of wild nut corner.

48 Nut corner, initially kept clean and cultivated but now nut windbreak is established it has been planted up with berries, nettles and wildflowers to encourage predators. Like the pond it is far from the vegetables so the less mobile pests are effectively isolated. The nuts require little maintenance so are ideal tucked away here.

49 A rotting log pile, hedgehog box and a concrete and rubble pile are placed here to give yet more habitats and winter shelters for predators. This area also holds another beehive.

50 Fruitcage, made from recycled materials and providing shelter at north end of vegetable bed, reinforced by polytunnel/shed complex. As this is visited often during the summer it is conveniently near to the house.

51 Grapevines in pots against a low corrugated iron wall and sheds gain from the warmth and shelter.

52 Propagating greenhouse in most sheltered site but close for access, water and electricity, made from recycled materials.

53 Mint bed under apples in shady site and near house for easy use.

54 Pathway running in shade of hedge, grass survives where little else would fare well.

55 Vines using warmth of wall.

6 THE ORNAMENTAL
organic garden

Gardens can be works of art – but tastes differ in art as in everything else. Some people prefer order and symmetry, while others like subtle shading and soft lines, or blazes of bright, contrasting colours. All are equally valid; but a mixture of diverse styles will not work, unless they are very skilfully handled.

What makes a pleasant garden is a feeling of naturalness, combined with a harmony of shapes, colours, scents and sounds. The gardener's art is to create beauty, not only in the front garden or in one particular bed, but in each and every part. A garden is complete only when every bed, view and vista – even the most functional and productive area – is a pleasure to the eye.

Moreover, even purely ornamental areas benefit the rest of the garden: they can be a source of fertility, contributing grass clippings, leaves and prunings for compost; and they can encourage and sustain many more forms of life. Most of all, ornamental areas make it possible to have the wide variety of plants needed to create a balanced ecosystem, helping to control pests and diseases in all parts of the garden.

An ornamental border in midsummer with lupins in the foreground, a mulberry tree in the middle of the bed, foxgloves and yellow asphodelines towards the back of the picture and kniphofias in front of *Cordyline australis* far right

planning the elements

framework The framework of a garden, its structure or skeleton, remains more or less unchanged throughout the year, so it is especially important to get it right. The view from the windows is particularly important: the outlines,

Golden variegated balm in the foreground, sweet cicely, angelica and red sage provide interesting foliage early in the year before the border fills with flowers

shapes and views formed by the permanent features need to look good when there is little leaf or flower to help decorate them – which can mean almost half the year. The shapes and edges of beds, borders and paths are most important, but pergolas, walls, hedges, tree trunks and evergreens also help create the permanent design, so great care needs to be taken with their layout and position. Plan carefully, using garden canes and string to try out different permutations before doing any work on the ground.

Ideally, the garden as a whole should not be visible from any one point – there should always be a hint of more to discover. Create a hidden corner by extending the edge of a bed or border, or plant an island bed, so that there is an invitation to explore. Long, thin gardens can be made more interesting by breaking them up into a series of 'rooms', with a meandering path that gives glimpses of spaces beyond. Paths can be tapered and curved to change perspective. They should always lead to something, if only an urn of flowers. Paths that bend so that they disappear round a corner invite more exploration, and *trompe l'oeil* steps at a boundary can give an impression of size and of more garden to discover. Arches, gateways and pergolas add vertical interest and help heighten the feeling of rooms within rooms. They allow a smooth transition from one part of the garden to another with a different flavour; they also block out unsightly objects and views – remember that the closer the screen, the less height needed for it to work.

The colours and materials that make up the solid part of the framework tend to be more pleasing if they are compatible with their surroundings, and with each other. It helps to have all timberwork stained to the same colour, and to use local materials throughout the garden.

foliage Deciduous foliage, although welcomed in the spring and appreciated in the autumn, is otherwise only noticed as a backdrop to flowers. Yet foliage is important in its own right; the many different forms, textures, colours and scents adding interest to any planting. Carefully selecting and combining these creates a more unified appearance than concentrating on flowers alone. You could even dispense with flowers completely, as many plants have beautiful leaf colours – and not only in the autumn. Some, such as the poplar (*P. c.* Aurora) and the jasmine (*J.* x *stephanense*) have brilliantly coloured new leaves in the spring and there are countless plants with variegated leaves in many patterns and shades. Many evergreens, such as elaeagnus, euonymous and holly, have forms with white and yellow variegated and coloured leaves, which are useful for brightening dull winter days and dark corners.

evergreens contribute much to the feeling of permanence in a garden. They need to be considered along with the framework to give year-round interest, especially in winter, when browns tend to predominate. The many shades and varieties of evergreens, the golds, reds and blues of conifers and heathers, enable you to create colourful gardens that remain almost unchanged throughout the year. Once established, these gardens require little maintenance, though they are hard to blend in with many settings. Evergreens, especially ivy, are useful for providing shelter, nest and hibernation sites for insects and animals in winter, and for this reason alone some should be included in each part of the garden.

The effect of foliage is enhanced by multiple planting, particularly of young herbaceous plants. Single specimens can give a spotty appearance which is reinforced when the flowers come out: most plants look best when grouped, especially in threes, fives and sevens. Obviously this is not always practical or desirable, but in a bed with say three dozen plants, the effect will be better with two groups of seven, two of five and four of three plants, than with 36 different ones. Repetition can become monotonous, but using one favourite plant frequently in various areas can contribute to the garden's unity.

flowers

For most people, flowers are the main purpose of ornamental areas. They contribute beauty and charm, and provide nectar and pollen for beneficial insects. Organic gardeners, who want to increase the amount of wildlife in the garden, try to ensure a constant succession of flowers, using as great a variety of plants as possible to sustain the number and variety of creatures. The value of plants is increased if their flowers are followed by seeds and berries, which then feed insects and animals. These fruits may be as attractive as the flowers, as with holly berries and Gladwyn iris. Few berries last for long but those in unusual colours, like yellow, pyracantha, seem to last longer than others.

Choosing flowers is a matter of personal taste. There are plenty of theories on composing colour mixtures with emphasis on the harmony of colours, or using single shade borders, for example with all white flowers. However, some people seem to like discords and splattered paintbox effects; others go for pastel shades and gentle gradations, while many just want masses of colour. There is only one way to find out what works for you, and that is to try and do it. Make notes of what works and what does not, and change the plants around as soon as they can be moved. No garden is ever finished — it can always be improved!

features

Features can be anything from classical statuary to an old wheelbarrow full of gnomes. Ponds and water in any form,

pergolas and timberwork, rustic arbours, urns and containers, special beds and specimen plants can all be features; it is their setting and positioning that makes them effective. If a garden has too many features though, it will become a junkyard. One main feature in each area or 'room' is usually sufficient. Particularly pleasing vistas are very much improved by a seat for viewing them. In fact, no garden is complete without seats — though the toiling gardener may seldom use them, they help to give an atmosphere of relaxation.

themes

are subtle features which particular areas, or the garden as a whole, has in common. A water garden or a wild garden is a theme; as are scented gardens, historical gardens, Bible plants, silver borders and herb beds. The danger with themes, as with features, is that they can become overpowering or constraining if followed too rigidly. Set the theme broadly and leave yourself room to manoeuvre. A wildlife garden that uses only native plants will have to leave out such useful ones as cotoneasters, buddleias and pyracanthas. A garden of all black flowers is going to be harder to achieve than a single border

top The salmon-pink rambler *Rosa* Albertine compliments the dark red of the shed creating a pretty corner in the ornamental part of the garden. A clump of *Alchemilla mollis* softens the edge of the water butt while mounds of thyme add interest at ground level
above The selection of fragrant thymes planted beneath the log seat make it an especially pleasant place to take a break

of silver foliage; and a bed can have more variation and colour if it is to attract both bees *and* butterflies than one or the other.

In the organic garden (which is a theme itself) some features and themes are especially pertinent as they benefit the life in the garden so much, for example, ponds and water, wildflower gardens, native plants, bee-hives and bee gardens. Other themes may be worthy in their own right, such as wildlife sanctuaries and gardens of endangered plants such as wildflowers, rare fruits or old varieties of vegetables.

Using particular forms of plants can create a theme without being too obvious. The spiky leaves of yuccas and crocosmia can give a drier, more tropical appearance, as can Chusan palms, bamboos and large-leaved plants such as figs. I've even had an Opuntia (prickly pear cactus) outside in a sunny spot for several years now, and I use only a cloche over it in the depth of winter. Conifers, heathers and silver birches give a colder, heath-like effect. Rampant climbers rapidly create an enclosed feeling. Of all themes, scent is my favourite: I have deliberately selected as many scented plants as possible so that my garden provides a feast for the nose as much as for the eye.

the cottage garden

The myth of cottage gardens, perpetuated by expensive follies at flower shows, has done much to mislead gardeners. Wonderful mixtures of flowers combined with fruits and vegetables look terrific when staged for the cameras but can be incredibly time-consuming to weed and maintain. In practice, many of the plants choke each other and birds eat most of the produce. Cottage-dwellers did not run their gardens for food; they lived on beer, bread and roots grown elsewhere. The cottage gardens were planted with herbs for flavouring and medicinal uses, together with some fruit trees and bushes.

Providing that plants are well chosen, there is great advantage in having a wide variety, as this supplies the diversity that makes for a stable ecology, so that pests and diseases become less of a problem. This mixing is highly suitable for non-productive areas, but vegetables require the best of conditions before they grow well (*see page 112*). Although they benefit from being grown with flowers and other plants, they must never be crowded or they will fail. Some vegetables, such as runner beans and marrows, can trail over other plants and produce usable crops, but their season is short. Salad crops can make quite attractive bedding in open spots but unless you grow a cut-and-come-again variety, harvesting will leave a gap. Many fruit bushes can be grown among flowers, but they are unlikely to do as well as in a specially prepared bed. Also, it can be difficult to protect fruits from the birds when they are growing among other plants (though bushes can be netted individually).

So although mixing food crops and flowers is generally a good idea, the food crops must be given priority of position and flowering plants added in any niche left spare. Basically, this means giving the vegetable patch an appealing design, adding companion plants and flowers, and surrounding it with trained fruit. Trying to do it the other way round – growing food crops in among existing ornamental plants – will nearly always give poor results because of the competition from the established plants. Of course, there is the alternative of growing edible ornamental plants, and delightful gardens can be made composed mainly of herbs (*see Chapter 9*).

finish It is the finishing touches that make the perfect garden; neglecting them spoils the overall effect disproportionately. Most important is to get rid of every bit of litter and junk. Have a glory hole where you can hide things away if you cannot bring yourself to dispose of them entirely. Junk includes anything that is not intended as a feature, so garden tools, pots, canes and buckets are best tidied into a shed rather than left exposed. The edging of turfed areas

below Single colour combinations like this one work well, partly because they highlight the shape and form of the blooms and leaves of each plant
bottom Sweet peas, larkspur and rudbeckia grown for cutting among the vegetables in the raised beds

is critical, and the removal of tufts of grass growing up against trunks and fences will improve appearances greatly.

Uniformity, or at least consistency, also helps: one plastic cloche made from a lemonade bottle can look unsightly; three dozen look neat. When adding to anything in the garden or repairing, say, a fence try and blend the new with the old by painting them all. As mentioned above, most timberwork can be stained to a similar hue, and black bituminous paint will give an enduring, inexpensive black finish to metal.

starting work

First prepare the area well, removing all weeds and rubbish and improving the soil as outlined in Chapter 2. Once the site is marked out and ready, plant trees, preferably fruiting as well as purely ornamental ones, and ensure that each has ample room to develop. After these have established for a year, plant shrubs and fruit bushes between, again leaving each plenty of room. After another year, plant herbaceous plants, ground cover and bulbs in the spaces left available. Finally, climbers can be grown to ramble over the trees and shrubs when these have attained sufficient size. The area needs

careful weed control until full cover is attained, but thick mulches will minimize this and aid growth. The temptation to plant up the apparently enormous gaps in the first two years should be resisted in order to give each form of plant room to establish itself.

This is obviously a counsel of perfection. Many people will have neither the time nor the patience to fulfil the plan year by year, waiting until first the trees and then the shrubs are established, and putting up with the gaps in the meantime. If you do want to do it all at once, at least put the trees in first, and try to let them have enough room to establish properly.

Often a bed or border is not empty in the first place. This makes it difficult to establish new plants, especially of related families or forms, because of competition from the existing ones. In this situation plants need even better weed control and watering until established than if they were in a clean bed.

Of course, often no conscious plan is made for planting up a bed. What happens is that the first plants to arrive get the best positions, and each wave of later arrivals has to be squeezed into any gaps left. This becomes more complicated as different plants outgrow their positions and neighbours, and the time comes to reorganize the bed. When this happens, the oldest trees and shrubs, if wanted, have to be left in place, but most common small shrubs can be lifted and replanted in a better position. Most herbaceous plants are invigorated by lifting and splitting every few years, in any case, which provides the ideal opportunity. It is much more effective to put the same plant together in small groups rather than scatter them around. Reworking a bed and splitting up plants gives a good opportunity to do this.

borders In the design for a border it is obviously expedient to have shorter plants closer

left Putting away pots, tools and other gardening equipment in a shed or outhouse improves the look of any garden. Here, the shed also harbours a grapevine
below A well-established planting of the climbing rose, Handel with jasmine and Regal lilies

top The ornamental beds in the middle of winter

above In midsummer the beds are in full bloom with Florentine iris, foxgloves, lupins and asphodelines. The trim lawn edges and lavender border enable the border plants to be seen at their best

right A formal silver border combines santolina in the front with lavender directly behind

inclined to be leggy, such as lavender or broom; to prune those that flower early in the year immediately after flowering; to prune those that flower later as soon as the leaves drop; and to prune evergreens, tender plants and those with hollow stems such as buddleia in spring, and the prunus family in midsummer. All shrubs benefit from soil enrichment and watering but they are mostly very tolerant of different soils. Climbers can add another layer with shrubs but herbaceous plants seldom flourish with them for long because of their competition.

herbaceous borders are often believed to need a lot of work, but with careful planning and dwarf plants the only regular chore is tidying back the withered growths in autumn, and weed control. Well spaced groups of plants makes weeding between them much easier, and heavy mulches are an immense benefit. When cutting back in autumn, wait until the stems have withered so that all the nutrients have been reabsorbed, then cut them off about 15cm (6in) high. This leaves the old stem bases to support and protect the young shoots as they emerge, and marks their position. Herbaceous plants combine well with bulbs which have a similar habit but obviously climbers can be added only if a timber framework is provided for them. Many shrubs can be grown with herbaceous plants to make a mixed bed, but they soon predominate and can be effectively combined only with dwarf varieties, or if they are given enough space.

Herbaceous beds, even with bulbs and annual flowers, tend to be rather empty much of the year and need to be placed where they will be appreciated in summer

towards you than taller, but do not regiment the heights too much. Allow some tall plants to have forward positions. Taller, late-growing herbaceous plants can come in front of early flowerers that look drab and need hiding, such as spring bulbs. The latter can also be grown under deciduous shrubs that are late to come into leaf because they can use the winter light and be dormant in the dark dry shade of summer. Shrub borders need the least maintenance, especially if they contain many evergreens. The dense shade of large shrubs keeps most weeds under control and few ornamental shrubs need much pruning if they are well spaced.

A general guide is to leave most plants unpruned unless they get too big, or are

but not so noticable from windows in winter. Their area can have year-round interest if they are backed by winter and early spring-flowering shrubs which will draw the eye before becoming obscured by the spring and summer growth.

bedding plants especially if bought ones, are wasteful of cash and resources because they are started off with heat, peat and plastic containers and so rate badly in ecological terms. They are expensive because they need replacing annually, and in order to get continuous colour and interest the bed needs to be replanted at least two or three times each year. Nevertheless, some bedding plants such as sweet alyssum, zonal pelargoniums, impatiens and fuchsias, are ideal for creating small features throughout the summer and are ideal for pots and containers.

French marigolds are one of the best companion plants and should be grown by everyone. They attract beneficial insects, discourage many pests and flower for months. French marigolds should never be transplanted once in flower, so nip out all flowers and buds beforehand, to ensure success later.

annuals Many bedding plants are not annuals, but are merely grown for one season only and then discarded. Many true annuals may be used as bedding plants and are useful fillers where gaps and losses leave space in beds but several have to be sown in position to do at all well. Annuals offer some of the brightest blazes of colour, and often grow well in poor soil and sites, particularly when direct sown. Some have outstanding value and should be included in almost every garden – for example, sweet peas, night-scented stock, pot marigolds and *Limnanthes douglasii*.

One problem with bedding plants is that most need to be started off early in the year under cover, competing for space and time with the vegetables. There are several ways to avoid this, other than having permanent herbaceous or shrub beds. Annuals can be sown in their final flowering position. This saves space, but they need very careful weeding and do not flower until late spring at the earliest. Hardy annuals sown in the autumn overwinter and flower earlier than

spring-sown plants, though they may also finish sooner and then need replacing.

biennials are the best solution. These are sown in late spring and summer in a seedbed after the brassicas have been planted out and no longer need the space. They are then planted out in their flowering position in autumn or early the following spring. Sweet rocket, sweet william, foxgloves, wallflowers and stocks are all very useful in this way and give a lot of effect for little labour.

Flowers for cutting are better grown on the vegetable beds where their loss will be less noticeable than from the middle of your best border and by growing them on the vegetable plot they break the rotation and benefit the crops as well as bringing in beneficial insects.

buying & propagating plants

It is better to plan a bed or border on paper first, with the aid of several catalogues, than to make it up as you go along. Catalogues give glowing descriptions of plants but it is

still hard to visualize them – sometimes even when a photo is provided. Going to visit garden centres and gardens, especially those that are well labelled, gives a much better idea of what plants look like.

If you order plants through the post, be prepared to send back anything that is of poor quality. At a garden centre you can choose which plants you want. Do not always go for the biggest, as these may not grow away so easily; look for healthy plants,

Bergamot and golden feverfew in the front of the border with a pear tree on the right and a mix of phloxes behind

Lawns are time-consuming to maintain but they look good with most plants and the colour and texture is more sympathetic than hard stone paths

with plenty of young strong shoots, and avoid any that look thin, spindly or sick, no matter how cheap. Plants that have been on the shelf too long will have roots coming out the bottom of the pot, and often a mat of weed on top. Buying weeds with your plants is like getting litter with your shopping: remove and leave them there, at the till if you are assertive enough.

propagating Much the best way of acquiring plants is to grow your own. Most can be grown from seed, in much the same way as vegetables, though some need to spend time in a nursery bed before they are big enough to plant out. For some trees this can be a long time, and these may be better bought, but many shrubs are ready quite quickly Named varieties have to be grown from cuttings as seed rarely comes true. *See pages 40-1 for propagation from cuttings.* Herbaceous plants can nearly all be propagated by root division when dormant and can be rapidly multiplied in good conditions, even from tiny pieces, providing each has a bud. Discard the centres of large old clumps in favour of vigorous young shoots from the edges, as these will grow better anyway.

With patience, a garden can be stocked in this way with little expense. Most gardeners are only too willing to donate cuttings and seeds, and few begrudge bits off herbaceous

plants, even if they are not prepared to dig up and divide the whole clump for you.

the backdrop Lawns, paths and hedges are a major part of the framework of a garden, and their appearance and maintenance is therefore crucial to the overall effect. If they are in poor condition they draw attention to themselves instead of enhancing the rest of the garden. Their shape and positioning needs careful planning combined with a good start to reduce or ease maintenance work later.

lawns and grass paths make up much of the typical garden. Their emerald green does show off other plants to perfection, but these areas take a tremendous amount of work, cash and resources to maintain. In very small gardens serious consideration should be given to dispensing with grass altogether: this can save the need for a grass cutter and its storage, as well as liberating ground space. Areas for sitting or sunbathing could be hard-surfaced or gravelled instead (though remember that these materials will also make it a lot hotter) and surrounded or patch-planted with low-growing plants such as chamomile and thymes.

For large gardens grass is the most sensible ground cover. It is relatively easy to keep neat and tidy, even if it is time-consuming. Grassed areas compete with the plants around them but their clippings can be used as a mulch to favour these plants. Grassed areas can be established in three ways: by seeding, by turfing and by cutting the natural cover regularly.

seeding is not expensive, but is quite hard work. The area needs to be dug, weeded, levelled and raked to make a seedbed, removing all stones and rubbish. Incorporate ground rock dusts, ground seaweed and lime or calcified seaweed to enrich the soil. The first flushes of weeds can be raked or flame-gunned. The area is then sown in spring or autumn with grass seed.

Tough-wearing recreational ryegrass mixtures are a better choice than the less competitive fine grasses intended for bowling greens. The fine grasses look good, but do not take hard wear, and they prefer acid conditions, which encourage mosses and weeds.

A good idea is to sow a mixture of companion plants along with the grass, such as clovers, chamomile, creeping thyme, daisies, yarrow and other scented and pretty turf plants. Of course pure grass can be grown, but mixtures are more interesting and ecologically sound, as well as staying greener when there is a drought. After sowing the seed, rake it in, firm it down and hang up bird scarers. Give the young grass a cut and roll when 5cm (2in) high and keep the usage light for a growing season.

turfing is the most expensive way to grass an area, but requires less work than seeding and gives more rapid results. It can only be done well in early spring or early autumn with damp conditions and/or frequent watering. The area still needs to be dug, enriched and levelled, but much less thoroughly. Stubborn perennial weeds like docks and dandelions must be dug out, but annual weeds can effectively be ignored as they will mostly be killed. Turfing theoretically gives a choice of turf, but this may be difficult in practice. Organic gardeners should be aware that much turf comes from old meadow land and is frequently pretreated with inorganic fertilizers and herbicides.

natural cover Cutting the natural ground cover regularly is the slower method of getting a good sward, but produces the most ecologically balanced mixture of plants with the minimum of work and expense. The process is the same as for regularly maintaining or improving an existing sward, and basically consists of making the conditions most suitable for grasses and unsuitable for most other plants. If the area is too rough initially for a mower, then use a strimmer or brushcutter for the initial attacks. Once the growth is down to a rough sward just keep cutting once a week from early spring to late autumn, returning the clippings and slowly reducing the height of cut. This kills almost all tall weeds. Acid-loving weeds are discouraged and the tougher grasses can be aided by liming twice a year with calcified seaweed or

dolomitic lime. Patches of clover which stand out green in a drought are blended in by sowing clover seed in the remaining areas: clovers improve the lushness of the sward.

scarifying in the autumn or spring with a wire rake is hard work but benefits the lawn; it is less hard work to hire a machine. Scarifying produces a mass of thatch for use as a mulch or for composting, but needs to be moistened with dilute urine or liquid feed to rot down quickly. Follow scarifying by raking in a mixture of ground seaweed, rock dusts and grass seed (with sharp sand for heavy soils) and calcified seaweed. This same feed can be used annually each spring, but it is better to use diluted urine sprinkled over the turf instead. It is absorbed rapidly, giving lush growth – use the clippings as a mulch. Rosette weeds such as plantains and thistles may survive scarifying, cutting and soil improvement treatments, but they can be hand-pulled with a sharp knife, severing deep underneath to stop regrowth.

grass-cutting The regular cutting of grass is an effective weed-control measure best done with a rotary mower that can collect the clippings. Cylinder mowers are not as good in damp conditions or with longer growths. Mowers that leave the clippings build up too much thatch. Ideally, cut the grass weekly, but vary the height through the season to control the growth. The first and last cuts should be high: 5-8cm (2-3in). Return the clippings to the surface as worms are actively eating them in spring and autumn. The spring cuts should decrease in height to 2-3cm (1-1½in) by mid spring, and remain there till midsummer, removing and returning the clippings alternately. From midsummer raise the height to 3-5cm (1½-2in) to keep the grass greener and more drought-resistant, and then to 5-8cm (2-3in) from late autumn, removing the clippings until the last leaves fall. Keep the mower blades sharp!

Spreading lawn mowings on a bed of potatoes is an efficient way of topping up the soil's fertility

cutting techniques Lawns and grass paths should have a pleasing design, but they also need regular cutting to remain neat. Near the house cutting should be done weekly; further away and in orchards, fortnightly, and in wild areas once or twice a year. This is time-consuming work, so careful planning and redesigning can be well worthwhile. If a low branch or object grazes your head or needs careful cutting around, then remove it. The same applies to those odd little corners where you have to push the mower in and out several times. Long paths should be made to fit a given number of passes, without leaving an odd strip to go back. Arrange your plantings so that there is some shrub or fruit bush deserving a mulch near to hand each time the grass box gets full. If grass cuttings have to be emptied some distance away, a wheelbarrow will combine several loads in one trip.

strimmers Using a strimmer adds neatness: it can do the edges, around tree trunks, and awkward and difficult spots the mower cannot reach. It is also good for trimming grass to different heights. For example, either side of a mown path in a wild area or orchard, the grass can be kept about 30cm (12in) high, so it does not fall over the path. Cutting grass with a strimmer can provide a good environment for bulbs, primroses, cowslips and violets, as the area can be kept neat without becoming overgrown and choking these treasures. The height should be varied by cutting hard around them while in full leaf or flower, and then cutting higher and uniformly as the summer progresses. (Never cut bulb leaves until they wither or you will spoil the flowering the following year.)

hedges Like turfed areas, hedges need planning and consideration. They warm the garden, and provide a nesting habitat as well as decoration so evergreen or beech hedges which hold their leaves through the winter are the most helpful for encouraging wildlife. Informal mixed hedges are not cut and are effectively just long narrow shrub borders which produce a beautiful flowering screen with little trouble. Scented hedges, fruit hedges and rose hedges are all possible and make particular sense in a small garden where the hedge might be the only place left to grow the plants that you like. A formal hedge takes up much less space as it is regularly cut, preferably twice a year. See pages 93-4 for recommended hedging plants.

Because hedges need to grow densely the ground must be well prepared, and they need weed control for the first two or three years until well established. Planting through a strip of carpet or plastic is ideal. For the thickest hedges, plant a double staggered row. Sloping the plants over at 45 degrees gives a lower, thicker base, and interweaving can increase this, giving a very low dense hedge from fewer plants.

Young hedges benefit from a temporary screen to reduce wind damage, but do not make this too close or too dark or it may kill back the foliage. Cut back the sides and top hard each winter until the hedge is nearly the required size, then cut back in late spring and again in late summer for the neatest effect. Taper hedges in at the top slightly to allow light and rain to reach the base. Like everything in the garden, hedges benefit from a monthly spraying with seaweed solution during the growing season.

The leylandii hedge provides a dense, dark backdrop to the flower borders and a sheltered place for a small bench from which to admire the garden

PLANT SELECTION

There are countless plants in cultivation: *The Hillier Manual of Trees and Shrubs* lists over 8,000. Here are a few of my favourites. I have chosen them for their ease of culture, pest and disease resistance, benefits to wildlife, beauty and wherever possible for their scent. I consider a plant as a tree if it is shrubby, with a single stem, and can be used as a specimen. Most shrubs can be treated as small trees in the manner of standard roses, and vice versa.

The letters *spp* after a genus means there are several interesting and similar species you may like to grow, but because of space I have selected only one. The information relates to my favourite species or variety in entries where one is mentioned and, where none is mentioned, to the genus as a whole.

specimen trees

It is important to choose trees that are not going to grow too large for your garden. Find out the final height and spread before you buy, and remember that a large tree can shade a whole garden, and will take up a lot of water and nutrients from the soil. Trees should not be planted too near the house, as they can damage drains and foundations – 12m (40ft) is a safe distance.

I have included here in the ornamental section a number of my favourite fruit trees: they are as beautiful as the purely ornamental varieties, are not too large for most gardens, and attract birds and other wildlife. For individual varieties of fruit trees, their needs and treatment, see pages 153-9.

planting   Trees are usually bought bare-rooted, or in containers, though sometimes they will be offered with the roots balled, or wrapped in sacking. Bare-rooted or balled trees should be planted in winter, while dormant. Check that the bare-rooted tree has a large, healthy-looking root system, and that the roots have not dried out (if the roots seem dry, soak for a day before planting). Follow the detailed instructions for planting

trees (see *page 147*), and remember that the soil should be well prepared beforehand. Try to order trees well in advance, so that you have time to prepare. Never plant trees in frozen or waterlogged soil. If conditions are bad, heel the plants in – dig a shallow trench, lay the tree in on its side, and cover the roots with moist peat or soil.

aftercare   Feed trees every spring, spray with seaweed solution monthly and mulch every autumn with well-rotted manure or compost.

information given: height and spread after 5 years/ scent if any/ flower colour/ time of flowering/ soil/ site/ when to prune

birch

betula pendula   3.7 x 2.4m (12 x 8ft)/ -/ -/ -/ most/ open/ midsummer to mid autumn
Silver birches look best in small informal groups; other birches have yellow foliage or attractive bark. Wine used to be made from silver birch spring sap.

In spring, a sweet cherry, a flowering cherry and a magnolia compete for attention at tree level while a laurel (*Prunus laurocerasus* Otto Luyken) adds interest lower down

top The medlar is a pretty
tree which is perfect to grow
as a specimen in a small
garden (see page 158); it also
bears fruit which can be
made into jelly
above Pear blossom
below The large white flowers
of a quince

maple

acer japonicum Vitifolium 1.5 x 1.2m (5
x 4ft)/ -/ red/ mid to late spring/ moist/
sheltered/ no

Japanese maples have lovely shape and form,
and are noted for their beautiful leaves, with
wonderful autumn colours of red, bronze
and purple.

rowan

sorbus aucuparia 3 x 2.4m (10 x 8ft)/ -/
white/ late spring to early summer/ acid/
most/ early to midwinter

Mountain ash or rowan is very attractive in
form and foliage and the numerous red
berries are much loved by birds. I prefer the
native to other ornamental forms.

false acacia

robinia pseudoacacia 6 x 3m (20 x 10ft)/
-/ white/ early summer/ dry, fertile/ open/
mid-spring

An ideal tree for the town garden. It has
attractive leaves which split into many leaflets,
and trails of pea-like flowers. The branches
are brittle and can suffer from wind damage
in exposed sites.

cherry

prunus cerasus 3 x 2.4m (10 x 8ft)/ -/
white/ mid-spring/ most/ open/ mid to late
summer

Fruiting cherry trees are very beautiful in
flower so plant these to benefit bees and
other beneficial insects . Choose trees on the
semi-dwarfing stocks and avoid the larger-
growing flowering cherries. Try Stella on Colt
stock.

snowy mespilus

amelanchier canadensis 6 x 3m (20
x10ft)/ -/ white/ mid spring/ well-drained/
open/ spring

Wonderful shows of flowers in spring followed by juicy black berries and red autumn
leaves.

judas tree

cercis siliquastrum 8 x 3m (25 x 10ft)/ -/
rosy-purple/ late spring/ well-drained/

pear

pyrus communis 3 x 1.8m (10
x 6ft)/ -/ white/ early to mid-
spring/ rich moist/ sun/ mid-
autumn to late winter and early
to midsummer

The fruiting varieties on dwarf
stocks stay small, giving masses
of white flowers unequalled by
any ornamental tree. The early
blossom is helpful to beneficial
insects. Pears suffer from fewer
problems than apples – try
Conference.

hawthorn

craetagus oxycantha 3.7 x 2.4m (12 x
8ft)/ -/ red/ late spring to early summer/
any/ any/ mid-autumn to late winter

The commoner C. monogyna has pink or
white fishy-scented flowers, is thorny and
produces berries freely. C. oxycantha Paul's
Scarlet is a double-flowered dark red, of
slightly less value to insects but very beautiful.

quince

cydonia vulgaris 2.7 x 1.8m (9
x 6ft)/ -/ pinky-white/ mid to
late spring/ most/ moist/ mid
autumn to late winter

One of the best specimen trees,
with a good framework, large
white flowers, spring and autumn
leaf colour and attractive yellow
fruits which can be left hanging
till early winter.

sunny/ any time

Glorious pea-like flowers spring from the bark and twigs in late spring, followed by purple seed-pods. Likes full sun.

strawberry tree

arbutus unedo 6 x3m (20 x10ft)/ -/ pink/ autumn/ any/ sheltered/ winter

Native to Portugal and Eire. The tree has attractive shredding bark and heather-like flower clusters and orange-red fruits in the autumn.

eucalyptus

e. gunnii 4.6 x 1.8m (15 x 6ft)/ -/ -/ -/ most/ sheltered/ early to mid-spring

Grown for its beautiful blue-green foliage. Protect from cold winds while young. Fast-growing: cut back hard in early spring to control size.

plum

prunus domestica 3.7 x 2.4m (12 x 8ft)/ -/ white/ early to mid-spring/ rich, lime/ open/ early to late summer

Least floriferous of the stone fruit trees, but very early blossom for beneficial insects. Grow Victoria, or Coe's Golden Drop in a warm spot.

apple

malus pumila 3.7 x 2.4m (12 x 8ft)/ -/ white, red & pink/ mid to late spring/ most/ most/ mid-autumn to late winter; mid to late summer

The fruiting varieties make good specimens and fruit, while most ornamental varieties are pollinators for fruiters, with beautiful flowers and bright red or yellow crab apples. Try John Downie or Golden Hornet.

hedges

Hedges are an ideal way of sheltering your garden from the wind – essential if it is in a very exposed position. A hedge will also give you privacy, as well as providing a home for an assortment of wildlife, from birds to hedgehogs, frogs and toads. Almost any shrub can be used to make an informal hedge, which is left to grow of its own accord, but if you are using flowering shrubs, plan the colour scheme before planting. Formal hedges are clipped regularly to form a dense wall of foliage. If you want to keep out animals (or burglars), brambles, briars and climbers trained over posts and wires can rapidly make an impenetrable barrier.

planting Most hedge plants are best spaced 30-60cm (1-2ft) apart, closer for small hedges such as hawthorn and privet, and wider, 60-90cm (2-3ft), for tall ones such as leylandii or holly.

trimming Hedges are shaped so that they are wider at the base than the top – sloping inwards on both sides – to allow light and rain to reach the base of the hedge. Start trimming the hedge immediately, to help to thicken it, especially conifers. They are trimmed once or twice a year, in summer and autumn, but fast-growing hedges like privet and leylandii may need cutting more often throughout the growing season. Informal hedges will only need stray branches tidied up. In a small to medium-sized garden keep the hedge at 2-3m (6½-10ft) high.

Information given: height after 5 years in good conditions.

cypress

cupressocyparis leylandii 3-4m (10-12ft)

Leylandii are a mixed blessing: they are dense evergreens which are very fast-growing indeed (1.2m/4ft per year) and take a lot of cutting. They rob the soil all around and can overwhelm a small garden, though they can

above Eucalyptus gunnii and *Jasminum* x *stephanense* flowering in early summer
bottom The densely packed leylandii hedge creates a separate 'room' which has a tranquil atmosphere away from the hustle and bustle of the rest of the garden

be kept to 60cm (2ft) thick with two cuts per year. The golden form is attractive and less vigorous. They do shelter wildlife: I hide old wellies, boots, pots and tubes in my leylandii hedge as nesting sites.

beech
fagus sylvatica 2.1-2.4m (7-8ft)

Beech is not evergreen but in mild climates the leaves stay on through the winter, dropping gradually, which creates work if they are near patios and drives. Beech will grow in any soil other than very heavy clay or waterlogged ground. There is an attractive copper-coloured form. Either can be kept to 1.5-1.8m (5-6ft) high.

box
buxus sempervirens Suffruticosa 30-90cm (1-3ft)

Dwarf box is the most popular hedging for parterres and formal gardens. It is a neat, very slow-growing evergreen and can be kept to only 15 x 15cm (6 x 6in). Common box, *B. sempervirens*, makes a very dense evergreen hedge which reaches 4.5m (15ft) eventually and is excellent for topiary work. It thrives on chalky soils, if not too thin.

honeysuckle
lonicera nitida 1.5m (5ft)

A tidy evergreen for low hedges, this has tiny leaves and is good for topiary. Planted 30cm (12in) apart it can be kept to 30cm (12in) thick. It will grow in dry spots and on most soils if well established.

myrobalan plum
prunus cerasifera 1.8-2.1m+ (6-7ft+)

This is most useful grown as an informal hedge, as it then produces cherry plums which make wonderful jam. The pure white flowers appear in early spring; trim once a year after these have finished, leaving some stems on top to fruit. Myrobalan prefers rich soil.

privet
ligustrum ovalifolium 1.5-1.8m (5-6ft)

Privets rob the soil nearby but make neat, quick-growing hedges and most are semi-evergreen. The golden forms are less vigorous and hardy, but make attractive hedges. Common privet berries freely if untrimmed. Privet can be kept to 30cm (12in) thick and grows in most soils, even in shade. Prune back hard after planting to help it to thicken.

quickthorn
crataegus monogyna 1.8-2.1m (6-7ft)

One of the traditional hedge plants, used to enclose cattle, this grows almost anywhere, though it does not like acid soil. When well cut and shaped it looks as tight as tweed. Prune hard in early spring after planting.

rose
rosa spp 1-2.4m (3-8ft)

Vigorous upright-growing and shrub roses make an attractive, impenetrable hedge with glorious flowers and hips to follow. Plant 45-120cm (1½-4ft) apart, depending on vigour, in enriched soil. *Rosa rugosa* makes a poor wide lax hedge, far better is Queen Elisabeth, Ispahan or Blanc Double de Coubert if you can find it.

western red cedar
thuja plicata 1.5-1.8m (5-6ft)

Less vigorous and of neater habit than leylandii, this dark green conifer makes a slower-growing hedge with less trimming needed. It resists the cold well and can tolerate chalk soils.

worcesterberry
ribes divaricatum 1.5m (5ft)

With its large, sharp, mean thorns this is the ideal boundary hedge to deter intruders. It produces edible, reddish-black berries. Layering and suckering, it is impenetrable except to small wildlife. Plant 1m (3ft) apart on boundaries and leave well alone.

shrubs

When choosing shrubs, make sure they have a healthy root system. If they seem dry at the roots, soak in water for a few hours before planting. If buying container-grown shrubs, check the roots at the base: if they are curled in a spiral, this can prevent the plant becoming established. Try to uncurl the roots before planting, and spread them out in the planting hole. Poor soils are best improved with well-rotted compost or bonemeal before planting, but soil that is too rich will give a lot of leafy growth at the expense of the flowers. However, requirements do vary – see under the individual shrubs listed below. Some shrubs need an acid soil – check before making a choice. Also check the final size of the shrub before you buy: it can be a constant battle to keep a large, vigorous shrub under control in a small garden.

planting Bare-rooted deciduous shrubs should be planted from late autumn to early spring, while they are dormant. Shrubs in containers can be planted all year round, provided they are well watered while they establish. Evergreen shrubs are best planted in late spring. Container evergreens can be planted at any time, except winter. As with trees, do not plant if the ground is frozen or water-logged. Heel in the plants and wait two to three weeks if necessary.

If planting in the summer, avoid the hottest part of the day. Spacing depends on the final size of the shrub. A general rule is that the space between two shrubs should be half the sum of their heights. Plant the shrub at the same depth as it was in the nursery (indicated by the soil mark) and fill in the hole with a mixture of soil and well-rotted compost. Water in, then mulch after planting. Provide a windbreak in exposed sites to prevent dehydration.

aftercare Ensure that the plant does not dry out immediately after planting – this is particularly important for container-grown shrubs – and pay particular attention to watering in the first year. Mulch every year in late spring with well-rotted compost. Extra nutrient such as bonemeal may be needed for shrubs that have to make a lot of new growth every year.

pruning is only needed to remove diseased or dead wood, to thin out overcrowded branches and keep the shrub in shape. In general, spring-flowering shrubs should be pruned immediately after flowering; summer-flowering ones are pruned in late winter. Evergreens are pruned in early summer, so that new growth has time to harden before the winter.

roses are planted as other shrubs, but they need to be sheltered from the wind to flower well. Most are sold already pruned.

information given: height and spread after 5 years/ scent if any/ flower colour/ time of flowering/ soil/ site/ when to prune

evergreen shrubs are best planted in spring, and should be kept well watered until established. They should rarely be pruned heavily but if they must be, then it is best done in spring or summer.

daphne

daphne spp; D. odora Aureo-marginata 1 x 1m (3 x 3ft)/ scent/ purple/ late winter to mid-spring/ rich/ shade/ no
The whole family are poisonous but have exquisitely scented flowers from early spring. Often difficult to establish, needing well-drained soil rich in humus, but very attractive and compact; most are evergreen.

californian lilac

ceanothus spp 3 x 2.7m (10 x 9ft) blue/ early to midsummer/ most/ wall/ mid-spring
Beautiful blue flowers, but most are not very hardy, especially the evergreen varieties. (Gloire de Versailles is a very popular deciduous variety.)

laurel

prunus laurocerasus Otto Luyken 1.2 x 1.5m (4 x 5ft)/ scent/ white/ mid-spring/ most/ most/ any
Laurel is a tough glossy-leaved evergreen which makes a thick screen anywhere. This versatile

below *Daphne* x *burkwoodii* Somerset
bottom *Prunus laurocerasus* Otto Luyken with variegated holly at ground level.

above Pineapple broom
(*Cytisus battandeiri*)
below The honey-scented
Buddleia Globosa is
good for attracting insects

ornamental cherry laurel is a dwarf variety which provides good ground cover.

elaeagnus

elaeagnus spp 1.2 x 1.5m (4 x 5ft)/ scent/ white/ mid-autumn to early winter/ any/ any/ late autumn to early winter

These fast-growing shrubs provide good shelter for wildlife. Variegated forms but nondescript flowers. *E. pungens* Maculata has a bright yellow leaf spot.

hebe

hebe spp 1.2 x 1m (4 x 3ft)/ scent/ blue/ early to late summer/ most/ sun/ no

Mostly evergreen, these have excellent foliage and attractive flowers but they need a sheltered spot, especially the variegated ones, to do well. The hybrid Midsummer Beauty is attractive and fairly hardy.

mexican orange blossom

choisya ternata 1.5m (5ft)/ scent/ white/ late spring/ most/ sheltered/ late spring to early summer

Needs shelter to protect its aromatic foliage, especially the yellow form. The scented flowers often return in late summer or autumn.

buddleia

buddleia spp; B. davidii varieties 3 x 1.8m (10 x 6ft)/ scent/ purple, lilac, red or white/ mid-summer to mid autumn/ most/ most/ early spring

B. globosa is semi-evergreen and makes a quick screen with orange ball-shaped flower clusters. *B. davidii*, the butterfly bush, draws them to long strongly scented racemes in a wide choice of colours. Prune back these vigorous shrubs hard in

spring. The cuttings root very readily.

mahonia

mahonia spp 1.8 x 1.2m (6 x 4ft)/ scent/ yellow/ mid-spring/ most/ most/ mid spring

Attractive holly-like leaves, black berries and yellow flowers are typical of this accommodating genus. *M. aquifolium* flowers in late winter but *M. japonica* is sweeter.

osmanthus

osmanthus spp; O. delavayi 1.5 x 2.1m (5 x 7ft)/ scent/ white/ mid-spring/ most/ shelter/ mid spring

This slow-growing shrub looks like holly or privet, but is more compact, and has sweet-scented flowers.

rhododendron

rhododendron spp; R. yunnanense 3.5 x 3.5m (12 x 12ft)/ -/ pink/ late spring/ acid/ most/ no

Magnificent displays of flower and foliage in a wide variety of colours and sizes. Must have lime-free soil, though they can be kept in big pots. *R. yunnanense* produces many flowers.

skimmia

skimmia spp; S. japonica Rubella (male) 1.5 x 1.5m (5 x 5ft)/ scent/ white/ early to mid spring/ most/ shade/ no

These are neat, attractive shrubs, producing bright red berries if both male and female plants are grown.

scented shrubs   Scent is the glory of the garden and I revel in it, both flower and leaf. These are some of the best.

broom

cytisus spp 3 x 1.5m (10 x 5ft)/ scent/ yellow/ midsummer/ most/ dry & sunny/ early spring

The brooms like hot dry positions, and are generally short-lived and small with yellowish scented pea-flowers. I love the tall-growing *C. battandieri* with silky semi-evergreen laburnum leaves and pineapple-scented flowers from early to midsummer.

witch-hazel

hamamelis spp; **H. mollis** 2.4 x 1.5m (8 x 5ft)/ scent/ yellow/ early to late winter/ peaty/ most/ early spring

The witch-hazels are nondescript in leaf, but in winter, when most needed, the long-lasting flowers smell divine.

honeysuckle

lonicera fragrantissima; L. syringantha 1.5 x 1.2m (5 x 4ft)/ scent/ lilac-pink/ late spring to early summer/ any/ most/ mid-autumn to late winter

Shrubby honeysuckle is a straggly mess but the flowers come from midwinter till early spring and are gloriously sweet – find space for it. For the best summer scent grow L. syringantha which rivals and is named after lilac.

magnolia

magnolia spp; M. stellata 3 x 2.4m (10 x 8ft)/ scent/ white/ early to mid-spring/ peaty/ most/ midsummer

These can grow very large, like the wonderful evergreen M. grandiflora which has enormous scented flowers. They prefer loamy, lime-free soil. My favourite is this dwarf variety.

rose

rosa spp; R. centifolia Muscosa 1.5 x 1.2m (5 x 4ft)/ scent/ pink/ early to mid-summer/ rich/ most/ late autumn

The finest of scented flowers, there is such a choice: old cabbage roses, the Damask, the vigorous Mme Isaac Pereire, but I love this one for its mossiness.

spanish broom

spartium junceum 2.5 x 1.5m (8 x 5ft)/ scent/ yellow/ midsummer to early autumn/ most/ sunny/ early spring

This deciduous shrub has rush-like growth and sweet-scented pea-like flowers laden with pollen.

lilac

syringa spp; S. velutina 1.5 x 1.2m (5 x 4ft)/ scent/ lilac/ late spring to early summer/ most/ most/ mid to late autumn

There are many excellent lilacs from the common purple and whites to the divine Persian, Canadian Preston hybrids and several dwarf forms.

mock orange

philadelphus spp; P. x Belle Etoile 2.4 x 1.5m (8 x 5ft)/ scent/ white-purple/ early to midsummer/ lime/ any/ mid to late summer

Mock oranges all have glorious scents, flower profusely and are generally trouble-free.

viburnum

viburnum spp; V. x juddii 1.5 x 1.2m (5 x 4ft)/ scent/ pink/ mid to late spring/ most/ most/no

There are so many attractive scented varieties, yet the scentless V. tinus Eve Price and V opulus, the guelder rose, are the most common. Grow this compact variety.

tender shrubs

Although the following will grow in sheltered spots they will need to be well-established. Prepare the planting hole well and water often until they are making strong growth. Protect them in very cold weather.

erica

erica spp; Erica x darleyensis Silberschmelze 45 x 90cm (1½ x 3ft)/ scent/ white/ winter/ loamy/ any/ early winter to early spring

The winter-flowering heathers are more tolerant of lime soils but none grow on chalk no matter how much peat you add. They will suppress weeds once established but will not stop existing infestations. Silberschmelze produces new shoots with creamy tips in spring and white flowers.

top Mock orange (*Philadelphus coronarius*)
above *Viburnum x carlcephalum*

escallonia

escallonia spp; E. x langleyensis 2.1 x 1.8m (7 x 6ft)/ scent/ pink/ early to mid-summer/ most/ wall/ late summer
Many are evergreen or partly so, and some have aromatic foliage. Not very hardy: better grown by the sea and in very sheltered spots.

fuchsia

fuchsia spp; F. magellanica Versicolor 1.5 x 1.5m (5 x 5ft)/ -/ red & violet/ early to late summer/ most/ sheltered/ early spring
These are hardier than you would imagine if the roots are well protected. They are easily propagated from cuttings. There are good foliage forms, such as this one.

hyssop

hyssopus officinalis See under Herbs (*page 178*).

southernwood

artemisia abrotanum 1 x m (3 x 3ft)/ scent/ -/ -/ most/ most/ mid-spring
This attractive shrub has feathery ferny foliage and a delicious lemon pine scent.

mallow

lavatera maritima 1.5 x 1.2m (5 x 4ft)/ -/ pink/ midsummer to early autumn/ most/ sheltered/ mid-spring
This is not very hardy but is worth growing as it flowers long and late, benefiting insects.

lavender

lavandula spp See under Herbs (*page 174*).

cotton lavender

santolina incana 60 x 90cm (2 x 3ft) scent/ yellow/ mid-summer/ most/ sun/ early to mid-spring
This shrub is tough, low-growing, evergreen, aromatic and a lovely silver-grey.

tough shrubs
This selection includes very tolerant plants which are modest in their care requirements and do well in almost all situations.

berberis

berberis spp; B. thunbergii Atropurpurea 1.5 x 1.2m (5 x 4ft)/ -/ yellow/ mid-spring to early summer/ any/ any/ early spring
There are an enormous number of varieties of this thorny shrub with brilliant autumn colour. Produces prolific yellowy flowers and attractive autumn fruits.

japonica

chaenomeles spp; C. x superba Boule de Fer 1.5 x 1.8m (5 x 6ft) red/ late winter to mid-spring/ any/ any/ mid to late spring
Fiery red flowers very early in spring followed by iron-hard fruits on lax bushes. A bit thorny: best trained on walls, even shady ones.

flowering currant

ribes spp; R. odoratum 1.8 x 1.5m (6 x 5ft)/ -/ scent/ yellow/ mid-spring/ most/ most/ late spring
The flowers come early, so are good for beneficial insects. They are easily propagated and flower red, yellow or white.

forsythia

forsythia spp; F. intermedia Spectabilis 3 x 2.4m (10 x 8ft)/ -/ yellow/early to mid spring/ most/ most/ mid-spring
Very popular, grown for their wonderful mass of flowers in early spring.

potentilla

potentilla sp; P. fruticosa 1.5 x 1.2m (5 x 4ft)/ -/ yellow/ late spring to early autumn/ any/ any/ mid-spring
These are tough and very long flowering; avoid the red versions as they are poor.

firethorn

pyracantha spp; P. coccinea Lalandei 4.5 x 3m (15 x 10ft)/ white/ June/ any/ any/ July
Firethorns produce masses of flowers and fruit which attract bees and birds.

below Southernwood
bottom Pink-flowering currant and white-flowering currant with primroses in spring

elder

sambucus spp; S. nigra Aurea 2.1 x 1.2m (7 x 4ft)/ white/ early summer/ any/ sun/ late autumn to late winter

Wild elder feeds the birds with copious berries. Variegated, cut-leaved and golden varieties are pretty especially this gold one.

cotoneaster

cotoneaster spp; C. horizontalis 1 x 2.1m (3 x 7ft)/ -/ pink/ early summer/ any/ any/ mid autumn to late winter

Many cultivars, all loved by bees for their countless little flowers and by birds for the red berries. The branches arch gracefully or can be trained on walls.

spiraea

spiraea spp; S. arguta 1.8 x 1.5m (6 x 5ft)/ white/ mid to late spring/ most/ most/ late spring

Slender, graceful, small-leaved bushes which flower profusely, especially Bridal Wreath.

weigela

weigela spp; W. florida Variegata 2.4 x 1.8m (8 x 6ft)/ scent/ pink/ late spring to early summer/ most/ most/ midsummer

These produce foxglove-like flowers in great quantities, in reds through to yellow.

climbers

Climbers need to be well established, like any shrubby plant, and (apart from a few) must also have support in the form of wires, trellis or netting. They grow high, and catch the wind, so make the supports strong, durable and renewable. If they are given enough space initially, most climbers can be left to ramble, creating good nest and shelter sites. Be careful where you plant very vigorous climbers like Russian vine, which will soon overwhelm trees or other plants.

planting They are best planted in the spring. Install supports or trellis before planting. Climbers are usually in the driest spot in the garden, against a wall or fence, so the site has to be prepared well, to ensure there is enough food and moisture in the soil. Dig a hole at least 30cm (12in) from the wall or support, and enrich the soil with well-rotted manure or compost. Plant at the level of the soil mark, except for clematis, which should be planted about 10cm (5in) deeper. Spread out the stems in a fan over the support, and tie lightly with plastic ties or twine. After planting, mulch to prevent moisture loss and to suppress weeds. When planting clematis, place large stones or tiles around the base of the stem to keep the roots cool.

top A well-sited honeysuckle (*Lonicera periclymenum*)
above Sweet Jessamine (*Jasminum officinale*)

top An unknown variety of
rambling rose entwines
with *Clematis montana wilsonii*
above *Rosa* Handel

aftercare Water in dry spells.
Climbers against a house wall
may need extra watering if sheltered by the eaves. Mulch annually in the spring.

pruning Prune climbers annually to improve flowering. As a
rule of thumb, early-flowering
ones should be pruned immedi-
ately after flowering and late-flowering ones
should be pruned in the spring.

information given: scent/ flower colour/
flowering month/ soil/ site/ when to prune

jasmine
jasminum spp; J. officinale scent/
white/ early summer to mid-autumn/ most/
sun/ mid- autumn
J. nudiflorum is barely a climber. It has pale
yellow flowers in winter – cut out branches
that have flowered. *J. officinale* is obligatory:
no garden is complete without this sweet-
scented twining plant which is best left to
ramble unpruned.

buddleia
buddleia alternifolia scent/ lilac/ early
summer/ any/ sun/ midsummer
A lax shrub with long hanging swathes of
flowers, easily trained up a pergola or wall
and very attractive to butterflies.

rambler roses
***rosa spp;* Zéphirine Drouhin** scent/ pink/
early summer to early autumn/ most/ most
/ mid autumn to late winter
Rambler roses are much more vigorous than
climbers; all need enriched soil and copious
moisture. There are many wonderful ones –
my favourites include New Dawn, Rambling
Rector, Souvenir de Claudius Denoyel,
Maigold, Handel and most of all the scented,
long-flowering, thornless, Bourbon rose,
Zephirine Drouhin.

vine
vitis vinifera scent/ white/ insig./ mid-
summer/ any/ sun/ mid-autumn to early
winter
Vines give wonderful autumn colour with
bunches of grapes, if you can keep the birds
off. Leaves turn yellow or red in autumn. *Vitis
coignetiae* has enormous leaves. Siegerrebe
has rosé coloured grapes.

ivy
***hedera helix; H. h.* Goldheart** green/late
summer to late autumn/ any/ any / early to
midsummer
Ivy is much neglected but a valuable self-
climber which provides late flowers for
insects, berries and nest sites. Large-leaved
variegated forms are not as hardy; plants
rooted from fruiting bushes flower soonest.

hydrangea
hydrangea petiolaris white/ early sum-
mer/ any/ any/ midsummer
Very slow to get going, but vigorous once
established, this will grow almost anywhere,
even on a shady wall.

russian vine
polygonum baldschuanicum -/ white/ midsummer to mid autumn/ any/ any/ late autumn to early winter

This rampant vine is definitely not for small gardens; it covers enormous areas rapidly and can grow 1.8m (6ft) in two weeks. Do not grow on house walls as it will make its way through tiles and twine round gutters.

wisteria
wisteria sinensis scent/ blue-white/ late spring/ most/ sun/ late summer

Slow to flower, these are worthwhile for the patient gardener, with lovely stems when old. It needs a lot of space.

clematis
clematis spp; C. flammula -/ white/ late summer to mid-autumn/ most/ sun/ early spring

All need their roots in cool, rich, moist soil and their tops in the sun. The large-flowered forms have good colour, are rarely scented and can be hard to establish – these can be cut almost to the ground each year, except for the early flowerers. There are many species with small flowers which are well scented and need no regular pruning. C. armandii is a not completely hardy evergreen. C. montana cultivars are good wall-coverers.

honeysuckle
lonicera spp; L. periclymenum scent/ yellowish/ early to midsummer/ any/ any/ late summer

Honeysuckles are gorgeous, easy to grow, and nearly all have wonderful scent. I have over a dozen different varieties. They attract fewer aphids when grown in semi-shade and not overfed. Leave them unpruned.

herbaceous perennials

Herbaceous plants are more difficult to combine with other plants as they suffer from the competition, so they are usually best grown in their own bed or border. Of course, some smaller shrubs can be used and are regarded as herbaceous to all intents.

planting They can be bought as container-grown plants or bare-rooted. Plant in the spring when new growth is starting. Most prefer a good, well-drained soil – heavy soils should be lightened with well-rotted compost. Make sure that container-grown plants are watered in well, so that the root ball does not dry out. A mulch of shredded bark after watering-in will keep the ground weed-free. Aim for good spacing between groups of three, five or seven plants for the best effect: the width measurement of the clump is also the ideal distance apart for each group.

Most perennials need regular lifting and dividing every three to five years once established. Remove the centre of the clump and replant good young shoots from the outside of the plant.

information given: height x width of clump/ scent/ flower colour/ flowering month/ soil/ site

low-growing plants
Ground-covering plants which form compact clumps and are ideal for the front of the border.

bugle
ajuga reptans 15 x 30cm (6 x 12in)/ -/ blue/ late spring to early summer/ any/ any

Carpet-rooting mats of bugle make excellent ground cover and attract bees, but are very invasive.

lady's mantle
alchemilla mollis 46 x 46cm (18 x 18in)/ -/ yellowy-green/ midsummer to early autumn/ any/ any

This makes good ground cover with mounds of soft foliage and feathery flowers. It seeds everywhere.

from the top *Wisteria sinensis; Clematis* Jackmanii; and honeysuckle (*Lonicera etrusca*)

alyssum

alyssum saxatile 23 x 45cm+ (9 x 18in+)/ -/ yellow/ mid spring/ most/ most

Trailing clumps of grey leaves; good for rockery ground cover with masses of golden flowers, but rather vigorous and invasive. Cut back immediately after flowering.

campion

lychnis spp 38 x 25cm (15 x 10in)/ -/ red/ 7-8/ any/ any

L. chalcedonica is commonly grown but I prefer the double-flowered catchfly, L. viscaria Splendens Plena.

thrift

armeria maritima 10 x 15cm (4 x 6in)/ -/ pink/ early to midsummer/ any/ any

Thrift resembles evergreen cushions of grass till it flowers. Makes a good edging.

below Candeytuft (Iberis sempervirens)

bottom The opium poppy, Papaver somniferum

candytuft

iberis spp; I. sempervirens 25 x 60cm (10 x 24in)/ -/ white/ mid to late spring/ dry/ sun

These are really dwarf shrubs, with lax evergreen foliage and masses of white flowers.

aubrietia

aubrietia deltoidea 13 x 45cm+ (5 x 18in+)/ -/ red-blue/ early to late spring/ any/ sun

Similar to alyssum with thick mats of evergreen leaves and masses of flowers. Needs cutting back hard after flowering.

bergenia

bergenia spp; B. cordifolia 30 x 30cm (12 x 12in)/ -/ pink/ early to late spring/ any/ any

Tough evergreen ground cover with large leaves, this plant survives almost anywhere and flowers early.

helianthemum

helianthemum spp; H. nummalarium 15 x 60cm (6 x 24in)/ -/ red-yellow/ early summer/ dry/ sun

Evergreen but short-lived, sun roses are very similar to cistus the rock rose and are really shrubs, ideal for dry walls or banks. Prune hard after flowering.

hellebore

helleborus spp; H. foetidus 60 x 60cm (24 x 24in)/ -/ pale yellow/ late winter to mid-spring / moist/ shade

The Christmas and Lent roses provide early flowers for beneficial insects and their handsome evergreen foliage makes good ground cover.

baby's breath

gypsophila; spp G. paniculata Rosy veil 46 x 60cm (18 x 24in)/ -/ pink/ 7-9/ lime/ sun

These form hummocks of tiny flowers, loved by insects.

brunnera

brunnera spp; B. macrophyla 38 x 38cm (15 x 15in)/ -/ blue/ late spring to early summer/ most/ most

Perennial forget-me-nots with heart-shaped leaves make tough ground cover anywhere.

medium-sized plants
These mostly stand up on their own or look best when left to form their own shape. In windy areas support may be necessary; tie them up early.

poppy

papaver orientale Mrs Perry 90 x 50cm (36 x 20in)/ -/ orange-scarlet/ early to mid-summer/ light/ most

Brilliant flower colour, and copious pollen for the bees.

michaelmas daisies

aster spp; A. novi-belgii Royal Velvet 1m x 38cm (31/2ft x 15in)/ -/ violet/early to mid-autumn/ most/ sun

Reliably provide late flowers for insects in reds and blues.

yellow loosestrife

lysimachia punctata 80 x 80cm (30 x 30in)/ -/ yellow/ early summer to early autumn/ any/ any

This plant is very invasive, and will grow anywhere. Benefits insects for many months.

campanula

campanula spp; C. glomerata Superba 46 x 46cm (18 x 18in)/ -/ blue/ early summer/ moist/ most

Bellflowers provide the best blues in the gardens unless you can grow gentians.

geum

geum spp; G. chiloense Mrs Bradshaw 51 x 30cm (20 x 12in)/ -/ red/ mid to late summer / any/ most

These tough plants make excellent ground cover with wiry clumps of vibrant flowers, scarlet in the case of Mrs Bradshaw.

sedum

sedum spectabile 46 x 46cm (18 x 18in)/ -/ pink/ early autumn/ any/ any

Most of this family are invasive but this one is delightfully controllable, with wonderful pink flower heads. It is loved by insects and has good shape and foliage.

iris

iris spp; I. foetidissima 60 x 60cm (24 x 24in)/ -/ insig/ -/ any/ any

Bearded iris are tough, beautiful and thrive even in dry spots. *I. unguicularis* is a scented winter gem; *I. foetidissima* is evergreen with magnificent orange berries.

catnip

nepeta spp; N. mussinii 38 x 38cm (15 x 15in)/ scent/ blue/ early to late summer/ any/ sun

N. cataria is loved by feline herbivores, the less loved *N. mussinii* is bigger with more pointed leaves; both are loved by bees.

tradescantia

tradescantia spp; T. virginiana Isis 60 x 46cm (24 x 18in)/ -/ blue/ early to late summer/ any/ most

Attractive odd rush-like foliage and royal blue-purple flowers all summer.

crane's-bill

geranium spp; G. endressii Wargrave Pink 51 x 46cm (20 x 18in)/ -/ pink/ midsummer to early autumn/ any/ any

Crane's-bill makes excellent ground cover and flourishes almost anywhere.

yarrow

achillea spp; A. ptarmica The Pearl 60 x 50cm (24 x 20in) -/ white/ mid to late summer/ any/ sun

The feathery foliage and flat flowers attract beneficial insects for a long season.

columbine

aquilegia vulgaris McKana hybrids 90 x 50cm (36 x 20in) -/many/ early to midsummer/ any/ sun

This is one of the essential cottage garden plants, with beautiful low fern-like foliage and tall graceful spurred flowers in many colours and combinations.

red valerian

centranthus ruber 80 x 60cm (30 x 24in)/ -/ red/ mid to late summer/ any soil/ anywhere

The red, star-shaped flowers attract insects. It thrives in poor conditions, but beware the plant does self-seed!

Yellow loosestrife (*Lysimachia punctata*) planted beside *Hosta plantaginea* with the leaves of *Helleborus foetida* showing bottom right

tickweed

***coreopsis grandiflora* Badengold** 90 x 60cm (36 x 24in)/ yellow/ early to late summer/ most/ sun

Good for cutting and for attracting insects. This plant must not be overfed or it will produce too much foliage.

sea holly

***eryngium spp; E. alpinum* Donard** 60 x 50cm (24 x 20in)/ -/ blue/ early to late summer/ dry/ sun

Sea holly is loved by beneficial insects. The metallic-blue flowerheads rise out of striking spiky, blue-green, holly-like foliage.

coneflower

below Coneflower (*Rudbeckia hirta*)

bottom Foxtail lily (*Eremurus bungei*)

***rudbeckia purpurea* Robert Bloom** 90 x 60cm (36 x 24in)/ scent/ purple/ late summer to early autumn/ rich/ sun

Coneflowers are loved by insects and come usefully late in the year.

red hot poker

***kniphofia spp; K. uvaria* Royal Standard** 90 x 90cm (36 x 36in) red/ mid to late summer/ dry/ sun

Red-hot pokers make attractive grassy clumps and are surprisingly tough.

lupin

***lupinus polyphyllus* Russell hybrids** 90 x 60cm (36 x 24in)/ scent/ many/ early to midsummer/ rich/ sun

Wonderful flowers and foliage but they need dividing every third year.

tall plants

Do not regiment a border from short at the front to high at the back – have it coming and going in waves, with some of these tall plants towards the front of a border. They will probably need tying up to supports.

delphinium

***delphinium spp; D. x hybrid* Blue Bees** up to 1.8m x 60cm (6 x 2ft)/ -/ blue/ midsummer/ rich/ sun

These wonderful flower spikes are loved by bees – and slugs (see *page 43 for slug control*).

hollyhock

***althaea rosea* up to 2.4 m x 60 cm** (8 x 2 ft)/ -/ red-yellow/ midsummer/ rich/ sun

Hollyhocks are one of the traditional cottage garden plants. Sadly, they suffer from rust (see *page 50*) but flower regardless if given rich soil at the back of a border. They should have an open site, but masked by other plants so that the oldest, and worst, leaves are hidden.

asphodel

asphodeline lutea 90 x 46cm (36 x 18in)/ -/ yellow/ midsummer to early autumn/ most/ sun

Spiky, blue-grey almost evergreen leaves erupt into tall spikes of yellow, starry flowers.

shasta daisy

chrysanthemum spp; C. maximum 90 x 60cm (3 x 2ft)/ -/ white/ early to late summer/ any/ most

Shasta daisies can be invasive, but their flowers attract many insects and their dark foliage makes a good backdrop for other plants.

globe thistle

echinops spp; E. ritro 90 x 60cm (36 x 24in)/ -/ blue/ mid to late summer/ any/ any

This thistle, statuesque with metallic blue flower heads, is one of the best bee plants.

foxtail lily

***eremurus spp; E. bungei* 1.1m x 51cm** (45 x 20in)/ scent/ yellow/ late spring to early summer/ rich/ sun

Tall spikes of tightly packed flowers with grass-like foliage.

sunflower

***helianthus spp; H. decapetalus* Loddon Gold** 1.5m x 60cm (5ft x 25in)/ -/ yellow/

midsummer to early autumn/ most/ sun
These perennial sunflowers are as good bee and butterfly flowers as the annuals.

leycesteria

leycesteria formosa 1.8 x 1.5m (6 x 5ft)/ -/ white/ mid to late summer/ rich/ most
Exotic shrubby 'bamboo' with ferny foliage and jewel-like flowers with red bracts. Can be grown as a shrub or pruned back to the ground each spring.

chinese lanterns

physalis franchetii 90 x 30cm (36 x 12in)/ -/ -/ -/ most/ sun
Invaluable for winter colour and decoration. I grow mine in front of, and up into, a passion flower which has the same orange-coloured fruits.

mullein

verbascum hybridum 1m x 60cm (40 x 24in)/ -/ yellow/ early to midsummer/ chalky/ sun
Beloved by insects, this stately plant is another cottage garden 'must'.

scented plants These gems need to be readily accessible – in the front of a border, around garden seats or under an open window.

lily-of-the-valley

convallaria majalis 15cm x 1m (6in x 3ft)/ scent/ white/ late spring to early summer/ leafy/ shade
This is hard to establish, but a weed once growing. It loves rich, mulched soil.

day lily

hemerocallis spp; H. thunbergii 90 x 60cm (36 x 24in)/ scent/ yellow/ late summer to early autumn/ most/ any
The flowers only bloom for a day, but the plant keeps on producing more.

hosta

hosta spp; Royal Standard 60 x 1.2m (24 in x 4ft)/ scent/ white/ moist/ shade

Better known for its striking foliage and susceptibility to slugs but it has a pleasant light scent.

lemon-scented balm

melissa officinalis 60 x 50cm (24 x 20in)/ scent/ insig/ -/ any/ most
Loved by the bees; the golden-splashed version is best.

phlox

phlox spp; P. paniculata hybrids 76 x 38cm (30 x 15in) scent/ lilacs/ mid to late summer/ most/ shade
Strange, spicy, musty scent. Long-flowering clusters of blooms on very upright stems.

paeonia

paeonia spp; Karl Rosenfeld 80 x 60cm (30 x 24in) scent/ red/ midsummer/ rich/ sun
Paeonies are exquisite, with bold, showy blooms and good foliage.

violet

viola spp; V. odorata 13 x 13cm (5 x 5in)/ scent/ violet/ early to mid-spring/ leafy/ shade
Not all violets are scented, but this one is. Underplant roses with it as both like rich soil.

primula

primula spp; P. denticulata 30 x 30cm (12 x 12in)/ scent/ violet/ early to mid-spring/ moist rich/ any
This sweet-smelling primula is easily established and is suitable for the side of a pool.

bergamot

monarda didyma 90 x 46cm (36 x 18in)/ scent/ reds/ midsummer to early autumn/ most/ most
This has strongly aromatic foliage with honeysuckle-like flowers loved by insects.

pinks

dianthus spp; D. x allwoodii

above The vibrant gold sunflower makes a strong statement and adds height to a border
below Cowslips and violets flower together in spring
bottom Primroses with flowering currants behind

Lilian 25 x 25cm (10 x 10in)/ scent/ white/ early summer/ friable/ sun

All this family are delightfully clove or sweet-scented, but the best of all are these hybrid pinks. These need propagating every two or three years or they can become straggly. Propagate by softwood cuttings in early spring. Pinks are perfect for growing in large quantities for cutting. There are also smaller species suitable for the rock garden. Dead-head repeat flowerers.

annuals

These are invariably better sown in position, but it is often more convenient to sow in small pots and plant out later, when they can also be used to fill gaps.

above Clove pinks in front of catnip
below Sweet rocket
bottom Night-scented stock

planting If using bedding plants, plant out after all danger of frost is past. Water plants in well. It is best to plant in the evening, when it is cooler. Water daily until established.

information given: height/ scent/ flower colour/ flowering time/ soil/ site/ when to sow

sweet rocket
hesperis matronalis 60-90cm (2-3ft)/ scent/ bluey/ early summer/ most/ late spring to early summer

This is an old-fashioned plant, easy and undemanding, with tall stock-like flowers. Dies out but will self-seed everywhere.

phacelia
phacelia tanacetifolia 60cm (24in)/ -/ lavender blue/ early summer to early autumn/ most/ most/ mid spring or late summer

This is a wonderful bee plant and a good space filler with absolutely masses of flowers.

gilia
gilia tricolor 60cm (24in)/ scent/ mid to late summer/ most/ sun/ early spring

Beautiful flowers, white edged with blue, yellow-eyed with strange scent and attractive foliage.

sweet pea
lathyrus odoratus 1.5-1.8m (5-6ft) scent/ many/ early spring to early autumn/ rich/ sun/ mid spring and early autumn

Obligatory – what is summer without them? Grow the old-fashioned ones with delicate colours and strong scent. Sow in position, and in pots in autumn and again in spring for a constant supply.

stock
matthiola spp 23-60cm (9-24in)/ scent/ many/ mid spring to early autumn/ most/ most/ mid-spring to early autumn

Ten Week stocks are opulently scented, East Lothian similarly so, but for best colour and the most divine evening scent sow a mixture of Virginian and night-scented stocks.

tobacco plant
nicotiana spp; N. sylvestris 90cm (36in)/ scent/ white/ midsummer to mid-autumn/ rich/ sun/ mid-spring

This variety of the tobacco plant has spikes of fragrant white trumpet-shaped flowers that open in the evenings and on dull days.

sweet alyssum
alyssum maritimum 15cm (6in) scent/ white/ most/ most/ sun/ mid-spring

Sweet, honey-scented flowers loved by insects. The rose-purple and dwarf forms are more attractive and compact, but less well scented.

marigold
tagetes spp; T. patula 25cm (10in)/ scent/ orange/ midsummer to mid autumn/ most/ sun/ mid spring

French marigolds are a good colour, long-flowering and attractive to beneficial insects; grow them everywhere possible for their benefits.

convolvulus

convolvulus tricolor 38cm (15in)/ -/ white, blue and yellow/ late spring to early autumn/ most/ most/ early spring to late summer

Like a petunia but hardy, so does not require greenhouse space. Pretty trumpet-shaped flowers attract bees, hoverflies and other beneficial insects.

nasturtium

tropaeolum spp 15-30cm (6-12in)/ -/many/ midsummer to early autumn/ poor/ sun/ mid-spring

The flowers and foliage are edible. Sow direct in mid-spring and do not over-feed or they will be all leaves. Dwarf forms are often well scented; trailers can cover large areas with flowers.

biennials

Start these off in a seedbed in early summer and plant out in their final position in autumn.

sweet william

dianthus barbatus 41cm (16in)/ scent/ purple-red/ early summer to early autumn/ most/ most/ late spring to early summer

Classic cottage garden plants. I love the hybrid strain Sweet Wivelsfield which has larger flower heads.

foxglove

digitalis spp 1.5m (5ft)/ many/ early to midsummer/ light/ shade/ late spring

Self-seeded plants are always best. They have no scent, but they feed bees, thrive in woodland settings and can be fitted into most odd corners easily.

wallflower

cheiranthus spp 46cm (18in)/ scent/ orangey/ early to late spring/ anywhere/ sun/ midsummer

Wallflowers are really perennial, but better discarded once straggly. They give more scent value than most plants, and are especially welcome as they provide colour and scent so early in the year.

matthiola

matthiola spp 38cm (15in)/ scent/ many/ mid spring to midsummer/ drained/ most/ mid to late summer

Brompton and East Lothian stocks sown in mid to late summer give gorgeous heads of scented flowers the next spring, but many are lost over winter even if cloched.

bulbs & corms

These can be grown like herbaceous plants, as clumps in a border, and most can also be naturalized in grass or under deciduous shrubs. They can be planted in any soil, so long as it is well-drained – bulbs will quickly rot in a badly-drained soil. If your soil is heavy or wet, plant the bulbs on a layer of sharp sand or grit. When planting in grass, use a bulb planter, which removes a core of soil; then put in the bulb and replace the soil 'plug'. Generally, the size of the bulb decides how deep it should be planted; plant twice as deep as the bulb height.

On lawns, you must leave the grass uncut for six weeks after the flowers have faded: this is essential to allow the foliage to die back, returning nutrients to the bulbs, otherwise their vigour and flowering will be reduced. In borders, the leaves should be allowed to wither. If you have to lift bulbs after flowering, heel them in somewhere and let the foliage die back. Store the bulbs in a cool dry place and replant the following season.

information given: height/ scent/ colour/ flowering time/ soil/ site/depth to plant

crocus

crocus spp 10cm (4in)/ -/ many/ early to mid spring/ any/ any/ 8cm (3in)

Often grown though grass, but they die out if the leaves are

below Foxgloves look particularly good in shady, woodland settings

above There are many varieties of allium suitable for the ornamental border; this one is a flowering leek (*Allium porrum*)

below Daffodils often look at their best when left to naturalize at the foot of a shrub or tree

removed too soon. The common Dutch varieties are inexpensive and useful to beneficial insects in early spring. They are best grown in groups, and need black cotton to stop birds damaging them. Other varieties flower in the autumn and winter.

cyclamen

cyclamen spp; C. europaeum 8-10cm (3-4in)/ -/ rosy/ well-drained/ light shade/ 10cm (4in)

Beautiful flowers: with many varieties it is possible to have flowers almost all year. Most have attractive foliage as well.

celandine

ficaria verna 8cm (3in)/ -/ yellow/ early to mid spring/ any/ any/ 5cm (2in)

This can be more of a weed, spreading by tiny little tubers, but it brings early cheer with sheets of gold for beneficial insects.

snowdrop

galanthus spp; G. nivalis Flore Plena 10cm (4in)/ -/ white/ mid to late winter/ any/ shade/ 8 cm (3in)

Snowdrops are best moved or bought when newly lifted, as dried bulbs die. Divide them annually and they increase rapidly. Double-bloomed varieties like Plena are especially attractive.

daffodil

narcissus spp; N. recurvus 43cm (17in)/ scent/ white/ red-eyed/ any/ most/ 15cm (6in)

Daffodils come in many forms, from the early dwarf *N. bulbocodium* with rush-like foliage, through the sheets of King Alfred at Easter, to the late-flowering, gloriously scented jonquils and *N. poeticus* or pheasant's eye which is ideal for naturalizing in a grassy area.

hyacinth

hyacinthus spp; H. orientalis 20-25cm (8-10in)/ scent/ red, white, blue/ rich/ sun/ 8cm (3in)

Hyacinths have powerful scent and bright colour, but they are expensive. Hyacinths forced for indoor use can be hardened off and planted out, but after a few years degenerate to resemble bluebells. Grape hyacinths (*Muscari*) which also flower in spring are much tougher and seed freely.

onion

allium spp; A. porrum 1m (40in)/ -/ white-purple/ midsummer to early autumn/ moist, rich/ sun/ 13cm (5in)

The onion family are tough and reliable, with ball flowers loved by beneficial insects. Some, such as garlic and chives, are believed to benefit other plants, especially roses. *A. moly* has lovely yellow flowers.

lily

lilium spp; L. regale 1.2m (4ft)/ scent/ white/ midsummer/ most/ sun/ 20cm (8in)

There are many wonderful lilies; most are not difficult though they need well-drained, rich soils. Some need acid conditions and most prefer full sun or partial shade. The easiest are *L. martagon* (Turk's-cap lily) and the regal lily, which is outstanding; it can even be grown from seed to flower in two years.

nerine

nerine bowdenii 41cm (16in)/ -/ pink/ early autumn/ dry/ wall/ 13cm (5in)

Only hardy in dry sheltered spots at the base of sunny walls, but gives a superb show of flamingo-pink blooms in early autumn when flowers are few. Protect from hard frost.

tulipa

tulipa spp 50cm (20in)/ -/ yellow-scarlet/ late spring/ most/ sun/ 13cm (5in)

The strong colours make them overpowering in some settings but give them tremendous impact on drab spring days. Plant the bulbs in large groups, never singly. Cottage tulips can be naturalized in rough grass.

aquatic & marginal plants

No organic garden is complete without a pond, however tiny, and the wide variety of plants you can grow in and around it make it doubly pleasing.

Information given: height or spread/ colour/ flowering time

deep-water plants

Place these in the pond in late spring, when the water has warmed up. Plants are usually supplied in perforated containers: cover the surface with stones to weigh it down and lower gently into the water.

water-lilies

nymphaea 30-90cm (1-3ft)/ pinky-yellow-white/ earlysummer to early autumn

The enormous flowers are beautiful, and their leaves enable insects to gain access to the water. They thrive in containers of chopped turf in water 30-90cm (1-3ft) deep. Propagate by division in early spring.

water crowfoot

rananculus aquatilis 15-30cm (6-12in)/ white/ late spring-summer/

This does well in still or running water.

under-water plants

These are absolutely essential; they provide food and habitat for many creatures, and prevent algae taking over.

canadian pondweed

elodia canadensis -/ green/ -

Invasive and has to be dragged out occasionally, but provides good compost material.

marginal plants

These are mostly bog plants: plant on the pond 'shelf' or in a special bog garden for plants which like to grow in shallow water. Bog gardens have the added advantage of providing a hidden, moist habitat for many creatures.

marsh marigold or kingcup

caltha palustrsis 30-90cm (1-3ft)/ golden-yellow/ spring

These will grow in water up to 15cm (6in) deep and give a beautiful blaze of gold in late spring.

monkey-flower

mimulus luteus 30cm (12in) / yellow/ spring to early autumn

Flowers for a long time, but it can prove invasive.

lobelia

lobelia cardinalis 60-90cm (2-3ft) / red/ summer to autumn

This will grow in shallow water and provides a brilliant show of colour to mid autumn, but take care the slugs don't get it.

waterside plants

These plants will grow at the water's edge, in damp soil, but cannot stand being waterlogged.

goat's beard

astilbe spp 90cm (3ft)/ red/ summer

These plants are ideal for the pond edge. They have attractive palmate foliage and feathery plumes throughout the summer.

below Regal lilies have a wonderful scent, beautiful flowers and are easy to grow from seed

bottom A landing pad for dragonflies and bees, the waterlily also adds a touch of serenity to a still-water pond

7 VEGETABLES
in an organic garden

There are many advantages to growing your own vegetables. Not only are they really fresh, but the varieties available are far superior to the commercial ones, which are chosen for their high yields rather than their flavour and vitamin content. Of course, growing your own also gives you fresh air, exercise and a rewarding hobby that saves money on food bills. However, if the vegetable garden is to be productive, it needs planning and care to function well. Whereas many ornamental areas can be kept looking reasonable most of the time with little attention, a neglected vegetable plot will rapidly become a weedy eyesore, and little of value will grow in it. Vegetables require the best in soil, sun and situation to crop at all, let alone well.

One reason is that vegetables are often extremely over-bred, the olympic athletes of the plant world. Many, such as onions and carrots, are naturally biennials, storing up nutrients to flower and set seed the following year, except that we eat them before then. Given the best conditions they will grow well, but the slightest check to growth or poor growing conditions leads them to bolt – flowering too soon. The vegetables grown for their fruit or seed, such as peas and beans, are easier, but still need good conditions to crop well. Hardest of all are the highly unnatural cauliflowers and broccolis. The part we eat is an enormous multiple flower bud which gardeners want to keep immature and succulent, while the plant wants it to open into blossom and be pollinated.

Midsummer vegetable harvest. Freshly pulled vegetables lie in the garden shed prior to blanching, freezing, drying and storing for use throughout the winter

111

Similarly, a cabbage is actually an enormous, swollen terminal bud, and Brussels sprouts are overgrown buds in the leaf axils – which all require optimum conditions. Crops such as tomatoes and sweetcorn come from hotter climes with longer growing seasons. Although they will ripen over the summer in a temperate climate, they must be started off early enough, with protection and warmth, to do so in time.

conditions for success

Vegetables thus need the best conditions to give good results: rich soil so they can draw on sufficient nutrients; plenty of sunlight to provide the energy that makes them work; copious water which is the basic raw material; and enough unchecked growing time to finish the job. A common failing is crowding too many plants in together, which makes three of the four vital ingredients rapidly dwindle into short supply. It makes little difference if the crowding is from plants or weeds, as they all compete to the death. It is better to grow a few plants well rather than many poorly! This applies to each and every sowing and to the garden as a whole. Certainly for the less experienced it is always a good idea to concentrate initially on just a few vegetables, adding to the range in following years. I have seen enthusiastic new gardeners become despondent, having spent a fortune on seed for every vegetable in the catalogue and then failing to produce crops from them. So decide which crops you really want, and leave the others for later years.

comparative value of different crops

Why grow anything you don't like, or grow more than you need? Many vegetables are grown because they are traditional; look round any allotment and you will see rows of leathery beetroot, rotting cabbages, withered runner beans and bolted lettuces. So before wasting time and effort, decide why you are growing vegetables. If it is for the fresh air and exercise then fine, grow anything, but if it is to save money, produce pollution-free food and fresh salads, or to get maximum nutritional value, then you must choose carefully what you are to grow. A good exercise is to list the vegetables you already buy each week.

Time is often limited, and is even more restrictive than space. A large town garden or allotment can feed a family all year if unlimited time is available, but will provide very little if few hours are spent on it. Growing a few crops in quantity takes much less time than growing a little of many.

yields Tables of expected yields like the one opposite cannot be taken as more than guidelines, as yields can vary enormously. Some years a whole crop fails, while another year you will have a glut. Still, some comparison of expected yields does help with initial planning, so you can decide roughly how much ground to give to each crop.

economy It is impossible to judge which vegetables are the best money-savers as you cannot give a value to each crop. The price of vegetables fluctuates, with the earliest of any crop being most valuable and the price dropping as maincrops mature. Generally, crops such as courgettes, broccoli and French beans are very expensive to buy compared to the cost of growing them, while roots and maincrop potatoes are incredibly cheap to buy, even organic ones. Peas and sweetcorn are expensive and time-consuming to grow, but bought ones are never as good as your own. Ultimately, quality, especially freshness, is only obtainable from your own garden and is particularly important for runner beans, sweetcorn, peas and new potatoes. Lettuces, spinach and saladings also rapidly lose their freshness. In many ways these are the best vegetables to grow, while onions, roots and maincrop potatoes could perhaps be left out unless time and ground are amply available.

nutrition from vegetables depends on the variety, treatment and freshness. Anything grown organically at home of a good variety will always have more nutritional value then shop-bought produce, as well as less chemical residues. However, to get the maximum vitamin value from a small space, concentrate on carrots, spinach and chards for Vitamin A, peas, onions and potatoes for Vitamin B1, broccoli for Vitamin B2, potatoes and peas

opposite Ease of growing relates to how easy the crop is to grow to shop-bought quality; the work required column refers to the crop's resistance to pest, disease and so on; finally, the cost calculation is based primarily on cost of seed, obviously where seed is self-saved the cost will be minimal

CROP VALUES
including yields per 3-m (10-ft) row

crop	yield K/LB	ease of growing			work required			cost	
		EASY	MOD	HARD	MUCH	MOD	LITTLE	DEAR	CHEAP
beans, broad	3.6/8	☛					☛	☛	
beans, french	5.9/13		☛			☛		☛	
beans, runner	9/20	☛			☛			☛	
beetroots	5.4/12		☛			☛			☛
broccoli	2.7/6			☛		☛			☛
brussels sprouts	3.6/8			☛	☛				☛
cabbages	4.5/10	☛				☛			☛
cauliflowers	3.6/8			☛		☛			☛
carrots	5/11			☛	☛				☛
celery	4.5/10			☛	☛				☛
courgettes	4.5/10	☛					☛		☛
cucumbers, ridge	4.5/10		☛				☛	☛	
garlic or **shallots**	3.6/8	☛					☛	☛	
kohlrabi	4/9	☛				☛			☛
leeks	3.6/8			☛		☛			☛
lettuces	2.2/5		☛			☛			☛
onions	4.5/10		☛		☛			☛	
parsnips	4/9		☛			☛		☛	
peas	2.7/6	☛			☛			☛	
potatoes	9/20	☛			☛			☛	
radishes	2.7/6		☛				☛		☛
spinaches	3.6/8		☛		☛				☛
sweetcorn	2.2/5	☛			☛			☛	
tomatoes	9/20		☛		☛				☛

for Vitamin B3 and broccoli, Brussels sprouts and kale for Vitamin C. Where space is at a premium then the best all-round value comes from carrots, salad vegetables and climbing peas and beans. If time is very limited then courgettes, radishes, broad beans and early potatoes can be grown with little work and attention. Onion sets, garlic and shallots are also easy.

laying out a vegetable plot

the site The vegetable plot needs careful positioning and laying out – if any choice is possible. Preferably, it should be in full sun, with no overhanging trees, and as far away from trees, walls or hedges on its sunny side as practical. Wet boggy sites and low areas should be avoided, as they will cause winter losses and frost damage in the spring, though they may be ideal for summer salad crops, leeks and celery. The plot should be kept well away from big hedges, especially Leylandii and privet, which will steal any goodness. These can be isolated by a slit trench cutting the roots and sealing them out by setting in plastic sheet. The plot should not be too far from the kitchen, a water point and the tool/potting shed or much time will be wasted going to and fro. The most frequently-used path should be hard surfaced or gravelled, to make it more pleasant in wet conditions. Grass paths dividing up a plot are a serious mistake. They look nice initially, but are difficult to keep cut and edged, encourage slugs and other pests and soon get smeared by wear, mud and compost. One easy way to get more from less is to replace paths with stepping stones.

The shape is best square or rectangular, as others make harder work, and it must be designed so that rows or beds run north-south so that the sun can shine evenly and not cause dense shade behind taller crops. For this reason a long rectangular plot is best running east-west with short rows or beds going north-south. If this means the plot is best aligned askew to the main garden then surround it with triangular borders to complete the whole square, and disguise them with screens of fruit or low hedges – but do not make these too tall or dense as air must be able to circulate. Borders and beds around the main vegetable plot will be useful for perennial crops such as asparagus or artichokes, and for seed, nursery and salad beds which need even more intensive care than the main plot. In the smallest garden, choice is rarely possible and the best use has to be made of what is available. Of course, with less area, time and money can be applied more intensively. Thick mulches, deep digging, heavy feeding and cunning cropping can be used to squeeze more out of the smallest sunny space.

the soil As explained earlier, vegetables need the very best growing conditions, which means a deep, rich soil that has been well-fed with organic material. If the soil is poor, a great deal of work will have to be done before it is worthwhile even trying to grow vegetables (*see pages 19-27*).

crop rotation Rotation is important, as explained in the pests and diseases chapter (*page 45*), but it is not necessary to divide the plot up into four quarters as shown in many books, religiously following the potatoes-legumes-brassicas-roots cycle. What is critical is that you do not grow the same crop, or its near relations, on the same piece of ground year after year. Move the crop around – or leave it out entirely for a year or two. It is not that important what follows

what, though some combinations can be less satisfactory. For example, potatoes do not happily follow brassicas or legumes if the soil was limed for them. The most important point is to ensure that potatoes, tomatoes and brassicas do not return to the same spot for as long as possible, and that the other vegetables are not grown on the same site as the year before. Of course, the more elaborate your rotation and the longer the gaps then the better the results. This is made easier if you grow a bigger variety of crops in smaller amounts, and if break crops such as flowers, strawberries or artichokes come on the plot for a few years.

Rotation is much easier if accurate records are kept of what has been grown where. The fixed-bed system lends itself to this, though it is not difficult even with rows if permanent markers are used on the plot. Keep a book or a card file, and record not only the crop and position but also the variety, sowing dates and performance, to make future planning easier.

block planting Block and row planting are alternative ways of laying out crops. For those that need support, such as peas, then rows have the advantage as long as they run north-south, not shading out a piece of ground. But rows are not essential, as you can grow beans and peas in a circle round a pole with strings to a wheel on top. Rows waste a lot of space and the paths between each row get compacted and require digging.

A simple card system helps with recording the history and rotation of each bed

For most crops, especially those that are close-planted such as carrots, block planting is better. Apart from saving space and reducing digging, it helps with weed control, as once the plants are half-grown their foliage meets, excluding light from the soil and choking out weed seedlings. This also forms a favourable microclimate and prevents moisture loss. Where netting or fleece is used to prevent pests reaching the plants then block planting is again more practical. For successful block planting you need loose, deep soil, to enable the roots to go deeper in search of nutrients.

raised beds Raised beds are becoming popular, and many of their advantages come from their being fixed beds. These are simply permanent sub-plots surrounded with narrow paths (packed soil is sufficient). As they are not walked on, they only need digging every seven or eight years, and they make block planting easy, though rows can still be run down the middle if they run north-south. The ideal width is about 1.25m (4ft) which is comfortable to reach from either side, and they should be no longer than say 5m (16ft) or there is a temptation

to walk over rather than around them. Having permanently fixed beds makes record-keeping and thus rotation simple and it further helps that each bed can be treated as a separate little plot.

Fixed beds slowly become raised beds naturally as mulches, compost and root residues build up. As well as being less back-breaking to work, this raising has several advantages: as the bed builds up, the surface area increases, not only giving some extra planting space but also increasing aeration and evaporation; raised beds give an earlier start in spring because they warm up sooner; and in winter the crops on top are in slightly warmer conditions as cold air runs off like water. However, raised beds also dry out more quickly in summer, and mulches tend to slide off or be pulled off by birds.

Still, on the whole their advantages outweigh their problems, especially if their shape is kept to the natural curve formed by the soil. This then provides several useful microclimates. The sunny end is a hot slope suitable for early cropping and tender herbs, while the shaded end suits saladings and leaf crops. The sides are protected from the wind and thus stay moist, suiting leeks, roots and

One of the many advantages of the raised bed system is that, in winter, the crops on the top of the raised area are in slightly warmer conditions than they would be if they were planted at 'ground level'

saladings. The top is open ground but especially well suited to onions, shallots, brassicas and legumes grown in rows, and for overwintering vegetables. Raising the beds artificially with planks, bricks or whatever round the sides reduces the area available, removes many of the useful microclimates, adds to costs with the materials required and provides hiding places for pests. Paths of packed soil are sufficient but get muddy in the wet, while straw and other mulches harbour pests and are hard to weed. Sharp sand or crushed gravel is much the best, and it doesn't matter if some gets mixed into the soil.

salad beds

A salad bed is a plot worked extra intensively for a few years and then best moved, leaving rich conditions for following crops. Where space is limited, concentrating on salads in their own bed is a good strategy, and if more salad crops are required with a larger garden, then a separate salad area is more productive than growing these crops in the main beds. As much organic material as you can spare should be worked into a salad bed with deep digging, plus extra dressings of seaweed meal to raise the fertility, aided by copious watering. This is to promote the rapid, lush growth that makes for sweet, succulent salads. If a permanent site is chosen then it is hard work but a good idea to raise the shaded end and graduate the whole bed down to create as steep a sun-facing slope as possible. This increases the amount of sunlight falling on the soil and gives a faster, earlier start in spring and longer cropping in the autumn.

seedbeds

do not need the high fertility of salad beds but do need the copious watering, and they also gain from being sloped to face the sun. A seedbed is used to grow plants until big enough to transplant into the main vegetable area. This keeps the main beds available for a prior crop and allows for easier

Golden Nugget winter pumpkin grown with a row of sweetcorn for the companion planting benefits

weeding and intercropping, while the small seedlings can be given better care and protection when concentrated in one place. Seedbeds are most useful for the brassicas, but also for growing bedding plants and biennials before moving them to their final sites.

nursery beds

are just seedbeds used for growing slower-growing plants and for propagating plants from cuttings until they are ready to be planted elsewhere in the garden. Using a nursery bed makes it easier to spread the harvesting period, as a crop receives a slight check when it is transplanted, and more so the bigger it has grown. Thus if one sowing of say Brussels sprouts or lettuce is divided into three batches, and transplanted to their final positions 10 days apart, each batch will mature at a slightly different time. Of course, for most vegetables, successive crops can be ensured by sowing in several batches over weeks or months, and by sowing different varieties that mature at different rates. The fastest are called earlies and produce less than the slower maincrops.

catch-cropping

Intercropping and catch-cropping are ways to get more out of a small plot, and are made easier if as many plants as possible are raised in seedbeds or in pots, though some such as root vegetables have to be sown direct. The idea is that many crops, especially the slower-growing ones, do not need all the space available to them all the time. Catch-cropping uses the quickest-growing crops, such as radishes, baby turnips and lettuces, to fill space before another crop is ready for planting or before it has grown very big. Intercropping is combining two crops together. When a main crop has grown large but still leaves some ground spare, or when it is standing waiting to be used (as with cabbages), another crop can be grown in between. When the main crop is lifted, the second crop is already established and rapidly grows to fill the space available. Care must be taken not to overdo this, as crowding will give poorer results, and crops will compete as badly as weeds unless the spacing and timing are well controlled.

companion planting Companion crops are those which can be combined together most successfully and give added benefits over simple intercropping. Again, care must be taken not to crowd plants, but provided sufficient air, light, nutrients and water are available, then some combinations of crops do particularly well together. For example, instead of three beds growing respectively peas, potatoes and sweetcorn, I find that growing all three crops on the three beds gives a total higher yield. On each bed I grow peas in a thin row down the middle and flank it on either side with alternate sweetcorn and potato plants. The peas provide shelter for the other young shoots, the potatoes keep the soil covered and moist which the sweetcorn and peas enjoy, while none shades out the others. Further and most important, combining and mixing crops significantly reduces the damage from pests and diseases. For example, I have found that beetroot grown between swedes and parsnips do not get attacked by the birds.

Similarly, many annual herbs are beneficial when grown with crops, especially as their strong scents help hide the plants from their pests. Perennial herbs such as rosemary, thyme, sage, chives, southernwood, hyssop and lavender are beneficial around the edges of the vegetable plot where their scents are effective pest deterrents and their flowers bring in predators and pollinators. Most useful of all are French marigolds, which should be planted in every plot and by paths and gates so you brush against them, releasing their pungent smell. On the following page is a table of the more important crops and which crops or herbs they can best be grown with or avoided.

sowing & growing methods

Methods vary for each crop but certain basics must be adhered to. Seeds are better sown thinly than too thickly, shallow rather than too deep, and late rather than too early. Seeds want to germinate and grow: give them the opportunity and they will do the job they are

Early Onward peas grown with sweetcorn and potatoes – ideal planting companions

meant for. Ensure that there is sufficient moisture under the seed when it is sown, rather than relying on applying it later, and keep weed competition down especially during the earliest stages of growth. Never let young seedlings dry out: don't forget that drying winds in mid and late spring can parch the topsoil bone-dry in hours, just when your seedlings have only shallow roots.

selecting seed Seeds are living things, and need to be kept in cool dry conditions, so store them in a sealed box and do not leave this in full sun, the greenhouse or kitchen. For the same reason it is not a good idea to buy seed from racks standing in full

a guide to
COMPANION PLANTING

plant	does **well** *with*	does **badly** *with*
beans, *broad/field*	brassicas, carrots, celery, cucurbits, potatoes, summer savoury & most herbs	onions & garlic
beans, *french*	celery, cucurbits, potatoes, strawberries, sweetcorn	onions & garlic
beans, *runner*	sweetcorn, summer savoury	beetroot & chards, kohlrabi
beetroot & **chards**	most beans, brassicas, onions & garlic, kohl rabi, parsnips, swedes	runner beans
brassicas & **cabbage** *family*	beetroot & chards, celery, dill, nasturtiums, onions & garlic, peas, potatoes	runner beans, strawberry
carrot	chives, leeks, lettuces, onions & garlic, peas, tomatoes	
celery & **celeriac**	brassicas, beans, leeks, tomatoes	
cucurbits: **cucumber, courgette, marrow, melons, pumpkin** & **squashes**	beans, nasturtiums, peas, sweetcorn	potatoes
leek	carrots, celery, onions	
lettuce	carrots, cucurbits, radishes, strawberries, chervil	
onions & **garlic**	beetroot & chards, lettuces, strawberries, summer savoury, tomatoes	beans, peas
peas	beans, carrots, cucurbits, sweetcorn, turnips	onions & garlic
potatoes	beans, brassicas, peas, sweetcorn	tomatoes, cucurbits
sweetcorn	beans, cucurbits, peas, potatoes	
tomato	asparagus, basil, carrots, onions & garlic, parsley	potatoes, kohlrabi
turnips & **swedes**	peas	

sun or in heated rooms. It is far better to buy from a seed catalogue, and you have a much wider choice. Seed catalogues are usually packed with information, though do take extravagant claims a bit sceptically, after all they want you to buy their own brand seeds rather than the more economical standards. If you get good quality seeds and keep them well, then almost all will still be viable after three or four years so never throw them away until you've used them up. Parsley and parsnip seed rarely keep for more than a year though larger seeds, especially the cucurbits like courgettes, may germinate after a decade while small seeds expire sooner.

Saving your own seed is remarkably easy for many vegetables – after all they do it naturally. The large seeds such as peas and beans are expensive and the easiest to save, especially as they tend to come true year after year (except for broad beans, which tend to cross). Let them ripen on the plants and store the dried pods in paper bags until required. Carrots, parsnips, celery, onions, tomatoes, leeks and lettuce are all fairly easy,

but then their seed is not so expensive. The marrow family are very promiscuous so if you have different ones flowering together the seed will not come true. F1 hybrids do not come true and we are told they cannot be saved, but I have often had excellent results from saved seeds so they may be worth trying, at least for the first year. Potatoes, garlic and shallots are all expensive to buy and easy to save seed from. It is true that you can build up diseases and get poorer yields but you can also save a lot of money, so save seed until yields drop or until you get a year with bad disease problems.

sowing When seeds are sown in rows a drill is usually drawn out with a hoe, but it is simpler and more accurate to press a thick straight cane into the soil. When plants are wanted at wide spacing, such as for parsnips, sow a few seeds at each station rather than evenly along the drill, and thin out to the best seedling as soon as they emerge. If seeds are sown in a block then use the cane to make a hatch pattern and get equidistant spacing; for

If you choose to save your own seed, allow the seeds to dry on the plants then store in a cool dark place for planting out the following spring

119

above **Multi-celled trays are convenient for sowing large numbers of seedlings**
below Home-made cloches provide insulation and drip watering system in one
bottom Protected sweetcorn plant approaches maturity

deeper holes mark with the cane and use a blunt dibber to make a hole at each station. In any case, water the drill or holes, preferably with rain water plus a dash of seaweed solution, let it soak in and only then sow the seed. (Larger seeds such as peas and beans will benefit if soaked for an hour or so beforehand.)

Cover the seed with dry soil or preferably any weed-seed-free material such as sharp sand and peat or leafmould, or old potting compost. This ensures that few weeds come up next to the crop. Big seeds such as peas, beans and sweetcorn can be filled in with ordinary soil then covered with a layer of grass clippings, which will keep them well mulched and suppress most weeds. Label with the date and variety – use the seed packet if it's empty, with a stone inside.

seedbeds Although the best plants always come from seed sown direct, often they do not make it at all, being eaten by pests or damaged by the weather, so it is safer to start them off in a seedbed or under cover whenever possible. Of course carrots and other roots have to be sown direct in their final bed, and the legumes are usually treated similarly, though French and runner beans are often transplanted in cooler areas. Brassicas do best grown in a seedbed, transplanted once when they are very young to break the tap-root and then transplanted to their final site when they are about 10cm (4in) tall with a good fibrous root system. Almost every-

thing else is more certain grown in little pots or multicelled trays and planted out when they and the site are ready. Start long-season and tender plants, like tomatoes, in this way (and in the warm) so that they have time to crop in a short growing season.

compost When growing in any container never use garden soil, but a good seed potting compost. Peat-based composts are effective if you don't mind using peat products. There are now peat-free composts on the market, but these have not been around long enough to be confident of their performance under varying conditions. Similarly, most organic composts have not been around long enough either, and give a variable performance. Start with a reputable brand but later try several and see what suits you most, or take the best points of each and make your own. Whatever compost you use it is only good when fresh, so buy from a reputable supplier with large, swiftly moving stocks.

pots and cells Almost all crops that are best started off in pots are better in multicelled trays, as this gives each plant it's own little space with minimum root disturbance. Also, the insulated trays are easy to fit in a propagator and move around. In pots or cells never risk letting seedlings crowd each other. The most common mistake is sowing thickly in one pot to prick out later, and leaving this for a day or two too long which causes severe losses of yield. However, beetroot and onions can be allowed to have two or three seedlings growing together: this produces smaller plants, which is desirable in their case. For other crops, sow two or three seeds in each cell or pot and thin out as soon as they emerge. When sowing in pots or cells care needs to be taken not to waterlog the seeds as well as preventing them drying out. It is best to pot in moist compost then to stand the pots in water till the top is wet, remove and drain well and do not rewater until the seedlings appear unless the compost starts to dry badly. Never use stale rainwater for seeds or seedlings as this can encourage damping-off disease. For valuable seeds even bottled water is not too great an expense, but tap water will usually do. Once the plants are growing strongly then rainwater is preferable as it contains no added chlorine and fewer pollutants.

hardy plants

sowing under cover A greenhouse is not needed for starting off hardy vegetables in cells or pots as they will be more than happy in a coldframe or sheltered spot until they are ready to go out. However, it is easier to provide better conditions earlier, especially enough light and warmth, with a greenhouse and this can then be used later for growing tender crops to fruition. Cloches are nearly as good but do not have as much space and are difficult to use, while a polytunnel gives the best value for money though they are not very nice to look at. Whatever you choose be careful to keep the glass or plastic clean, as light is more important than heat for most plants, especially hardy vegetables. Ventilation is also important as it is easy to cook small seedlings if the full sun comes out on them while they are tightly sealed up – either be vigilant or invest in an automatic vent opener.

hardening off Once hardy vegetables have started growing well in pots then they can be planted out into the main plot, but they must be hardened off first. This simply means getting them used to tougher conditions by standing them outside each day, but putting them back under cover at night for three or four days. Do not skimp on this important exercise unless cloches or clear plastic bottles are used to protect plants outside, in which case they can be planted out with a little less initial hardening off.

cloches Gallon water bottles are excellent cloches for growing plants to quite a large size, but even the smaller ones work well: cut the bottom off and discard the cap. It is easy to make big cloches by using several bottles held together to make a box with waterproof clear tape and a lid of glass or plastic. Do not cut the bottoms off as a little water in the bottom of each will prevent the cloche blowing away and if you fill them to the brim initially then the water acts as a heat reser-

voir from the day. On cold nights they can be filled up with warm water from the house to give extra protection. Later in the season making a small hole near the bottom of each with a nail will allow trickle irrigation when the cap is removed.

If the main plot is not ready when the plants are big enough for planting out, or the weather is bad, then the plants must be put into larger containers or they will stop growing. Look at the root system to find out if it is wound round in a ball; if it is, the plant needs more space. It is not necessary to continue using bought-in potting compost once the plants are growing well. Instead, sieve well-made garden compost with some potting compost, use this mixture to fill the pot up, and then top off with bought-in compost which is weed-seed-free and keeps the surface clean.

planting out When planting out hardened-off or seedbed-grown seedlings, water them well the day before. Ideally, you should also prepare the planting holes the day before and water them well. Certainly, water the holes long enough before planting to allow the water, with a dash of seaweed solution, to drain away; do not plant in mud. Make the holes bigger than necessary and for the hungry feeders – brassicas, sweetcorn, tomatoes and cucurbits – mix a handful of sieved garden compost in with the soil before you replace it firmly around the rootball. As most seedling transplants are succulent, protect them from bird damage with black cotton wound around canes.

tender plants

sowing from seed Growing tender plants from seed is difficult, as most of them need starting off in warmth early in the year when light levels are low and they easily get leggy. They also need repotting several times, as

top Protected propagation. Tender and half-hardy plants are started off in this propagating cold frame which is electrically heated. It stands in the middle of the greenhouse, which is kept frost-free by means of a paraffin stove
above As the plants get bigger, the most hardy are moved onto the staging in the greenhouse, leaving the tender plants with enough space to grow larger

121

above The freezer coldframe. Once I have finished using it for propagating tender plants, I use this coldframe for cucumber plants which respond well to the additional heat
below *Nicotiana sylvestris* has sticky leaves which trap any whitefly and thrips that the marigolds at the entrance fail to discourage

they cannot be planted out even under cover before late spring without extra heat. In fact, the biggest problem is not germinating them — any little propagator on a sunny windowsill will do that — but where to keep them in the warm while they get bigger and bigger in larger and larger pots. Constructing a coldframe in the greenhouse is one way; heating the greenhouse is an excellent if expensive option; but I find the best solution is a disused deep-freeze.

the freezer coldframe This is best stood in a greenhouse but will work against a sunny wall or even sunk in the ground. What you have is a well insulated box with a lid. Fitted with a ventilated glass or plastic cover for daytime use it is a superb coldframe and at night the lid is shut, keeping the warmth in. A false floor is needed to bring the plants up near the light and if this is covered in sand a soil warming cable can be run in it to keep it warmer still for use as a giant propagator. Without electrical heat, extra warmth can be supplied by putting in bricks warmed on a radiator or bottles full of hot water. Once the weather is warm

enough for moving the plants into a coldframe, polytunnel or greenhouse the freezer coldframe can be used for growing melons or even watermelons.

growing sequence I start off all my tender plants in a freezer coldframe and move the toughest out first into a coldframe in the greenhouse, one section of which is heated. As they get bigger and tougher they move to the unheated section and then to the greenhouse proper, and some of them eventually are hardened off and go outside. As each plant moves through the sequence it leaves space for the next so I can raise dozens of plants with very little space or electricity. The order is: outdoor tomatoes move from the warmth first, followed by indoor tomatoes, sweetcorn, ridge cucumbers, peppers, courgettes, squashes and aubergines, leaving cucumbers, melons, watermelons and okra which stay indoors all summer.

growing in the greenhouse

In the greenhouse or polytunnel it is preferable to grow plants to fruition directly in the soil rather than in containers, as it saves on watering and compost. But even with rotation, moving the plants around each year and adding copious amounts of garden compost, the yields start to drop after five years or so. The answer is simply to dig out the topsoil and replace it with compost and fresh soil dug from a clean part of the garden. This is hard work, but does not need doing very often and is less work than filling up and watering loads of containers every year. It is very beneficial to grow French marigolds in the greenhouse or tunnel especially by the door where you brush against them as these keep whitefly out but attract bees and hoverflies. I also find sweet tobacco (*Nicotiana* spp) and wild tobacco (*Nicotiana sylvestris*) beneficial as their sticky stems trap many little insects like thrips. I use old carpet and cardboard to cover bare soil and for paths as this has several advantages. It prevents weeds and moisture loss, it stops splashing of soil on to crops, it is more pleasant to work on, and rolling the strips back allows me to pick off slugs and other pests hiding there.

PLANT SELECTION

This section deals with the individual needs and uses of each vegetable. (Plants used more as additions to salads or as flavourings, will be found in Chapter 9.) The information given is to help you produce usable crops organically for household consumption with the least effort – not to give record yields or win prizes at shows. The methods I recommend have been found satisfactory for producing reasonable crops with least work. I have given sowing periods, but these are only guidelines, as they vary according to region and season; depths for sowing are maximums and planting distances are for vegetables grown in blocks to optimum size, but again these may be varied tremendously, depending on whether you want small, young or larger-growing specimens; seed packets carry instructions for larger and smaller varieties and distances for row planting. Despite the loss of old varieties (a situation starting to be remedied by the HDRA Heritage Seeds programme) there are still many varieties to choose from, and although I recommend the ones I have found exceptionally good for organic growing or flavour they may not be suit you. It is always worth trying different varieties to see which suit your soil, situation and taste.

shoots & buds

globe artichokes

Artichokes are large attractive plants that can be used in an ornamental area, but do better given their own bed of rich soil and rotated every third year or so. Recommended if space is available.

cultivation Sow in pots in mid-spring, and plant out seedlings the following summer at 1m (3ft) apart each way. They are also grown by planting suckers, with roots attached, taken from mature plants. Water well in dry weather. They are easy to grow, but may be lost in hard, wet winters unless protected with straw or cloches.

varieties Purple artichokes taste better than the green but have small thorns on the buds

problems and solutions Rarely affected by pests and diseases.

harvesting and storage Cut artichoke heads when fully developed but before scales open. If aphids or earwigs get in the buds remove by soaking in salt water before cooking. The hearts can be frozen for winter use.

asparagus

A real luxury which requires three years before it becomes productive. It has attractive foliage so can be used in ornamental areas. Best in a permanent bed on its own as it takes a lot of space to yield any quantity. It can be grown under fruit, especially grapes, to save space.

cultivation Plant one-year-old crowns in early spring. Prepare a trench 25cm (10in) deep and work in plenty of well-rotted manure or compost. Soak crowns in water for one hour then plant in the trench 15cm

above By succession sowing a wide range of vegetables, you avoid a midsummer glut and instead have the reward of a varied harvest like this one
below A ready-to-pick artichoke head makes a delicious treat for midsummer

above A good variety of asparagus is Connovers Colossal
below Seakale leaves show through the soil surface during the blanching process
bottom Seakale stalks after blanching

(6in) deep and 60cm (2ft) apart.

varieties New hybrids are offered that are all male and do not waste energy producing seed, otherwise there is little to choose between varieties. Highly recommended where space is available.

problems and solutions Rarely suffers from pests and diseases.

harvesting and storage Harvest from the third year. Cut from mid-spring to midsummer when spears are 12-15cm (5-6in) above ground. Do not remove foliage till dried up. Mulch in autumn with well-rotted manure or compost.

celery & celeriac

These need careful tending and a permanently moist – if not boggy – rich soil to grow at all well. Not easy. If you only want celery for its flavour, grow it like parsley, let it self-sow and use the leaves.

cultivation Celery needs to be surface sown in tiny pots or cells in a propagator, in late winter or early spring. The seed is difficult to sow individually so thin early and pot up into 5-7.5cm (2-3in) pots. Harden off in a coldframe and plant in late spring. Plant out 30cm (12in) apart in trenches filled with well-rotted compost or manure. Protect with plastic bottles or cloches. Water thoroughly – the plants must never be allowed to dry out. Once they are three-quarters grown surround each one with a newspaper collar and earth up to blanch them. Continue earthing-up every three weeks as the plants grow. Do not believe claims of self-blanching types.

Celeriac is started the same way as celery and requires the same moist rich soil, but is more forgiving . No trenches are needed, but well-rotted manure should be dug in during the winter. Plant out 30cm (12in) apart and keep well watered. It can be persuaded to produce the swollen root by most gardeners and no blanching is needed. Strip off lower leaves as roots starts to swell

varieties Celery comes in many varieties. Two popular ones are Giant Pink and Giant Red. Balder is about the only celeriac variety commonly available.

problems and solutions It is essential to take precautions against slugs. Celery fly (see page 46) and carrot fly may also attack plants (see page 47).

harvesting and storage Lift individual celery plants with a fork or trowel during autumn and winter as required. Protect remaining plants against frost with straw. Celeriac is harvested in the autumn. In mild areas it can be left in the ground until needed, covered with straw to protect against frost. Otherwise lift once mature and store in a cool, frost-free place. Celeriac can be used grated raw in salads, braised or in other ways where celery flavour is required.

florence fennel

Grown for its bulb-like leaf bases which have an aniseed flavour. Native to the Mediterranean region but can be grown in more temperate regions given a sunny site and a moist, rich soil.

cultivation It is best sown late spring to late summer, either in the open or in cells sown in the greenhouse and planted out when small at 30cm (12in) apart each way. Keep well watered at all times – do not let the plants dry out or they will bolt and run to seed. Earth up the bases when they begin to swell and continue earthing up for 3-4 weeks.

problems and solutions Slugs may be a problem (see page 43).

harvesting and storage Cut the bases just above the roots. The leaf can be also be used for a fennel flavour in salads.

seakale

This is rarely grown, despite being unaffected by pests and diseases and producing a tasty, nutritious crop in early spring. It is attractive enough to be grown in ornamental areas.

cultivation Seakale needs a rich soil – dig in plenty of well-rotted manure or compost before planting. Sow in a seedbed and grow for a year, then transplant to a permanent position in late winter. Plant out in an open, sunny position, giving 45cm (18in) each way, and grow on till autumn. They are easier grown from 'thongs' or crowns (if available). Do not crop for two years after planting. To crop, in the winter put bottomless buckets over the crowns during dry weather and cover to a depth of 23cm (9in) with a mixture of peat or leafmould and sand.

varieties Lily White is still available. A luxury for the enthusiastic gardener.

problems and solutions Generally free from problems, except possibly slugs (see page 43).

harvesting and storage When the shoots appear in spring remove the bucket and filling and cut the head off at ground level. Mulch with compost or manure. The crown will crop for many years. Steam the shoots and serve with Hollandaise sauce or butter.

fruits

aubergines

Recommended if warmth and protection is available.

cultivation These are definitely a greenhouse crop and need continuous warm, moist conditions. Sow in pots in a propagator or on a sunny windowsill in early spring. Repot monthly, then plant under cover in mid-spring (heated greenhouse) or late spring (unheated greenhouse). Plant in border soil 45cm (18in) apart and support with canes. Water and liquid feed regularly. Allow 5-6 fruits per plant and pinch out tops when 30cm (12in) high.

varieties Try Long Purple.

problems and solutions These are very prone to red spider mite and aphids, so need regular spraying with soft soap or biological control (see page 55).

harvesting and storage Harvest fruits before seeds form. Any surplus can be frozen, either sliced or in ratatouille.

peppers, sweet & chilli

cultivation They need warm, moist conditions, preferably in a greenhouse, though they may just succeed planted out, or in large pots, against a warm wall. Sow in pots in a propagator or on a warm windowsill in late winter to early spring. Repot monthly, then plant under cover mid to late spring (if it is cold only in a heated greenhouse) in 23cm

(9in) pots. Support with canes. Pinch out growing point when plants are 15cm (6in) tall. Water regularly and feed with liquid seaweed.

varieties Highly recommended, especially Bell Boy. Chilli varieties get surprisingly hot!

problems and solutions They need spraying with soft soap against aphids, and watch for slug damage to ripening fruit (see page 43). Interplant with basil which likes the same conditions.

harvesting and storage Peppers can be harvested while green, or when red (fully ripe). Surplus fruits can be frozen.

courgettes, marrows, squashes & pumpkins

These are all closely related. They need a very rich, well-manured soil to do well, and flourish on the compost heap.

cultivation Sow in pots in the warm in mid-spring and plant out 90cm (3ft) apart each way in late spring once the last frost has gone. They can also be sown direct under a cloche or plastic bottles in late spring. Most varieties of marrow produce long stems which can be trained up fences or along wires. They can be grown under and over sweetcorn if it is well established or wound up sunflower stems. Keep well watered, especially in dry weather, and give a liquid feed when the fruits begin to appear. As they grow large marrows, squashes and pumpkins should be propped up on bricks or pieces of wood to keep them off the soil and so prevent rotting.

varieties It is not worth saving their seed as they cross-pollinate too freely. Courgettes are highly recommended, especially All Green Bush and Ambassador. There are yellow varieties such as Golden Zucchini which are little different but add colour to dishes. For marrows, Long Green Trailing is probably the best, while Green Bush is a compact

top A tender aubergine ready for picking
above A large, succulent green pepper bears fruit in the polytunnel
below Pick courgettes regularly to encourage further fruiting

variety more like a courgette plant. Custard White or Patty Pan has round flat fruit on compact plants. Golden Nugget is the best and tastiest of the pumpkins, with a compact habit. Uchiki Kuri is a similar Japanese form and has sweeter, nutty fruits. These can be added to soups and stews or baked. Mammoth grows big, takes even more space and has little culinary value unless you want to eat pumpkin pie for months on end. Grow courgettes instead!

problems and solutions Watch out for slug damage (see page 43) but otherwise they have few problems.

harvesting and storage Courgettes give large numbers of fruit which should be picked when 15cm (6in). If you stop picking them they produce fewer, and those left grow to be marrows. They only keep a few days and don't freeze well. Use a surplus in ratatouille, which does freeze well. Marrows should be picked with a short stalk when fully ripe in early autumn before the frosts. They can be stored hung from a garage roof in old stockings or tights. Squashes and pumpkins are left on the plant to ripen in the sun for as long as possible. Store in a frost-free shed.

cucumbers

These need continuous warmth and moisture under cover with a really rich soil for the best varieties, though there are inferior types that will crop in frames or out of doors in good seasons.

cultivation Greenhouse cucumbers need to be sown in pots in a heated propagator late winter to early spring, and are then potted up until planted in mid to late spring. They must have continuous high temperatures of 21°-24°C (70°-75°F) and very high humidity. If the greenhouse is unheated do not plant out until late spring. Plant in border soil or growbags (allow two plants per bag) or plant individually in 23cm (9in) pots. Support the plants by tying to bamboo canes or twisting gently around strings attached to the roof. Pinch out the growing point when the plant reaches the roof and regularly trim sideshoots to two leaves. Cucumbers must have male flowers removed (no tiny cucumber behind them) before opening so that the females are not pollinated, or bitter fruit will result. Keep well watered and spray plants and paths with water to keep humidity high. Give a liquid feed regularly to promote growth. In very warm sites or with electric heating they can be planted in coldframes but are never easy to grow well. If you must, try Conqueror, which is tolerant of cooler conditions, or Petita.

Ridge or outdoor cucumbers and gherkins are lower quality and often have little prickles. They benefit from a coldframe or cloches and are often better grown in a cold greenhouse or tunnel. Dig in well-rotted manure or compost before sowing. Sow in pots in a propagator in mid-spring, keep warm and pot up until planted out 60cm (2ft) apart each way under cover in late spring. Alternatively, sow under cloches in late spring to early summer. Do not remove male flowers. They trail like marrows so can also be grown up fences or over a trellis once they are vigorous enough to fill the cloche or coldframe. Syringe regularly and mulch to conserve moisture. Give a liquid feed regularly.

varieties The Japanese varieties Yamoto and Kyoto are excellent. Masterpiece is worth trying. Gherkin varieties for pickling are more reliable, and can be eaten as small cucumbers anyway and vice versa.

problem and solutions They are prone to red spider mite (see page 49) and mildew (see page 50)

harvesting and storage Cut off with a sharp knife when they reach the right size.

tomatoes

cultivation These need well enriched soil. Sow in pots in a propagator in late winter and early spring for indoor crops and mid-spring for outdoor. Pot up twice and keep warm until hardened off and planted out at

below Golden Nugget have an excellent flavour combined with a compact habit
bottom Greenhouse-grown Petita cucumbers enjoy the added protection of the 'freezer coldframe'

60cm (2ft) apart each way, in mid-spring under cover or late spring/early summer outdoors.

Most varieties are normally grown as single cordons tied to canes, with all the side shoots rubbed off. I grow some plants as double and triple cordons though, as these give bigger, early crops. Early removed sideshoots can be potted up, as they easily root to make more plants. Indeterminate types or non-deshooted plants produce many sprawling stems: to keep these and the fruit off the soil I place old wire baskets over the young plants which grow up through them. These can also be covered with plastic sheet to act as cloches while the plants establish. Out of doors they always benefit from cloches, or at least wind protection with nets on stakes: these can be used later to protect the plants from birds.

Growing under cover gives bigger yields which come earlier. Plant the tomatoes directly into the soil in the greenhouse or tunnel rather than using pots. The extra watering and feeding can never replace a free root-run. The soil will become tired if tomatoes are grown in it year after year, so dig it out and refill the top with enriched fresh topsoil every few years.

Feeding is not really necessary in rich loamy soil, but is needed by plants in poor soils, or in pots or containers. Comfrey liquid (see page 24) is ideal for feeding tomatoes. For early crops be careful not to overfeed as this produces growth instead of fruit, and I find the fruit from underfed plants tastes better, though starved ones just do badly. Even for main crops do not overfeed. Water well but not too often for plants in the ground, without allowing them to be checked, which causes blossom end rot. In pots or containers it is harder to get an even water balance: water frequently, and keep the medium constantly moist once growth starts vigorously. Tomatoes ripen best on the plant – leave a ripe one or a banana in the greenhouse to help the others to ripen.

varieties Grow several varieties for different uses and flavour. Gardener's Delight is the best. Marmande beefsteaks produce large ones, tasty and good for salads, but to get really big ones limit them to 3-4 per plant at a time. San Marzano and plum-type ones taste poor raw but wonderful cooked, especially fried. Golden Sunrise are yellow and add colour to salads, but also make a good jam with lemon juice.

problems and solutions
Tomatoes rarely suffer badly from pests and diseases, especially if grown with French marigolds and basil. Soft soap and predators (see pages 53-5) will eradicate any whitefly attacks in the greenhouse. For general greenhouse pests and diseases see pages 53-4.

harvesting and storage At the end of the season pull the plants up and hang upside down in a warm airy place to ripen the remaining fruits. Tomatoes freeze easily without blanching for use in soups and stews.

pods & seeds

okra

cultivation Very difficult to grow unless permanently heated conditions are available, or in warm, sheltered areas with long, hot summers. Treat as for aubergines (see page 125) but space 60cm (2ft) apart. Support with canes. Pinch out tops when 30cm (12in) high to encourage bushy growth.

problems and solutions Red spider mite, aphids and whitefly may cause problems (see pages 49, 55, 51).

harvesting and storage Pick pods while young and tender. Harvest regularly for a succession of pods over several weeks.

sweetcorn

A real luxury, this needs to be cooked within half an hour of picking or it is not as sweet. Recommended for all but the smallest plot.

cultivation I find toilet-roll tubes ideal for sowing under cover in mid-spring and sow a second crop direct 2.5cm (1in) deep and 60cm (2ft) apart each way in late spring. For sowing from seedlings, follow the step-by-step sequence (right). When sowing in situ,

top Marmande tomatoes start to ripen in the sun

bottom The yellow variety Golden Sunrise have good flavour

127

each site is dug and improved and the seed sown 10cm (4in) deep but covered with only an inch of fill; then follow steps (7) onwards in the step-by-step sequence. Sweetcorn is best grown in a block to ensure pollination and I find that potatoes are a good intercrop, keeping the soil moist and providing the young shoots with more shelter. Do not grow extra-sweet varieties near ordinary ones as they cross-pollinate with poorer results. A good watering once the cobs start to swell is worthwhile.

varieties Grow several varieties to give a succession. I love Kelvedon Glory and Honeycomb. Earliking is my favourite early and Sweet 77 the best extra-sweet.

problems and solutions Trouble-free.

harvesting and storage The cobs are ready when the tassels turn brownish-black. Pull off the cob with a twisting, downwards movement. Sweetcorn is bulky but freezes well so strip it from the cob for use in soups.

broad beans

These are very nutritious and easy to grow. Highly recommended.

cultivation Extra early crops of longpod varieties may be raised from late autumn sowings in mild conditions. Best on fertile, well-drained soil. Avoid cold, wet conditions for over-wintering or seeds may rot. Sow 5-8cm (2-3in) deep from late winter to mid-spring 15cm (6in) apart each way. Provide support as they develop.

varieties Aquadulce Claudia (early), Express and for small gardens The Sutton.

problems and solutions Can be affected by blackfly, bean weevils and chocolate spot (see pages 54, 51, 50). Pinch out the tips once they start flowering to prevent black aphid attacks or use soft soap later. Broad beans intercrop well with potatoes and summer savory helps discourage black aphids.

harvesting and storage Pick before they become tough and leathery. They freeze well and can even be dried for use in soups.

french beans

cultivation Sow under cloches in mid-spring, and in the open from late spring to

midsummer. Sow 5cm (2in) deep and 30cm (12in) apart each way. They are prone to late frosts, cold winds and slug and bird damage so benefit immensely from plastic bottle cloches. Mulch after sowing with grass clippings to preserve moisture. Water in dry weather.

varieties Highly recommended especially Canadian Wonder, Baffin and Tendergreen. For drying as haricots try Brown Dutch but any variety can be used. There are climbing varieties that grow like runner beans but have the finer texture and flavour of French beans and I strongly suggest you try these, especially Blue Lake.

Planting out sweetcorn seedlings **1** Dig each planting hole deep and wide; **2** water with diluted seaweed solution, and **3** add sieved compost and seaweed meal. **4** Take the seedlings which were grown under cover and **5** plant in the holes, with more sieved compost; **6** firm well and **7** add a bottle cloche for protection. **8** When the plant is about 30cm (12in) high **9** remove the cloche. **10** Now is the time to add more sieved compost earthing up the plant to encourage rooting; **11** firm well and add a mulch of grass cuttings to minimize moisture loss

problems and solutions May be attacked by slugs and aphids (see pages 43, 55).

harvesting and storage Keep them well picked or they stop producing and pick the beans young before they become stringy. After harvesting, leave the roots in the soil to release their nitrogen. A nutritious crop which freezes well, and the seeds can be dried for winter use.

runner beans

An easy crop to grow, and the varieties with coloured flowers and purple beans look good in ornamental areas. They are highly productive, but have a coarser texture and flavour than French beans.

cultivation If your soil is very poor it will be worth improving conditions by digging in well-rotted compost before planting, but generally these beans are highly productive without any special preparation. Seeds can be started off under cover in early spring, one seed per pot. Plant out in late spring after hardening off. Otherwise sow in late spring 5cm (2in) deep, 22cm (9in) apart. They need to be well mulched, watered and picked to do well.

Runner beans need to be supported on poles, wires, or strings; netting is better and wire-netting best of all. All of these can be suspended from posts, walls or fences. Try growing the shorter varieties up and over sweetcorn if this has been started off earlier in pots and planted out. Pinch out the plants when they reach top of their supports to encourage bushy growth.

varieties Grow Desirée, Kelvedon Marvel, Scarlet Emperor or Butler.

problems and solutions They may suffer from slugs and aphids while small (see pages 43, 55).

harvesting and storage They can be frozen and the dried seeds can be used in stews.

peas, mangetout, sugar snap & asparagus peas

Peas are more work than most vegetables, but are so delicious fresh that I can never give up growing them, and as legumes they enrich the soil for other crops (see page 25). One of the few crops better grown in rows, I have modified the way they are usually sown and supported to save as much work as possible (see step-by-step sequence, right).

cultivation First, grow short varieties. Although they produce less they do not need as much or as strong support and do not shade out other crops as much. In dry conditions peas are quicker to germinate if soaked for an hour or so before sowing, and adding a dash of seaweed solution helps disguise their smell from mice. As peas need support grow them down the middle of a bed and grow potatoes, brassicas, carrots or sweetcorn on either side. For succession, peas can be sown from late winter to midsummer. They can even be sown in late autumn for overwintering, but these rarely do very well. I have found one good watering when the flowers are just finishing will improve yields substantially.

varieties The round-seeded varieties are the hardiest but not as sweet: Meteor is probably the best. The wrinkle-seeded varieties are sweeter, so for later sowings grow Early Onward, Greenshaft, Kelvedon Wonder and Onward. Petits pois are just small, very sweet, wrinkle-seeded peas that take a lot of podding, so grow Waverex or Cobri. Mangetout peas have edible pods so podding is not necessary when they are young and tender, but they are usually very tall and rapidly get too tough to eat. Sugar-snap peas are similar but better with thicker, sweeter edible pods, but they also tend to be tall except for the variety Sugar Rae. Asparagus peas are more like a vetch than peas. The pods can be eaten when very small and tender. The best that

top The climbing French bean, Blue Lake grows in the same manner as a runner bean and is convenient for small vegetable plots
above Runner beans benefit from regular picking, these are just the right size for maximum flavour and tenderness

can be said of them is that they will grow in poor conditions and have pretty flowers.

problems and solutions Pea guards keep birds from eating the seeds and young leaves but not mice, so use traps if these are a great problem. If maggots in the peas bother you spray with derris once most of the flowers have just finished, but wait till the bees have gone home in the evening. Do not worry about mildew as it rarely affects yields.

harvesting and storage I cook the peas in the pods and serve them whole so you can eat them as a starter, like asparagus. Surplus peas can be dried on the vines and saved for winter soups and stews though they need soaking overnight before use. They can also be frozen.

leaves

swiss chard (seakale beet)

Chards are beetroots, grown for their leaf stems instead of the roots, and are treated similarly. Highly recommended as one of the most productive crops for small gardens – it will carry on producing until hard winter frosts.

cultivation Sow 30cm (12in) apart each way in mid-spring, and make another sowing in midsummer for winter use .

varieties Ruby chard is brightly coloured and looks good in the ornamental garden.

problems and solutions Water well in dry weather. Slugs are the only problem (*see page 43*) but Ruby chard may suffer from blackfly.

harvesting and storage Pull or snap off the leaves from the outside as required and it will keep on growing. The stems of Swiss chard are delicious braised in a cheese sauce, and the green leaves are treated as spinach. Chard wilts quickly once picked, but can be cooked and frozen as spinach.

lettuces, endive & chicory

cultivation Lettuces are one of the easiest crops to grow well, and yet are often badly grown. Never sow a lot of seed at once. They can be sown in situ 1cm (½in) deep and 15-25cm (6-10in) apart, or grown in a

1

2

3

4

5

6

7

8

9

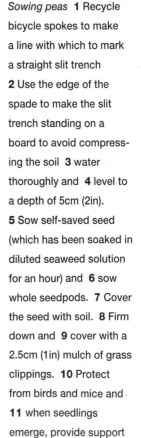

10

11

seedbed and planted out, but without any doubt the best way is to use multicelled packs. Sow a few cells each of several varieties every few weeks through most of the year. Thin to one plant per cell and plant out as intercrops. The biggest problem is slow growth, which makes them bitter, so water thoroughly. Salad bowl and cutting varieties are not uprooted but eaten on a cut-and-come-again basis, so make the best use of the ground. Cos lettuces are tall and need tying up to blanch them or they may be bitter. Over-wintered lettuces need to be grown under cover, not so much for the warmth as for protection from the weather

Sowing peas **1** Recycle bicycle spokes to make a line with which to mark a straight slit trench **2** Use the edge of the spade to make the slit trench standing on a board to avoid compressing the soil **3** water thoroughly and **4** level to a depth of 5cm (2in). **5** Sow self-saved seed (which has been soaked in diluted seaweed solution for an hour) and **6** sow whole seedpods. **7** Cover the seed with soil. **8** Firm down and **9** cover with a 2.5cm (1in) mulch of grass clippings. **10** Protect from birds and mice and **11** when seedlings emerge, provide support

and hungry creatures. The popular radicchio, which is dark red, adds colour and a subtle bitterness to salads. This is sown 1cm (½in) deep or started in cells like lettuce and planted out 25cm (10in) apart each way from late spring to midsummer.

Endives are grown just like lettuce but must be blanched or they are too bitter. They can be cropped on the cut-and-come-again basis so are economical on the ground. Sow from late spring to late summer 1cm (½in) deep and 30 cm (12in) apart each way, or better still start them in cells like lettuce.

Chicory produces heads that are grown like lettuces – they may be solid like a cos or round and looser. They can be left unharvested until late autumn, when the roots are lifted, their foliage cut off and stored in a cool place. Then when wanted they are packed in sand in a box and kept in a warm dark place where they start to produce solid shoots called chicons which are a superb addition to winter salads. If not lifted chicory may overwinter and produce early leaves for cutting before bolting.

varieties There is a tremendous range of lettuce varieties so try many different ones to see which you enjoy most. I grow Tom Thumb as it is very quick from early sowings, All The Year Round, Great Lakes, May King, red and green Salad Bowl, Webb's Wonderful for summer use, Little Gem and Lobjoit's cos lettuce and for over winter Kwiek and Kellys (under cover). Grow Radicchio (Rossa de Verona) for all purposes and Brussels Witloef for forcing.

problems and solutions Keep birds off with black cotton and use slug controls (see page 43).

spinach
cultivation Leaf beet, called perpetual spinach, is much easier to grow and more nutritious than real spinach. However, for those who want the real thing, sow at intervals from early spring to late summer. Sow thinly 2.5cm (1in) deep and thin to 18cm (7in) apart each way, although it can also be started in cells or pots if planted out while still very small. It is worth feeding the soil

beforehand with a handful per square metre of seaweed meal or a bucketful of sieved compost as it needs rich conditions, otherwise it bolts. Water well to encourage growth and prevent bolting. One of the best crops to grow through a plastic mulch as it keeps the soil off the leaves and aids growth.

For winter and early spring, prickly-seeded spinach can be grown. Sow in the same way during late summer. Cloches will protect the plants but may encourage mildew.

New Zealand spinach is another non-spinach that is used and grown the same way. It survives much better in hot dry conditions and is more reluctant to bolt but needs more space. It is better started in pots, and planted out 60cm (2ft) apart each way. Again, water well.

varieties Monstrous Viroflay, Monatol and Medania are the best summer or round-seeded spinaches. For winter try Sigmaleaf, which is really a summer spinach, and Broad Leaf Prickly. Bergola can be sown under cover from autumn to spring.

problems and solutions Protect from birds with black cotton and use slug traps (see page 51). Never ever allow plants to dry out or they will bolt.

harvesting and storage Pick regularly, taking only a few outside leaves at a time from each plant. Spinach should be used immediately after picking, or it can be frozen.

brassicas
As the brassica family are exceptionally good for our health they are all highly recommended.

cultivation Although brassicas can be started in small pots, the most reliable crops are sown direct in a seedbed. Follow the step-by-step sequence (right) for details. Dill gets on well with brassicas, and I intercrop onions with them.

problems and solutions They all suffer from bird damage, so use black cotton. To prevent cabbage-root fly attacks when they

Swiss chard just touched by the first frosts. The succulent midrib and the green spinach-like leaf will still make a tasty winter meal

are transplanted use 15cm (6in) square pieces of old carpet, underlay, or roofing felt with a slit cut in one side. Push round the stem of the seedling, and lay it flat on the ground, thus preventing the fly laying its eggs in the soil. Seedlings can also suffer from root fly in pots and seedbeds. The dreaded caterpillars can be handpicked, or spray with *Bacillus thuringiensis* (see page 54). Whitefly can be controlled with soft soap if they start to increase, as can aphids. Flea beetles make little pinholes in the leaves; keep the area wet to discourage them. (*See page 54*).

The worst problem brassicas suffer from is clubroot disease, which once it gets in your soil is ineradicable. The best 'cure' is prevention, so never buy in brassica plants. If you must, then only buy ones grown in sterile compost, never soil. (Wallflowers and stocks can carry the disease, and it may be introduced with animal manure, which must always be composted before use.) It can be decreased in virulence by heavily liming the plot before the brassicas are planted, and crops can be grown in pots, then transplanted to holes filled with sterile compost, so that the infected soil does not touch the young roots. Strict rotation of crops (see page 45) is essential where brassicas are concerned, to prevent build-up of the disease.

sprouting broccoli

This is one of the over-wintering crops available in the spring when little else is growing. It is also very nutritious and so should be in every garden.

cultivation Sow mid to late spring in a seedbed, and transplant 75cm (30in) each way by midsummer.

varieties Grow Early Purple, Late Purple and White Sprouting for succession.

harvesting and storage When the heads start to sprout, keep cutting, or they will quickly flower. Cut the central head first, and this will encourage side-shoots to develop. The shoots can be frozen.

calabrese

cultivation This is really an autumn broccoli, but is not hardy. To do well it needs to be

sown direct from mid to late spring, but with care can be started off in 7.5cm (3in) pots if planted out 45cm (18in) apart each way well before the root system fills the compost. It needs even richer, moister soil than most brassicas. Mulch well with compost and water well in dry weather.

varieties All varieties are excellent. Mercedes is very productive, Emperor is the most forgiving and disease-resistant. Romanesco is really delicious, with a superb texture and flavour, but difficult to grow well.

harvesting and storage It must be kept cut once sprouting, or it flowers. Any surplus can be frozen.

Transplanting brassicas
1 Seedlings protected against cats. **2** When 7.5cm (3in) high, lift to break the tap root and **3** replant in seedbed 7.5cm (3in) apart. Step **4** shows a strong lifted seedling (*right*) and a puny non-lifted seedling. **5** When about 15cm (6in) high, transplant the seedlings: make a deep hole at recommended spacing for individual brassicas. **6** Add diluted seaweed solution and **7** seived compost, seaweed meal and calcified seaweed. **8** Plant seedling to the depth of the lowest leaves and **9** firm well. **10** and **11** Protect against cabbage root fly

brussels sprouts

cultivation These can be available from mid-autumn to early spring if several varieties are grown. Sow successive varieties from early to mid-spring, transplant 60cm (2ft) apart each way by midsummer in well-firmed soil and plant them extra deep.

varieties Grow Cor Valiant (early), Seven Hills (mid), Fortress and Rampart (late), Rasmunda (very late). If you love sprouts then try Noisette, which produces tiny nutty ones, and Rubine, which are red like red cabbage but also small. The tops can be eaten as spring greens.

harvesting and storage Pick the sprouts as soon as they are firm, working up from the bottom of the plant. Strip off the leaves as they turn yellow, in case they encourage fungus diseases. If you have a glut they can easily be frozen.

cabbage

cultivation Cabbages can be produced for use every day of the year. For early summer cabbages start in pots under glass from mid-winter onwards, harden off in a cold frame and plant out 45cm (18in) apart each way in early- to mid-spring. To follow on, sow from late winter to early spring in the seedbed and plant out 45cm (18in) apart each way in late spring. For early autumn cabbages sow in the seedbed mid to late spring and plant out 45cm (18in) each way in early summer. For late autumn and early winter cabbages sow in a seedbed late spring to early summer and plant out 60cm (2ft) each way in midsummer. For spring use, sow mid to late summer in the seedbed and plant out 30cm (12in) each way early to mid-autumn.

varieties Early summer: Greyhound, Primo or Spitfire, followed by Primo, Minicole or Stonehead. For early autumn sow Minicole, Winningstadt and Red Drumhead. For late autumn and into winter sow Holland White, Celtic, Christmas Drumhead and the crinkly-leaved Savoy Ormskirk. For spring use, sow Offenham and Spring Hero

harvesting and storage All cabbages may produce a bonus crop of little ones if the root is left in when the head is cut and a cross cut in the top of the stem. However, this is not worthwhile if the ground is needed for another crop. When hard frosts threaten, pull the winter cabbages up roots and all and hang them upside-down in a cool, frost-free shed.

cauliflower

cultivation Cauliflower can be available most of the year with successive sowings of different varieties, but they are much more difficult than cabbages to grow well. They need very rich, moist soil and their growth must never be checked at any stage or button-sized heads result. Make sure the level of lime is adequate (see page 21) and keep the soil moist and well-watered, especially in dry weather. Do not expect good results on light soils. When the curd starts to swell bend the side leaves over to keep the light from yellowing it.

For summer and autumn cauliflowers, sow in the seedbed early to late spring and plant out 60cm (2ft) apart each way from late spring to midsummer. For spring use, sow mid to late spring and plant out 60cm (2ft) each way in early summer. On light soils and in small gardens grow mini-caulis. These are close-planted 15cm (6in) apart and are best direct sown. They produce small heads, suitable for individual meals, and are good for freezing. In total mini-caulis give more weight per square metre.

varieties For summer and autumn cauliflowers, sow All the Year Round, Dok Elgon and Snowcap. For spring cauliflowers, sow Armado April and May Star, while Purple Cape is red, tasty and remarkably reliable. I find Garant is the most reliable mini-cauli.

harvesting and storage Cut the curds as they develop and remove the plant. If necessary summer cauliflowers can be

below Purple sprouting brocolli, one of the most reliable, nutritious and hardy of spring crops

bottom A variety of calabrese called Mercedes. This vegetable is similar to sprouting broccoli in growth but the flowerheads are larger and more densely packed

top The mini cauliflower
Garant which does well on my
sandy soil
above Curly kale, seen here
among the asparagus fern, is
hardy and reliable
below A variety of carrot
called Amsterdam Forcing

lifted and hung upside-down in a cool place where they will keep.

kale

cultivation Kale is the hardiest of all and will provide tasty greens in spring when all else fails. It is also very nutritious, fairly resistant to clubroot and cabbage-root fly and is not usually eaten by birds. Sow mid to late spring and plant out 45cm (18in) apart each way in early summer.

varieties Dwarf Green Curled and Pentland Brig are almost the only varieties available. A wonderful tasty old variety Asparagus Kale has been lost to us, which is a shame.

harvesting and storage Kale will withstand snow and frost, so there are no storage problems. Pull young leaves as needed from the centre of the plant, but do not strip it and it will produce more.

chinese cabbage

cultivation Chinese cabbage is grown alongside the other brassicas, but the soil must have well-rotted manure or compost dug in beforehand. It must be sown direct 1cm (½in) deep and 30cm (12in) apart each way in rich moist soil or it will bolt, as will most varieties sown before midsummer. All do best sown successively from midsummer to early autumn, though the later ones need cloching. Keep moist and well watered, as they tend to bolt in dry conditions.

varieties Tip Top is one bolt-resistant variety that may do well from as early as late spring.

problems and solutions In hot, dry conditions they suffer from flea beetle before they bolt and in wet conditions they are often attacked by slugs (see pages 43).

harvesting and storage Chinese cabbage does not store easily. Sow at two-week intervals in short rows for a succession of plants throughout the summer.

roots & tubers

carrots

cultivation Probably the most worthwhile crop but they must be grown under an old net curtain, fleece or fine netting to prevent carrot fly damage. Carrots need a light, stone-free soil to do well – heavy clay soils need lightening with organic material and sharp sand well mixed in. If digging in compost, make sure it is well-rotted and friable, to prevent roots forking.

Sow at 3-week intervals 1-2.5cm (1½in) deep from early spring to midsummer. Station sowing every 15cm (6in) is best if you want large carrots for storing, but for handfuls of baby carrots I prefer broadcast sowing. Rake the soil then water it heavily and let it drain away. Mix the seed with sand and then sow this, side to side and backwards and forwards. Cover the seed with 1cm (½in) of used, sterile potting compost, sharp sand and peat or similar, pat it down and cover with the net pegged down with old bicycle spokes. Carrots can be sown and intercropped with spring onions and leeks sown all together.

varieties It is worth trying many different carrot varieties. I find Amsterdam Forcing the best quick carrot. It freezes well and is excellent grown in a coldframe. Nantes Tip Top is nearly as good – it can be sown from late winter under cover right through to late summer for little ones for winter. Mokum is a good summer carrot with a sweet crunchiness rivalling shop-bought apples. Autumn King is superb, if a bit coarse, for winter storage. Rondo is useful for shallow soil or containers in the greenhouse, as it grows short and round like a radish. For maximum Vitamin A, Juwarot is superb, having double the average amount.

problems and solutions Carrot fly is the main problem (see page 47).

harvesting and storage Pull broadcast

and successive sowings while still young and tender. Lift maincrop carrots in late autumn and store in peat or sand in a frost-free shed. Do not leave in the ground unless there is no danger from frost, and they are protected from slugs.

jerusalem artichokes

These 1.8-2.5m (6-8ft) tall plants can be useful as quick, easy windbreaks. They are difficult to eradicate so are best confined to wild corners of the garden. Don't plant where they are likely to over-shadow other crops. Not recommended unless you are sure you like them.

cultivation They will grow even in poor soil, but for best results dig a trench, working in well-rotted manure or compost. Plant tubers 15cm (6in) deep and 60cm (2ft) apart each way. Water in dry spells.

varieties Fuseau is a new, smooth-skinned variety that is much easier to prepare.

problems and solutions They seem to be immune to pests and diseases.

harvesting and storage They are ready mid-autumn. They only keep well in the ground – dig as required. Protect tubers with straw in severe weather. After harvesting cut down the stems to about 15cm (6in).

kohlrabi

This odd-looking root (really brassica stem bases) is rarely grown, but it is very easy, highly nutritious, and untroubled by most pests and diseases. Somewhat like a turnip, which is not hot to taste, it can be cooked but is best used raw, grated or as crudités. I strongly recommend it.

cultivation It will grow in relatively poor conditions, though like all brassicas it prefers a rich, well-drained soil, and unlike turnips can be transplanted from seedbed, cells or pots. Sow 2.5cm (1in) deep and plant out 25cm (10in) apart each way from mid-spring to late summer. Water well in dry weather and mulch to conserve moisture.

varieties Purple Vienna is easily available but far better is Superschmelz from Holland which given space can get very big and still remain crisp and tender.

problems and solutions Usually trouble-free, but it is important to grow them without check, giving enough food and water, or they become hard and woody.

harvesting and storage Harvest when the size of a tennis-ball, before they get large and tough. Can be frozen, diced, like other root vegetables.

radishes

cultivation Sow these anywhere you like a few seeds at a time, every week from spring to autumn. Water in dry conditions. They will tolerate most soils. Very quick-growing, but not nice unless eaten young and tender as they get hot. Black Spanish and Japanese radishes are sown after midsummer and are more like turnips, so treat them as such – they are pleasant grated raw in salads.

varieties Grow Cherry Belle and Long White Icicle.

problems and solutions Flea beetle may attack (see page 54)

harvesting and storage Pull regularly while still young and tender. If ordinary radishes are allowed to go to flower they are good for beneficial insects and then produce pods which are tasty and nutritious.

beetroot

Very easy to grow and highly nutritious.

cultivation Likes a deep, rich soil, so dig in well-rotted manure or compost. Sow in pots or cells under cover in early spring. Plant out and sow in the open mid-spring to early summer, 2.5cm (1in) deep, 20cm (8in) apart each way. These work well sown one seed capsule to a pot or cell and left unthinned when planting out to give little beet for pickling; sown direct and thinned they can be grown larger for winter storage. Avoid damaging roots when weeding as they will bleed.

top Kohlrabi is useful as a quick-growing catch crop
above The yellow variety of beetroot, Burpees Golden on the left and the conventional round, red beetroot on the right

Beetroot and swede
provide valuable fresh produce
in winter

varieties Highly recommended, especially the yellow variety Burpees Golden; for conventional round reds grow Boltardy for early sowing, and for slicing and storage Forono, which is barrel-shaped. For winter storage grow Crimson King.

problems and solutions No common pests or diseases, but the birds eat the leaves, so protect with netting or black cotton.

harvesting and storage Early sowings can be thinned and used when golf-ball size. Main crop is ready mid to late autumn. To store, twist off leaves 2.5-5cm (1-2in) above root, but do not damage skin. Store in boxes of peat or sand in a frost-free shed.

parsnips & hamburg parsley

These roots are not difficult to grow but take up the ground for a long time and are not very valuable nutritionally. Not recommended where space is short.

cultivation They like a well-drained soil, but not one that has been recently manured. Avoid stony soil. Parsnips need station sowing: sow 3 seeds 2.5cm (1in) deep and 10cm (4in) apart each way for small varieties, but up to 25cm (10in) for larger. Sow from late winter to early spring, but avoid cold, wet conditions. It is often better to wait and make a later sowing in mid spring when the soil is warm. Parsnip seed is slow to germinate. The seed does not keep, so use fresh every year. Thin to one seedling once they emerge and forget about them until harvest.

Hamburg Parsley produces a parsnip-like root and is grown and used just the same, but tastes of parsley. The leaves can be used as parsley.

varieties Avonresister is good but small; Tender and True is the best large parsnip.

problems and solutions Some varieties suffer from canker. Avoid hoeing near the roots, as damage to the shoulders can encourage canker. They may be attacked by carrot fly (see page 47). Water regularly in dry weather or the roots may split.

harvesting and storage Harvest when the leaves die down. They can be left in the ground and dug as required – they taste better after the frost has got to them. Try them parboiled then made into French fries. They tend to go soft if stored.

turnips & swedes

cultivation These need a well-drained soil, rich in humus to help retain moisture. Turnips can be started in cells if planted out while still small but do best sown direct from early spring to late summer 2.5cm (1in) deep at 15cm (6in) apart each way. Keep well watered and mulch to conserve moisture, as they become tough and stringy if grown in dry conditions. Swedes are very like turnips, but are grown for autumn and winter use as they stand and store better than turnips. They are sown mid to late spring, either direct or in cells, and transplanted while small to 30cm (12in) apart each way. Water well, especially in dry weather, or they will become woody. Mulch to conserve moisture.

varieties Golden Ball is the best all-round turnip and will store in a cool place reasonably well. Snowball is quick to grow and more succulent. For swedes, Acme Purple Top and Marian are both recommended.

problems and solutions They are liable to attack from flea beetle, white aphids, cabbage-root fly, mildew and clubroot may occasionally cause problems (see pages 48-55).

harvesting and storage Harvest turnips while still small – tennis-ball size at most. They can be stored in peat. Swedes are hardy and can be left in the ground and dug as required, or stored in peat.

salsify & scorzonera

These roots are like long thin parsnips, but with better flavour. They are quite decorative, especially if left to flower, and suitable for ornamental areas. The young shoots can be blanched and eaten as salad leaves.

cultivation Like parsnips, they prefer a deep, rich soil. Grow them like parsnips, sowing 3 seeds to a station in mid to late spring, 2.5cm (1in) deep and 15cm (6in) apart each way. Thin to one seedling. Weed by hand –

the roots are easily damaged. Water regularly, especially in dry weather, and mulch to conserve moisture. To produce young shoots in the spring, cut off the leaves in the autumn and earth up to a depth of 15cm (6in).

varieties For salsify, try Mammoth, and for scorzonera try Habil.

problems and solutions Generally trouble-free so long as they are watered regularly.

harvesting and storage They can be left in the ground and dug as required. Lift carefully with a fork to avoid damaging roots. Boil them before peeling, slip the skins off then quickly fry in butter. To harvest blanched shoots, scrape off soil in mid-spring. The young shoots can be eaten raw in salads.

potatoes

cultivation These are easy to grow but need care to give worthwhile yields. They need a soil well enriched with organic material and can be a lot of work. To minimize labour and to cope with dry conditions I have modified the usual planting method (see the step-by-step sequence on page 138).

As they are very prone to diseases spread on the seed potato tubers it is best to buy new certified stock every year. However, to save the expense, grow self-saved tubers for a couple of years and buy new stock before yields drop or after a year troubled by disease. Only save tubers from healthy, typical plants and never from those that yield badly or look poor. Egg-sized tubers are best; green bits do not matter.

As soon as you can each year chit your seed by laying the tubers in a tray and keeping them in a frost-free slightly warm place with lots of light so they start to grow short green shoots. As soon as the weeds start to grow vigorously it is time to plant the seed. Earlies need to be planted 10-15cm (4-6in) deep and 30-45cm (12-18in) apart each way, maincrops need the same depth and 60cm (2ft) apart each way. To produce many small new potatoes leave all the shoots on, but for fewer, bigger tubers remove all shoots but one. To increase yields significantly give potatoes heavy waterings when the flowers appear (remove the poisonous seedheads

that come after the flowers).

varieties There are hundreds of varieties available from specialists but few are widely offered. I grow Sutton's Foremost, Epicure, Sharpe's Express and Pink Duke of York for my earlies. Wilja are superb for second earlies, and for maincrops I grow the wonderful baker but low-yielding Golden Wonder, for salads the divine waxy Pink Fir Apple, and Diana and Romano for baking and chipping.

problems and solutions Organic gardeners are advised to grow early varieties. These give lower yields but crop quickly and can thus be harvested before potato blight

A selection of my favourite potatoes: **1** Majestic; **2** Romano; **3** Diana; **4** Sutton's Foremost; **5** King Edward; **6** Arran Victory; **7** Wilja; **8** Pink Duke of York

becomes a problem, as it usually comes after midsummer during a warm wet summer. Second earlies similarly miss most blight attacks, but the more productive maincrops need to grow on into early autumn to give full yields. Scabby patches can be avoided by mixing in grass clippings with the soil and compost. Adding well wilted comfrey leaves is always advantageous. Tubers can also be affected by wireworm, eelworm, and blackleg (see pages 46, 48, 52).

harvesting and storage Once flowers appear search among the clippings and soft soil for tubers big enough to eat, but leave the smallest to grow on. This saves digging up a whole row for the first meal and increases overall yields. To get the best storing potatoes, cut the haulm off and leave the tubers for a fortnight before digging: this gives them tougher skins. But the most important factor is to dig them up in dry conditions. Be careful not to bruise them, and use small and damaged tubers first. Leave the best to dry in the sun for an hour, but no more, then store them in paper sacks in a cool frost-free place.

the onion family

garlic & shallots

These are among the easiest vegetables to grow, provided you have a sunny site and have dug in plenty of well-rotted manure or compost. Garlic can be planted from mid-autumn to late winter, and the earlier the better. Plant individual cloves, pointed end upwards, 2.5cm (1in) deep and 15cm (6in) apart each way. Shallots need very shallow holes and can be planted 1cm (½in) deep 23cm (9in) apart each way from midwinter to early spring. Keep the plants weeded at all times – by hand if necessary. Garlic and shallots can be grown in any spare patch in the ornamental garden where they will discourage pests and disease in other plants. Highly recommended.

problems and solutions Both may be pulled out of their holes by birds and worms and need replanting, but otherwise rarely suffer any problem.

varieties Long Keeper is one of the varieties

specially developed for cooler climates.

harvesting and storage Harvest in the summer when the leaves begin to yellow. Loosen bulbs with a fork and leave to dry and ripen in the sun. Store in nets in a frost-free shed. If you fail to dig up any they will show their position when they sprout. They can then be dug up, split and replanted for a new crop.

leeks

cultivation A very hardy crop that takes up little space. It rarely suffers any problems in a rich moist soil but may not do well in hot dry conditions. Dig in plenty of well-rotted manure or compost before planting. Sow 2.5cm (1in) deep under cover in early spring. Plant out in late spring 15cm (6in) apart each way. When transplanting make deep holes at least 15cm (6in) deep with a dibber. Insert the leek then water in well with dilute seaweed solution. Do not fill in the holes with earth. Hoe to keep down weeds. In dry

Sowing potatoes
1 Conventionally, the seed potato is planted in a trench but I make large saucepan-sized holes at the required distances using a kitchen saucepan and a trowel. **2** Once complete, add comfrey leaves followed by **3** sieved garden compost. **4** Plant the seed potatoes and **5** add grass clippings as protection against scab. **6** Replace soil in the hole and firm down.
7 Once the potatoes emerge, drag soil up around each plant to reach molehill size. A mulch of straw, leaves or grass clippings keeps the soil moist and protects the young tubers from the sun, which would turn them green; for main crops, first apply a 'collar' of newspaper so that if birds scratch away the grass, the tubers remain out of the light and then **8** add the grass clippings

weather water regularly and mulch to conserve moisture.

varieties For autumn leeks, sow The Lyon or Argenta; for winter use, Musselburgh is hard to beat and Alaska will stand and grow larger until late spring. The latter has blue foliage and looks good in ornamental areas.

problems and solutions Leeks are relatively free of pests and diseases, though rust is common (*see page 50*).

harvesting and storage Leeks are very hardy and can be left in the ground and dug as required. Leeks can be frozen, if only the white part is used; they also make excellent soup which can then be frozen. Unused leeks should be left to flower as they are loved by beneficial insects. Highly recommended.

onions

cultivation Onions like a richly organic soil – over winter, dig in plenty of well-rotted manure or compost. They do suffer from a few pests and diseases but most years they still produce good results if the weather is favourable – they need a sunny site. Keep young onions weeded and water regularly in dry weather. They can be grown in several different ways, which splits the risks and also extends their season of availability.

Easiest of all is to buy onion sets which are more expensive than seeds, but usually avoid many of the problems and give good results. These are planted from late winter to mid-spring, but the earlier the better if the ground is ready. Rake to a fine tilth then plant them in very shallow holes 20cm (8in) apart each way and keep putting them back as the birds and worms pull them out. These are convenient for intercropping where space is available, especially between brassicas and in ornamental areas, where they discourage pests and diseases.

Onion seed can be sown direct, but is best sown under cover mid to late winter in pots or cells. Don't worry about getting more than one plant per cell, as two or three grown together will produce smaller, harder onions that keep better. Harden off for a few days in a cold frame before planting. Plant out the seedlings in early to mid-spring. Use close planting at 10cm (4in) apart each way for small, long keepers and 18cm (7in) for big ones for earlier use.

In late summer, direct sow Japanese onions for overwintering. Rake the soil to a fine tilth and sow 1cm (½in) deep. Thin to 10cm (4in) apart each way. These are ready before midsummer, when onions are expensive to buy, but do not try to keep them after summer as they go off easily. Pickling onions are sown thickly so that they crowd each other. Paris Silverskin is the standard variety but I prefer pickling shallots. Spring onions are the slender ones you want for salads but are never ready in time: they need to be sown 1 cm (½in) deep and 1cm (½in) apart in early autumn for spring use, and again in late winter and early spring for succession. The spring sowings can be sown with carrots as an inter-crop.

varieties Sturon and Turbo are excellent for onion sets. Giant Zittau, Bedfordshire Champion and Southport Red Globe are my favourites for onions grown from seed. Senshyu Yellow and Express Yellow are the best Japanese onions for overwintering.

problems and solutions If onion fly is a problem in your area grow sets, which rarely suffer, or grow under netting or fleece. If the leaves get a grey mould dust them with wood ashes which checks the attack. If white rot or stem eelworm appears (*see page 48*) dig up and burn the infected plants. Be careful never to break or damage the leaves

or bulb when cultivating so it is best to weed round onions by hand.

harvesting and storage Once the bulbs start to ripen let the weeds grow as they will take up nutrients and help the ripening process. Never bend the leaves down to help ripening as this lets in disease. Most will fall over by themselves. Lift the onions from underneath with a fork and dry them off in the sun or under cover in an airy place, turning them regularly. Store on open trays in a well-ventilated, frost-free shed rather than tying them up in bunches.

top Southport Red Globe onions drying in the onion dryer
above Garlic bulbs ripening in the sun

8 FRUIT
in an organic garden

When conditions are good, growing organic fruit is easier and makes even more sense than growing vegetables, yet many people put a great deal of effort into cultivating a vegetable patch and never think about having a mini-orchard as well (or even instead). There are many advantages to growing your own: shop-bought fruit can never be really fresh, and the varieties available are invariably commercial ones chosen solely for their high yields. At home, you can choose old-fashioned varieties with exceptional flavour and high vitamin content. Ribston Pippin apples, for example, have nearly four times as much Vitamin C as Golden Delicious. Further-more, organic fruit picked when fully ripe has even more vitamins, flavour and goodness than fruit grown conventionally and picked underripe to enable it to be transported great distances.

The summer soft fruit harvest is a feast for the eye and the table. **Clockwise from the top right** Tayberries, gooseberries Langley Gage, white currants, gooseberries Keepsake, red currants, yellow raspberries, strawberries, blackcurrants and gooseberries London

the value of fruit

Economically, fruit can give much better returns in weight or value per square metre than most vegetables. One gooseberry bush can yield 4.5kg (10lb) of fruit or more, yet occupies little more space than a cauliflower. Although the initial cost may be higher for trees and bushes it is a one-off payment which you recoup in the first years of fruiting, whereas seed bills for vegetables are annual.

It is true that the returns are more immediate with vegetables, as these will be cropping the first

season, but many fruits are not far behind. Strawberries can be cropped less than a year after planting; autumn-fruiting raspberries similarly. All the currants and berries give good crops the second year after planting, and even top fruit such as apples, peaches and pears will often start to crop in their second or third year. The yields also increase annually, for most fruits reach peak production after five to ten years then maintain this for decades – with little annual expense.

Labourwise, fruit is easier than vegetables, taking far less work and some will grow in shady spots vegetables would spurn. Care is needed to establish the plants well, but thereafter little work is needed except for pruning, which is far less effort than digging. Fruit benefits from soil enrichment but many fruits are more tolerant of neglect in this quarter than are vegetables. When it comes to pests and diseases, fruit has its fair share but often, when a tree or bush is under attack, the crop is still usable. Another point to consider as our climate changes is that

although fruit will benefit from watering it tends to withstand droughts better, and still produce in seasons when vegetables fail.

Ecologically, it is wiser to grow fruits than vegetables. Trees and bushes are permanent, require less annual input and their initial production uses less scarce resources than vegetable seeds. Also, their season in leaf is longer, fixing more carbon dioxide, and their root systems go deep enough to use more of the soil's own resources. Once established, most tree fruits can be grassed around leaving no bare soil to erode or leach, and they all support wildlife with shelter, nest sites and food (especially if we are not over-careful to protect it).

Nutritionally, fruit is marginally less valuable than vegetables, but it is much easier to get children of all ages to eat more fruit and fruit juices than more vegetables. Strawberries have more vitamin C than cabbage, nuts provide more protein than vegetables, and watermelon supplies more nutrition than spinach!

One of the advantages of growing large quantities of fruit is that it can be stored through the winter in a number of different ways; the juice which is being made here can be frozen for use in winter when the flavour of summer fruit has a special value

Aesthetically, it is easier to make an attractive and productive garden using fruit trees, vines and bushes than it is with vegetables and of course the length of their season is longer. Fruit trees can have an attractive appearance even when out of leaf, the bare branches silhouetted against a winter sky, and the changing seasons bring leaf colours, flowers and fruits. Fruit trained as espaliers or fans can enhance a wall or be used as screens to divide up the garden or block unsightly views. Grapes and kiwi vines can be draped over trellises or pergolas, or used to cover sheds.

The ornamental value of many fruit trees such as pears and cherries is equal if not superior to ornamentals. Quinces and medlars have attractive shapes and leaves and are much more attractive than the Kilmarnock willow too often used as a feature on small front lawns – and they are cheaper as fruit trees carry no VAT. Fruit trees and bushes are also good competitors, and will still produce when grown amongst vigorous shrubs and in overcrowded borders. Fruit trees grown as standards with a clean trunk can be grassed underneath to leave a play area, and will hold a swing when big enough.

Harvesting and storage in general is more pleasant, with less bending and no mud. Apples, some pears and quinces can be stored for months on trays, or in perforated plastic bags, kept in the garage. Even better is to lay them in trays and put them in a disused deep freeze. An old freezer, the seal stripped off to allow some minimal ventilation, is a frost-free rodent-proof box that will keep apples in excellent condition for six months or more.

All fruits can be frozen without blanching, which saves a lot of time, effort and energy. After freezing, the texture softens, making most fruit more suited for cooking, but if the defrosting is timed carefully to catch the fruit while still softening then it is excellent eating especially with yoghurt or cream! Juicing is easy and the juices can be frozen in plastic

A recycled freezer in one of the outhouses maintains a fairly constant temperature making it a very serviceable apple store

bottles for use during the rest of the year. Modern equipment hired, or even bought for less than a video recorder, will convert apples into juice at about 9 litres (2 gals) per hour, and softer fruits even faster. The juice can be drunk or converted into wines, cider or vinegar with little added sugar. Fruit can also be bottled or made into jams and jellies, and if it does go mouldy will do little harm.

planning the site

soil You get better results with almost any plant from a deep rich moist soil full of organic material, so every effort should be made to improve the soil before planting. Needless to say it will be much more difficult later on. Equally, the ground must be cleared of weeds. Few plants other than bilberries and cranberries will thrive in soil prone to waterlogging, so drainage may be necessary, though raised beds or mounds are a better alternative. Cooking apples will stand wetter conditions than the dessert varieties, and in general all culinary fruits are more tolerant of adverse conditions than dessert. Thin dry soils, particularly over chalk, will also be unfavourable to many fruits, for example, raspberries and pears, though apples may just succeed. In general, all poor sites will need building up with copious quantities of organic material.

Top fruits need soils that are neither extremely acid nor alkaline, with apples preferring a slightly acid soil and the stone fruits such as cherries and plums preferring it more alkaline. Soft fruits generally prefer acid conditions, as do bilberries and cranberries which thrive in peat bogs. If they are initially well established, grapes and figs will grow in chalky conditions where other fruits fail.

site No fruits will grow well in heavy shade, especially from large trees, and the root competition will also make establishment and cropping poor. Light shade will not be harmful to most of the soft fruits as their native habitat is shady woodland, and they can thus be planted in less favourable positions, leaving the best sites for the trees. But

above Trained fruit trees surround the vegetable beds adding valuable protection from cold winds for earlier cropping

below Protection from frost is vital for fruit trees – even a light cloth can make sufficient difference for the blossom to pull through unharmed

raspberries and strawberries do best in full sun for at least half the day.

Windy, exposed sites will cause poor pollination, slow growth and loss of blossom as well as premature dropping of the fruits, so windbreaks are of immense benefit. Nutbushes, damsons and Myrobalan plums all make productive windbreaks. Cherries make large trees which can be planted upwind to protect more tender fruits, though they may lose their own fruit some years.

Frost damage probably causes more loss of fruit than every other problem put together. We cannot change the climate, but it is possible to improve the microclimate. The early flowering fruits can be grown against sunny walls, where they are only half as likely to be damaged, and if they are further protected by a cloth or fine net they will probably escape unharmed. Tree and bush crops can similarly be saved by throwing some form of cloth over them, to stop the heat escaping to the night sky. Warm,

sunny spots on walls and patios, and places with extra heat such as near a boiler flue, should be reserved for the most susceptible fruits such as pears, peaches and apricots. Soft fruit in a cage is often protected by the roofnet and this can be augmented with an old sheet, or even wet newspaper spread on top. Strawberries are easiest of all to cover.

Frost pockets are low-lying places that collect the coldest air, which flows downhill just like water. Avoid planting such low spots with strawberries, early flowering fruits and low bushes; it is better to grow taller forms such as half standards, to keep the flowers up out of the coldest air. Frost will damage young fruitlets as well as the flowers, so protect these too if a frost is predicted.

selecting plants

varieties When planning your fruit, remember to extend the season by choosing early and late fruiting varieties. This technique is especially rewarding with apples, which with careful storage can be available for six to ten months of the year. Extending the season also spreads the workload, so that picking and preserving do not all come at once, and with many different varieties there is less like-lihood of all the crop being lost to frost, pests or diseases. Where space is available then, grow as many varieties as possible; even if space is limited several varieties can be fitted in by growing cordons. An alternative is to grow what have become known as family trees, which have three or more varieties grafted on to one set of roots.

For favourite fruits it may also be worth-while extending the season of a particular variety by planting some in a warm sheltered spot and some in a cool shady place, thus spreading the cropping period by a week or two. It is also worth noting that the fruits on the sunny side of a tree are usually well ahead of those on the shady side, so do not pick them all at once. Please also note that fruit picked wet rots rapidly.

Old varieties versus new is always contro-versial, it all depends on what you want. Certainly some of the new varieties of fruit are higher yielding than the old and many offer some resistance to disease. But where flavour is concerned it is a matter of taste, and many of the old varieties are superb – that is why they were bred in the first place. Modern breeders, on the other hand, are usually after the commercial market, which wants the highest yields before all else. The best way to choose is to visit a nursery with a wide selection of fruit or a pick your own farm, and try them; otherwise, read the cata-logues carefully. Currants vary little in flavour, but apples, gooseberries and grapes vary tremendously. Over 6,000 varieties of apple are recorded and it is still possible to obtain several hundreds!

rootstocks Almost all trees sold in garden centres are on dwarfing or semi-dwarfing rootstocks to stop the trees getting too big and to ensure earlier cropping. For bigger trees and larger crops, or to cope with diffi-cult soils, different rootstocks may be prefer-able. Trees sold for specific purposes such as cordon training, and full standards, are nor-mally supplied with a suitable rootstock by the nursery. (The exact type of rootstock will be shown on the label if you use a reputable supplier.)

It is important to know the rootstock so you can give the tree the spacing it requires: this applies particularly to apples, which vary the most. Standard trees on the vigorous apple stocks M25 and M2 will need to be 6-9m (20-30 ft) apart, while those on the very dwarfing M27 and M9 will need only 1.8-2.5m (6-8ft) and permanent staking. For medium-sized gardens M26 and MM106 are best as they do not need staking once estab-lished and grow vigorously enough so you can use the space underneath. Plant M26 3-3.5m (10-12ft) apart and MM106 3.5-5 m (12-15ft) apart. Always check the rootstock and application with the supplier.

buying plants It is essential to plan tree and bush planting. Order several catalogues early and plan the planting on paper. Rather than buying from a garden centre with lim-ited choice, it is better (and less expensive) to buy from reputable mail-order nurseries. Their catalogues will give the rootstock and spacing for each type of tree, as well as offer-ing a wider choice. Buy young, bare-rooted, certified virus-free plants and order them by early autumn. Soft fruit does not have a choice of rootstock but similarly requires careful spacing. It is always better to have fewer, well-spaced plants than to crowd them, leading to poorer cropping, excessive pruning and disease problems.

The worst place to buy your fruit trees and bushes is from a cheap market stall or a 'supermarket' garden centre. Sadly, most of these only stock the fastest-moving lines and offer a poor choice of variety with no choice of rootstock. Do not buy special offer large or old plants as they never do as well as younger ones. Garden-centre plants are often grown in containers, which makes for a cramped root system. This is little problem for herbaceous plants, small shrubs or most soft fruit, but to plant a tree that could live a century or more with its first 90 cm (3 ft) of roots wound into a circle hardly makes for a good foundation or anchor.

propagation Growing your own is quite simple for most of the soft fruits if you can get cuttings from healthy bushes. If you

145

above Tayberry in flower
bottom right Hand-pollination of melon plants which I grow best in a cold frame on top of the compost heap for the additional heat benefit

want to have large numbers of one variety then buy one good, certified virus-free plant and take cuttings from it.

Hardwood cuttings of soft fruit about 30 cm (12in) taken in the autumn will usually produce excellent fruiting plants in two years at no cost. Rub off the buds from the lower half (blackcurrants excepted) and push the cuttings 7.5-13cm (3-5in) deep and 30cm (12in) apart into clean gritty soil in the open ground on a seed, vegetable or nursery bed. On heavy soils mix sharp sand into a slit trench and plant the cuttings in this, but be careful to firm the soil well. Keep the cuttings sheltered from cold winds, and cloched in hard winters, and the soil weeded and moist until they can be moved the following autumn. Blackcurrants are the easiest, and as they are best stooled with many growths from ground level, all the buds can be left on cuttings. Other currants are very easy. Gooseberries and grapes are fairly easy, but benefit more from cloching.

tip-layering All the blackberry family and hybrids can be grown from the tips of the canes, which are allowed to root into pots in late summer.

Shrubby plants can be rooted by bending a branch down, damaging the bark and burying the branch, pinned down, in the ground or in a pot of moist, gritty potting compost.

Strawberries and raspberries provide ample new plants themselves. The former are best rooted in pots from runners off deflowered vigorous young plants; they can

then be planted out early enough to fruit well the following year. Raspberries produce suckers all over the place: strong ones with many underground buds are best.

It is essential to use healthy plants, so avoid nondescript old blackcurrants, raspberries and strawberries as these are prone to more disease (virus) problems than the other fruits. Top fruit cuttings do not root easily and would not then be controlled by a suitable rootstock anyway. It is also inadvisable to grow most fruits from seed as they are unlikely to be very good.

replacement It is important to eradicate any old currant bushes you inherit with a garden and periodically replace old with new. Strawberries need to be replaced every third or fourth year, but I have found that you can replant with your own new plants for eight to ten years before buying in new. Blackcurrants and raspberries will need replacing every ten to fifteen years. Most other fruits will still be producing well long after we are but memories. Try to replace any plant on a different site to avoid replant disease.

pollination must also be considered when planning the fruit garden. Most soft fruit is self-fertile so there is little problem, though heavier crops will result where several varieties are grown. With top fruit, however, more care must be taken. If there are many other fruit trees nearby (within 45m /50 yds) you may get away without considering pollination, but otherwise if you want specific varieties you will also have to plant their suitable partners. Further, the pollinating

partner may not itself be pollinated in return, necessitating a third partner, as happens with triploid apples. Biennial bearers are also a bit risky as they may not flower, losing their own crop and that of the pollinating partner. For example, a common error is to plant just a Cox (a difficult fruit to grow well) or a Cox and a Bramley, which are not compatible. But add a James Grieve, and they are all pollinated. Many popular fruits such as Victoria plums and Conference pears are self-fertile, but like the soft fruit will give better, heavier crops if pollinated by others. Pollinating partners have to be compatible, but obviously they also have to be in flower together, so the biggest problems arise with very early or late flowering varieties. In practice it is not too complicated and most good nursery catalogues will recommend suitable combinations. Remember that fruit grown in the greenhouse will need to be pollinated by hand, using a soft brush.

Wild varieties of fruits (such as the common crab apple) are usually excellent pollinators for cultivated forms and can be grown in hedgerows to save space. Family trees also solve the pollination problem by having compatible varieties on the same rootstock.

planting Preparation of the planting holes a long time before your plants arrive is not a good idea as it may allow the soil to dry out, but it is better to dig the holes early and do a good job than to rush at the last minute.

Fruit trees and bushes are generally planted in the winter, but planting cannot be done when the soil is very wet or frosted. If conditions are too poor keep the plants in a frost-free place until the soil improves, or heel them in, digging a slit-shaped trench and cover the roots with soil. If the roots are at all dry, soak for an hour before planting. If conditions are very cold and windy, cover the roots with damp sacking while digging the hole, to prevent them drying out.

The hole for a tree or bush needs to be as big and as deep as you can make it, not just large enough to squeeze the roots in. Deeper is better than wider, but do not

bring up the deeper soil layers. Mix well-rotted compost or manure evenly throughout each layer, and add a handful each of rock phosphate and bone meal if the soil is poor. Never put in large amounts of anything without mixing it in well, especially peat. I have seen many promising trees killed by being given too much peat: a layer of peat isolates the roots and dries out the rootball so that the tree fails in its first summer as capillary moisture cannot reach it.

Having prepared a large hole mound up some soil in the middle and adjust with the plant in situ so that the dirty mark on the trunk showing its original planting depth is at or just above ground level. The exception is blackcurrants, which should be planted deeper. The bump which shows where the tree was grafted on to the rootstock should be at least 10cm (4in) above the soil.

Position a stake for the tree next to the trunk and passing between the roots, remove the tree and hammer in the stake. Now put back the tree, loosely tie the two together and start to fill in with the soil mixture. Take care to spread the roots widely and keep them in their original layers while working the soil in and around them firmly. Tread the soil as firmly as you can. After planting fix the tie more securely and surround the trunk with a mulch to retain warmth and moisture, but do not allow the mulch to touch the bark or cover any graft union. Keep the mulch in place with a piece of old carpet or plastic weighed down with bricks or skewered. This will help to keep weed-free conditions while the plant establishes. Keep the plant weed-free for a radius of 90cm-1.8m (3-6ft) for the first couple of years or optimum growth will never be achieved.

It is standard practice to prune fruit trees and shrubs after planting, to help the roots establish. However, I do not personally recommend cutting back either top growth or roots when planting unless these are damaged or diseased. Let the plant get established first, and then cut the top hard the following year, if necessary to form the shape.

container growing In the smallest gardens, where you may only have a patio, it is still

above Grape vines are grown in containers, which is problem-free as long as you do not neglect the watering

below A fruit cage increases soft fruit yields by keeping off the birds

possible to grow fruit trees, soft fruit and even vines, by confining them in containers. This cramps the root system, preventing them getting too big, and tends to bring them into fruit earlier. However, they are very prone to dropping their fruit and even dying unless extremely good care is taken to keep them well and regularly watered – this can mean three or four times a day in the summer. Similarly, attention is needed to prevent the roots freezing in winter. An advantage is that the whole pot can be taken under cover to prevent frost or bird damage, or to bring on earlier growth. Use the biggest container you can manage (plastic dustbins can be converted with holes in the base and are much cheaper than pots) fill with a good potting compost, use the most dwarfing rootstock, and arrange some form of automatic watering system.

first year Water new plantings heavily in late spring and early summer as it is then that they will be under most stress with drying winds sucking the new foliage before a large root system has formed. Drought in late summer is less of a problem as the tree will

then have a larger root system. Spraying with seaweed solution will help stimulate growth during the first year in leaf and should be done routinely at monthly intervals. Never let trees or bushes fruit the first year as this diverts energy from growth at a critical stage and they will do poorly ever after!

fruit cages A fruit cage increases yields of soft fruit by more than 100% as it keeps the birds off. Commercial cages are expensive but do recoup their outlay. It is much less expensive to build your own from posts, with chicken wire for the sides and a plastic net roof. Roof nets must be taken off for the winter to prevent snow breaking them; this also reduces weathering so the net lasts longer and allows the birds to eat pests during the winter. The fruits that benefit most from being caged are raspberries, strawberries, tayberries, red and white currants and grapes. Blackberries, blackcurrants and gooseberries suffer less from bird damage but still benefit from protection. Cherries need to be protected but tend to make too much growth to be contained in cages, though new dwarfing stocks now make this possible.

underplanting and intercropping fruit trees or bushes with flowers or vegetables can be practised where space is at a premium, but it is essential to keep a circle of at least 90cm-1.8m (3-6ft) clear around a tree or bush for the first few years to enable it to establish without competition. Less inevitably leads to poorer growth and lower yields. Trees compete more effectively than bushes and may produce even when grown in overcrowded borders, though picking can be difficult in this situation.

Companion plants will similarly compete initially but later can be of immense benefit in attracting and maintaining predators and pollinators. *Limnanthes douglasii*, *Convolvulus tricolor*, chives, nasturtiums, rosemary, thyme and sage will all be of benefit and when grassing down trees in later years add clovers and alfalfa to the grass seed mixture.

Grassing down must not be allowed under trees until they are well established but then may be done to improve the appearance and reduce labour. The grass will compete with

tallest trees on the northern side and the tenderer pears and peaches on the southern. Place any chicken hut next to the plums or peaches as they will benefit from the increased droppings thereabout and water troughs are best situated by the pears or peaches.

greenhouses In colder regions, tender crops including tropical fruit, can be grown in the greenhouse. This gives excellent bird and frost protection, and earlier crops, but on the down side tends to cause more pest and disease problems. There is no background ecology of predators and parasites, and diseases tend to spread more easily in the close, often humid conditions.

To combat pests try companion planting of flowers such as French marigolds (which attract aphid predators), spray with soft soap, or use biological pest control of whitefly and red spider mites by introducing parasites (*see pages 53*).

Common greenhouse diseases are mildew, blight, botrytis and leaf mould. See the section on pests and diseases (*pages 45-55*) for detailed information on combating greenhouse diseases. In general, they can be controlled by maintaining strict hygiene in the greenhouse, and any diseased or damaged plants should be removed immediately. Good ventilation is essential, to prevent plants suffering from moisture or heat stress.

above An underplanting of *Limnanthes douglasii* maintains a healthy supply of predators and pollinators in the fruit cage and provides food for honey bees
right Hens and gees in the orchard supply extra fertility and keep the grass down

the trees but if the clippings are returned their fertility will balance out and it prevents soil erosion. Grassing does increase the danger from spring frosts, as bare soil keeps the air above warmer at night – pears in particular and the soft fruits should not be grassed down as they are more badly affected than others.

orchards Large quantities of top fruits are best grown in an orchard. If they are on half standard or standard trunks then it can be a play area, paddock or wildlife meadow underneath. It is an exceptionally good idea to run chickens, ducks or geese underneath fruit trees as they will improve the fertility, control the grass and reduce pest problems to a minimum. (Cynically, it is said poultry are even more effective if you do not feed them much.) When planning an orchard put the

pruning & training methods

above A trained pear tree providing shelter to the raised vegetable beds

below An apple tree trained in a festoon in early spring

bottom An espalier-trained boysonberry just coming into leaf in early spring with blackcurrant bushes behind

Fruits can be grown either in border soil or in containers. The advantage of using containers in the greenhouse is that this restricts growth more easily than pruning. It also enables plants to be stood outside for the summer months, but they will then require even more careful watering. Container growing in a greenhouse is most suitable for grapes (wound up a bamboo cane in a spiral), peaches, and citrus fruits. Remember that fruit grown in a greenhouse will require pollination by hand.

Tree fruits are easiest grown as standards, half standards or bushes where pruning is at a minimum, with only ingrowing, rubbing and diseased growths needing removal. These forms take up space, and are slightly slower to start producing, so for small gardens or where many varieties are desired, trained forms are better. These require much more work and permanent supports but give earlier and superior fruit but they cannot be neglected without dire results.

training The initial formation of trained fruit trees is not difficult, and if left to the nurseryman will cost more than doing it your-self by buying unformed maiden (one-year-old) trees. Once the shape has been formed you must simply prune regularly, following instructions.

cordons are effectively one branch grafted on a dwarfing rootstock and are usually best grown at a 45° angle to make them as long as possible. They are grown against walls or fences, or in the open, and need posts and wires to support them. Cordons are very decorative, and are particularly suitable for small gardens as they can be planted at close intervals, 75cm (30in) apart, allowing many different varieties in a short run, say along the side of a path. Though each cordon produces much less than a bush or tree they produce more per square metre and the quality can be much better. Apples and pears are very suitable for cordon training, as are red and white currants and gooseberries.

espaliers are amongst the most attractive forms, enhancing a wall or being used as a screen. The tree is planted against a wall or fence and trained so that it consists of an upright stem, with branches growing horizontally at 38cm (15in) intervals. Plant espaliers 3.5m (12ft) apart. Espalier treatment is suitable for apples and pears, but the other tree fruits are more difficult to train and are better grown as fans.

stepovers are a one-tier version of the espalier, consisting of only one long branch grown along wires on either side of the stem. It is useful along paths and as a border edging where space is limited. Apples, pears and plums can all be grown like this.

dwarf pyramids are trained to produce a free-standing tree about 2.15m (7ft) high. The branches are pruned so that they taper towards the top, making picking and pruning very easy. Apples, pears and plums can all be grown by this method.

festoons are a method of training fruit trees and bushes by bending the branches into hoops, rather than pruning them. This has the effect of restricting the flow of sap, limiting growth and encouraging the tree to produce fruiting buds instead. The branches are tied down to the main stem, making an attractive small tree. Apples, pears and plums can all be grown as festoons.

fans are grown flat against a sunny wall, and have all the branches radiating from the top of a short trunk. They also need wire support

Winter pruning the tayberry
from the top Removing the
dead wood and tying in the
new; the pruned tayberry;
applying a feed and mulch of
seived garden compost
right I use a recycled bicycle
inner tube to support the new
growths of a Bedford Giant
blackberry until I am ready to
tie them in

and can be very attractive. They are more suited to the stone fruits – peaches, nectarines, plums, cherries – which are difficult to train as espaliers.

All these methods of training must be regularly pruned to control the growth and prevent crowding. Once the shape is formed then maintenance pruning is simpler.

pruning Winter pruning is done initially to form the shape of a tree as it stimulates replacement growth, though it is best avoided for the stone fruits such as plums as these may then be attacked by silverleaf disease (*see page 55*). Winter pruning is also done when major removal of boughs is necessary, as otherwise the tree may die of shock. When a tree has lost its vigour winter pruning can stimulate growth; too much replacement growth produces the hedgehog look seen in gardens from overuse of secateurs. Dead and unhealthy growth, which can be identified when the branches are bare, should be removed at this time. Do not use 'wound paints' or pruning compounds on cuts, as these contain chemicals.

Summer pruning is far more important for established trained trees and soft fruit. It does not stimulate growth, but fruiting. Basically summer pruning is removing half to three quarters of each new shoot once midsummer is past. This allows in air and light and checks growth, encouraging the formation of fruit buds. Of course, where the plant is still being allowed to expand, then shoots going in the desired direction are not cut off but may be shortened in winter, which encourages more sideshoots to develop.

Soft fruit pruning is easier than for top fruit and the plants are much quicker to respond, so it is ideal for gaining experience. Red and white currants are very forgiving and can be grown in almost any form; trained gooseberries make for easier picking. These all require young growth to be cut back by half to three-quarters in the summer, and then again by a bit more in the winter. They are all best grown as bushes on short legs so that the air can circulate, which helps keep them disease-free, but for prize berries grow as cordons.

Blackcurrants are grown as stools, with many shoots from ground level, the oldest third of these being cut out each year after fruiting. Blackberries and their hybrids and raspberries are normally grown as stools, with young growths being encouraged from ground level to replace the old on an annual basis. Simply cutting out the old and leaving the new removes most pest and disease problems simultaneously. Tying the fruiting canes down on either side and allowing the new to grow up through the middle keeps the new canes cleaner of disease spores dropped by the old. I use bicycle inner tubes fitted with wire hooks as giant elastic bands to hold new growths out of the way until I am ready to tie them in.

general care & maintenance

Where trees are established and growing well they may not flower or fruit, preferring to grow more first. If there are strongly growing vertical branches, then attach lines near the tips and pull the branches gently down from the vertical, securing the lines round the trunk (as with the festoon technique). I find that this checks the sap flow and induces fruiting more effectively than pruning.

If flowers are prolific but none set, and cold, windy weather is not to blame, suspect the lack of a suitable pollinator. If possible, acquire some sprays of blossom from a friend's tree and try hand-pollinating with these. If any of these set the fruit, you will then have to buy a tree in that pollination group.

Some fruit, especially apples, tend to biennial bearing where they only fruit in alternate

above clockwise from top left Thinning the peach tree before the fruits begin to swell significantly

below clockwise from top left *Applying sticky tree bands:* first wrap around the trunk a foil strip; next add the sticky band material; then wrap a band of corrugated cardboard and tie (any beneficial insects which find their way into the cardboard band can be shaken free)

seeds that exhausts a plant, taking proteins, fats and minerals, so reducing the seed numbers helps the plant. It will still give the same weight of fruit, only each one will be bigger. Thinning twice is better still, the second thinning being done a month later, leaving only perfect, well-positioned fruits.

Watering is not as necessary for fruit as for vegetables, but is always advantageous in dry years, especially for soft fruit, as two crops are threatened, this year's and next's. It is absolutely vital for fruit in containers, which will need watering three times daily in hot summers. Rainwater is much better than tap for any established plant, and especially for those in containers, as it contains less dissolved salts which will build up in the soil as the water evaporates. Fruits growing in borders next to walls (such as fans, cordons and espaliers) and in dry corners will benefit greatly from watering as rain does not always reach them.

The critical point with any plant is to water before it suffers or wilts. Fruitlets often drop in late spring when the soil first dries out, so apply mulches wherever possible and water well before the soil has started to dry out or the plant shows any sign of wilting.

years. The answer to this is simply to remove half or more of the fruits during the 'on' year so that the tree is not exhausted and does not need a year off.

Almost all the tree fruits, gooseberries and grapes will give bigger, better fruit if they are thinned every year. This is the simplest way of improving the quality, since all the diseased and pest-ridden fruits are removed and destroyed. Thinning is best done after the 'midsummer drop', but before fruits have started to swell significantly. Pears are best thinned to one fruit per cluster within six weeks of petal fall. It is the production of

regular maintenance Specific cultivation requirements are given under each fruit in the Plant Selection (*opposite*). All fruit trees and bushes benefit immensely from mulching. At least every third year they should be given a good mulch of garden compost. In the winter, rake mulches aside for a day or two so that birds can get at pests overwintering under it. Monthly spraying with diluted seaweed solution from early spring to midsummer is also highly recommended as this promotes vigour and disease resistance.

All trees and bushes benefit from banding with sticky tree bands as it is mainly pests that climb trunks. Do not forget to band the stakes or wires as well. Hygiene is important so remove all diseased material as soon as it is spotted and burn it. See the section on pest and diseases (*page 45-55*) for detailed methods of control.

PLANT SELECTION

tree fruit

apples

Apples are the most useful fruit to grow as they are easily stored for many months, and can be eaten raw, cooked in various ways or turned into delicious juice or cider. The apples that are most useful where space is limited are the extra earlies, late keepers and those with exquisite flavour. Avoid Coxes, as they are difficult to grow well, and Bramleys, unless you want a lot for cooking.

cultivation Apples are not fussy about soil or site, doing well almost anywhere, though very wet sites may encourage scab and canker. They do prefer a slightly acid soil. (*See page 143 for general advice on planning the site for fruit trees*). The section on pruning and training (*see page 150*) applies particularly to apples and of all the fruits they are the most forgiving. Most apples can be grown as cordons 60cm (2ft) apart, and as espaliers at 3m (12ft) apart to give high quality fruit and squeeze as many varieties as possible into a small space. They can also be grown as fans, stepovers and fes-toons (*see page 150*). Some known as tip bearers, such as Beauty of Bath and George Cave, are better grown as rarely pruned dwarf bushes. To grow apples in containers, use the most dwarfing rootstock M27 or the more vigorous rootstocks M26 or MM106. (*For advice on apple rootstocks see page 145*).

Any apples which are not quite up to standard for eating, because of attacks from wasps and the like, I make into juice. By mixing the varieties I get a blend with a perfect flavour. Frozen, this lasts me through the winter

Pollinating partners are best provided by growing several varieties which share a flowering period. A crab apple will pollinate most others also in flower.

varieties For earlies grow George Cave and Discovery, for late keepers Ashmead's Kernel, Winston, Wagener, and Tydeman's late orange. For outstanding mid-season flavour try James Grieve, Orleans Reinette, and Epicure. Bramley is the best cooker but Rev. Wilks and Howgate Wonder are also good. If you grow cordons then you can have great variety – searching the catalogues in mouthwatering in itself. Some of the newer varieties have merit; consider Fiesta, Greensleeves, Jonagold, Jupiter, Katja and Spartan. Even Golden Delicious tastes good when grown organically at home!

problems and solutions Apples suffer infestations of quite a few pests and diseases – woolly aphid, codling moth, apple sawfly, wasps, canker, scab, rot etc – but as they produce so freely there is nearly always plenty of good fruit, especially if the damaged ones are removed during successive thinnings (*see pages 45-55 for advice on pests and diseases*). Apply sticky tree bands in early autumn and keep them touched up throughout the winter to catch the majority of winter moths. Use pheromone traps to prevent codling moth maggots in valuable crops. Scabby patches on fruit are related to blisters and blotches on twigs and leaves – prune these out and allow more air and light, mulch and feed to stimulate growth and spray monthly with seaweed solution. This will also discourage canker 'ulcers' often found on poor growers. Brown

from the top The Souvenir de Congrés pear; pruning the espalier-trained Doyenne du Comice before, during and after

rotten patches on apples are caused by bruising or damage and then infection by spores overwintering in stems and soil. Again, hinder these with mulching and seaweed sprays which encourage healthy growth. Small trees and bushes can be netted to protect against birds.

harvesting and storage Early apples will not keep, and must be eaten off the tree, though they can be juiced or puréed and then frozen. Late keepers should be left until they start to drop, or come away easily, and then carefully picked, laid on hay or newspaper on trays and stored in a frost-free place, ideally in a disused deep-freeze, though a garage will do. Keep them away from potatoes and onions to prevent tainting and remove rotted ones regularly.

pear

These are relatively easy to grow, although late frosts can damage the blossoms.

cultivation Without doubt they are best grown as fans or espaliers on a sunny wall; Jargonelle and Williams will even grow on a cold wall. Pear rootstocks grow much too large for most gardens, so pears are usually grown on quince rootstocks, which make small to medium-sized trees. Grown as bushes 3.5-4.5m (12-15ft) apart on the Quince A (semi-dwarfing) rootstock they are trouble-free, and they also respond well to cordon training on Quince C (dwarfing) rootstock if a wide number of varieties are wanted – a good idea as it spreads the eating season. They do need pollinating partners, though some varieties such as Conference, Dr Jules Guyot and Durondeau are partly self-fertile they produce better fruits if pollinated. As with apples, the best answer is to grow sev-

eral. If this is not possible for any reason, select two or three from the same pollination group.

Pears need a fairly rich soil (see *page 22* for advice on enriching the soil before planting). They suffer badly from grass competition – be sure to clear perennial weeds before planting – and will not fruit well if dry at the roots, so need to be well mulched. Follow general instructions (see *page 151-2*) for feeding and watering.

varieties Doyenne du Comice (late autumn) is outstanding, but really does need a wall. It is pollinated by Beurre Hardy, Dr Jules Guyot or Glou Morceau. Beurre Hardy (mid-autumn), Williams Bon Chretien (early autumn), Clapp's Favourite (late summer) and Jargonelle (late summer) I find superb, and these can be grown as bushes. Glou Morceau (early winter) is probably the best flavoured keeper. Dr Jules Guyot (early autumn) and Conference (mid-autumn) are ideal for a two-pear garden while Beth (early autumn) is a new compact variety worth trying as it has good flavour.

problems and solutions Leaf blackening in spring is usually from harsh winds, but if the flowers and leaves wither and brown it may be fireblight. Prune this out and burn before it spreads. Leaf blistering is caused by mites, and can be cured with soft soap sprays. Sometimes the fruits blacken and drop with pear midge maggots inside: collect these up and destroy them. Pears can also suffer attacks from winter moth, woolly aphids, codling moth, sawfly, canker, scab, and brown rot. Wasps and birds can be a nuisance.

harvesting and storage Pears are ripe when they can be picked easily. Test for ripeness by twisting the stalk and tugging gently. Early or mid-season pears are best picked before fully ripe, as they tend to go soft and mealy. Pick when still firm and store in a cool place. Late pears can be left on the tree longer. They will mellow in store for two weeks and can then be brought indoors for final ripening. Pears will not keep longer – without carefully controlled temperature regulation – unless bottled, or frozen (they tend to darken). Pear juice is much like apple with a bit less of a bite, but pear cider is more difficult to make, requiring perry pears.

peach, nectarine & almond

Peaches, nectarines and almonds are all identical so far as cultivation is concerned. The trees are very beautiful in both flower and leaf, so can easily be grown in the ornamental garden.

cultivation Peaches grown as bushes 4.5m (15ft) apart are easy, self-fertile, and fruitful from early in their life provided they have a rich, moist soil and are kept well mulched. It helps to thin the fruits in cropping years as the remainder will then be much bigger and better. Pruning back hard in early spring every couple of years will ensure a plentiful supply of new wood and thus fruit. In more temperate regions peaches and nectarines can successfully be grown fan-trained against a sunny wall.

See page 147 for details of planting trees, remembering that soil is often particularly dry against a wall, and plenty of manure or compost should therefore be worked in. Again, the trees should be kept well mulched. On walls, fruiting can be more consistent because of the protection against frost, but then pruning must be more carefully and regularly done by cutting out old shoots that have fruited and tying in new ones. This can be quite arduous. (*See page 150 for details of training*).

Peaches and nectarines can also be grown in the greenhouse on the dwarfing Pixy rootstock, which makes them smaller than on the usual St Julien. In the greenhouse they are usually fan-trained against a wall in the same way as for outdoors. Trees in the greenhouse should also be well mulched, and fed during the growing season. Fruit in the greenhouse will have to be pollinated by hand. These fruits can also be grown in containers, using the Pixy dwarfing rootstock. This means they can be taken indoors over winter, which ensures freedom from leaf curl but tends to cause more problems with red spider mite. If moved outside again when in leaf they will avoid the latter and can fruit quite well.

varieties I highly recommend Peregrine or Rochester peaches grown as bushes, or even as specimen trees, where their beauty can be seen. Nectarines are basically fuzz-free, more tender peaches. They will not crop as bushes, needing the warmth of a sunny wall or greenhouse. Treat the same as peaches. Almonds

can be grown as bushes or trees and need the same treatment as peaches, but do not require thinning or pruning. They can be neglected with less dire results, and the flowers are even more beautiful.

problems and solutions The trees must be sprayed with Bordeaux mixture just before leaf-fall, and again in late winter to early spring to prevent peach-leaf curl attacks which pucker and colour the leaves, weakening the tree. Peach-leaf curl can be avoided if the trees are over-wintered indoors or a plastic sheet is hung over them. For fan-trained trees the sheet can be hung from the top of the wall to keep the branches dry all winter up to late spring, and this will also help with frost protection. Frosts take off the blossoms and fruitlets most years in temperate zones, so they must be covered on cold nights. On walls and under cover they also tend to be bothered by red spider mite. This is discouraged by frequent syringings with water and can be controlled by purchasing the predators *Phytoseiulus persimilis*. Plants in the greenhouse can also be affected by mildew and scale insects (*see the section on pests and diseases, pages 45-55*).

harvesting and storage These fruits are ripe when they come off the branch easily. Handle gently as they bruise easily. Peaches and nectarines will not store, but can be bottled, made into jam, or juiced. Almonds can be dried and stored in salt.

I highly recommend the Rochester peach tree, mine was laden with sweet flavourful fruit this summer

155

plum, bullace & damson

cultivation Though these can be grown as trained fruits on the new dwarfing Pixy rootstock they are much easier grown as bushes or half standards 4.5m (15ft) apart. They like richer conditions than apples or pears, and are well placed near the compost heap. Cropping is sporadic as they are easily frosted and often they wait several years before commencing but this can be speeded up by pulling the branches down from the vertical. Pollination partners are required for most, though some are self-fertile. Damsons and bullaces are self-fertile. As bushes or trees they can be left unpruned, except for remedial work which is best done in midsummer because of the risk of silver-leaf disease. Plums often crop very heavily, and it may be necessary to support the branches. Thin the fruit, especially if the crop is heavy, after the stones have formed.

Damsons and bullaces are grown in exactly the same way. They are hardier, with less vigorous growth. Bullaces are tough trees, good for windbreaks and hedgerows.

varieties Victoria (early autumn) is hard to beat for all-round performance, though it can be prone to disease. Coe's Golden Drop (early autumn) is a shy fruiter as tasty as an apricot; Reine Claude de Bavay (early autumn) is a consistent good cropper; Oullin's Gage (late summer) and Marjorie's Seedling (early autumn) are good for frosty areas, and the former can even be grown against a cold wall as can Jefferson (early autumn) which is delicious.

problems and solutions Plums suffer from several pests and diseases – rust, bacterial canker, silverleaf, plum sawfly, red spider mite and particularly mealy aphids, though I have found that these do not seem to affect the crop (see *pages 45-55 for specific information about pests and diseases*). It is

the birds and wasps that destroy most crops, and birds also take the buds off in winter so use black cotton after leaf fall and net if possible to protect the fruit. Fruit moth maggots can be prevented with pheromone traps and earwigs by banding the trunk. As with cherries, gummosis may cause oozing from the bark in badly drained or acid soils. Silver-leaf is prevented by not pruning except in summer, and by keeping the tree vigorous.

harvesting and storage Fruit is ripe when it is picked easily. All make wonderful jam – use underripe fruit, as this adds tartness. If freezing, stone them first as otherwise they have an off flavour. They can be juiced if simmered in water first and then strained.

apricot

These are surprisingly easy and I am amazed so few people grow them.

cultivation They will succeed as dwarf pyramids or bushes in sheltered spots or in tubs on a patio, but really prefer to be fan-trained at 4.5m (15ft) apiece on a sunny wall. Their main problem is frosts taking off the flowers or fruitlets: fans and bushes should be protected with netting when frost is expected, while containers are best taken into a greenhouse or conservatory. I have found cropping is erratic, but as they can fruit very heavily, thinning is required at intervals (see *page 152*). Pruning is best done twice, after the flowers have set and again when the fruits have swelled. Remove half to three-quarters of each young growth and all of any growth growing towards the wall.

varieties The best variety is Moorpark though others are worth trying.

problems and solutions They are rarely bothered by pests and diseases – see pages 45-55 for information if troubled by aphids, red spider mite, silver leaf etc. If growing poorly they may suffer dieback; cutting out the dead wood and feeding with liquid seaweed or seaweed meal should restore health.

harvesting and storage The fruit comes from mid-summer onwards. When ripe enough to drop it tastes better than you could ever imagine. Surpluses are good for jam and freezing.

below Delicious Purple Pershore plums for jamming
bottom I have my Moorpark apricot fan-trained on a wall which gets a good deal of sun

cherry

Morello cherries are dark bitter ones only suitable for cooking or jam, for which they are superb. They are self-fertile and will pollinate most sweet cherries, though too late for early flowerers.

cultivation Cherries do not like a heavy or badly drained soil. Prepare the site well (see page 147 for general advice on planting trees) and dig in well-rotted compost or manure before planting. Sweet cherries tend to make too much growth to fit in small fruit cages, though some new dwarfing rootstocks are now available. Otherwise they are better grown as fans against a large sunny wall which can be netted against birds. No net – no fruit! Where space is available (6-9m/20-30ft) grow them as half standard trees where they can be in full sun, perhaps beside a driveway or among shrubs. Avoid windy sites and frost pockets. Standard trees require little pruning.

The acid Morello cherries are not so vigorous, and do well in shade. They need to be heavily pruned after fruiting, removing the old shoots and leaving the new, and can thus be controlled to fit into a fruit cage or fan-trained on a wall, including shaded ones.

varieties Most sweet cherries need a pollination partner unless Morello (only to be relied on for the later flowerers) is grown as well, though Kentish Red and May Duke are partly self-fertile, and Stella and Sunburst are generally regarded as completely self-fertile. My favourite, and compatible, pair are Governor Wood and Napoleon Bigarreau.

problems and solutions They are best given only minimal pruning (in summer) to remove dead and diseased wood, thus avoiding silver leaf disease (see page 55), though fan-trained cherries will need more. Cherries have a tendency to root up to the surface, which makes them no friends to lawns, and so are better grown in paddocks and orchards. They crop well despite black aphid attacks, which usually do little real harm though they look appalling, and these breed up many ladybirds. Where netting is impractical pull nylon stockings over the branches of fruit but even then the birds will try and eat through them.

harvesting and storage Pick cherries before the birds get them! They will not juice, but make good jam – I jam the fruits in redcurrant jelly which makes them set and go further. If freezing, stone them first to prevent taint.

citrus fruits

cultivation In most temperate climates citrus fruits (lemons, limes, mandarins, grapefruit etc) can be grown under glass in a greenhouse or conservatory, provided it is frost-free. Trees or bushes grown in containers can usually be moved into the open for the summer. Grafted plants can be obtained which will fruit while small, and these can be grown in large containers, preferably terracotta or wood slat. They need an open, gritty potting compost and should be watered copiously then allowed to drain and almost dry out before rewatering.

varieties Lemons are the hardiest and can produce worthwhile quantities of fruit. Meyer's is the best. Satsumas are easier than oranges and produce delicious sweet fruits. Oranges and grapefruit require bigger pots to do well, but are still possible if given enough space.

problems and solutions Mealy bugs, aphids, whitefly and scale insects all attack citrus trees (see pages 45-55).

harvesting and storage Pick fruits as they ripen (temperature is more important than sunshine). Marmalade is easy to make, and I freeze all the skins to add to a jelly made from yellow tomatoes and whitecurrants.

fig

This is an easy fruit to grow and highly decorative, giving a tropical look to your garden

cultivation Figs must not be given too rich a soil or they make all growth and no fruit and they prefer chalky, well-drained soil. Traditionally the roots are restrained by planting the tree in a sunken brick box, approx. 1 × 1.5m (3 × 5ft), but it is far easier to use the drum from an old washing machine. This prevents the roots from getting too big, but allows water, air and fine roots to pass unhindered. Figs need a wall to do well and preferably a sunny one, at least 3m (10ft) high and wide. The young shoots and figs are prone to damage by frost, so protection is essential.

Pruning is best confined to thinning out the

from the top The medlar makes an attractive specimen tree although its fruit is an acquired taste

Young Cydonia quince, a fruit highly prized by more adventurous cooks

Cobnuts are easy to grow providing ready-to-eat nuts in early autumn

number of young shoots but it is important to remove every little fig you can find before midwinter. This prevents them sapping the growth, so that those formed in spring can ripen in early autumn.

Figs can also be grown in a greenhouse, either fan-trained against the wall of a 'lean-to' type greenhouse, or as bushes grown in containers. If grown in pots they will need careful watering.

varieties Brown Turkey or Brunswick are the best varieties.

problems and solutions Red spider mite in dry conditions, but syringings with water will control them, or try biological controls (see *page 54-5*).

harvesting and storage Eat figs when they start to soften and darken. Can be dried or frozen.

medlar

cultivation Usually grown as full or half standard, 13.5-6m (12-20ft) high. It has lovely large apple-like blossoms, beautiful contorted branches and attractive leaves. It is slow-growing, compact, and needs no pruning. It is self-fertile. It needs a sheltered spot as leaves and flowers are easily damaged by wind.

problems and solutions Few problems to worry about.

harvesting and storage Fruits ready to pick mid to late autumn. They are then 'bletted' – stored in a cool, dry place, eye downwards, not touching, for two to three weeks until the flesh softens.

mulberry

There are white and black mulberries and it is the latter we eat, which are a bit like black raspberries. They are slow to come into fruit (up to ten years) but make lovely if large specimens in the middle of a lawn, traditionally with a seat underneath.

cultivation As it is slow-growing, it is best to buy a 3-5-year-old tree. Fairly tolerant, but thrives best in rich, fertile, well-drained soil, and likes a warm, sunny site. In colder regions, it is best trained against a sunny wall. Self-fertile and requires no regular pruning.

harvesting and storage When the fruit eventually comes it is delicious, and is best shaken off the tree. It will only keep if bottled, but makes good jam or wine.

quince

There are two genera of quince. Chaenomeles or Japanese quinces have rock hard small fruits, spines and are usually grown in the ornamental garden for their flowers though they make a tasty jelly. Boule de Feu is highly productive, though all are easy, self-fertile and tolerant with no pests or diseases.

Cydonia quinces are an old fruit resembling a pear. They keep well and have an aromatic scent that will fill a kitchen. They cannot be eaten raw unless grown in a very sunny, warm climate, but added to apple or pear dishes they impart a delicious flavour. They make very decorative small trees with big apple-blossom flowers and can be used to good effect in ornamental areas. All are self-fertile and are tolerant of most soils and sites, though preferring moist ones. They do not thrive in colder areas. unless planted with the protection of a sunny wall. Plant 3 m (10 ft) apart.

varieties The Portuguese is the best variety, though the others are also worthwhile, but one tree is sufficient for most!

problems and solutions Cydonia quinces are susceptible to the same pests as apples – winter moth, woolly aphid, codling moth, canker, blight and scab (see *pages 45-55*).

harvesting and storage Usually ripen mid to late autumn, when they turn yellow. Leave on the tree as long as possible to develop their flavour. Store in a cool, dark place for one month – store by themselves as they have a strong aroma. They can be used to make jams and jellies as well as in apple pies.

hazel, filbert & cobnuts

cultivation These are remarkably easy and taste completely different and delicious when eaten fresh. They will grow anywhere, but crop badly on heavy damp sites while they do well on poor, stony or sandy sites. They flower very early and, to make nuts a viable prospect, need protection from cold winds in all but the warmest locations. They make big bushes which need 3m (10ft) apiece and as they can grow quite tall make excellent wind-breaks. Pruning can be forgotten about, except to remove suckers, and dead or over-crowded branches.

varieties Red Filberts are small but delicious. I recommend you grow them, and Cosford Cob, Kentish Cob or Webb's Prize. Grow several varieties to ensure cross-pollination.

problems and solutions They suffer from few pests and diseases except squirrels, so get the nuts in early!

harvesting and storage Once dried, the nuts can be stored in their shells in boxes with layers of salt for many years.

walnut

cultivation Another tree for the large gar-den. It is very slow (5-10 years) to fruit though when they come the nuts are very healthy for us to eat. Self-fertile and pest- and disease-free they also require no pruning. Not much grows very happily under a walnut so they are better planted as specimens 7.5m (25ft) apart along drives, or in meadows and orchards.

soft fruit

bilberries & blueberries
vaccinium myrtillus & v. corymbosum

The bilberry, a low-growing shrub native to Europe, is rarely cultivated, though the purple berries are delicious in tarts or made into jelly. The blueberry, native to the USA, is similar to the bilberry, though the fruit is a little larger, and is much more popular.

cultivation Both are grown as bushes, planted 1.5m (5ft) apart. They need moist, acid conditions and so should have peat – for the acidity – and well-rotted compost or manure, for the soil structure, incorporated into the soil when planting. The conditions need to be very acid, so if your soil is highly alkaline they may still not succeed. Mulch each spring with compost or leaf-mould, and water well in dry weather. Although self-fertile, they fruit better if different varieties are grown nearby. Pruning is not essential.

varieties Berkeley, Blue Crop and Earliblue are the easiest to find.

problems and solutions It is essential to net the bushes against birds once the berries have appeared. There are no pests or dis-eases of importance, though rust disease can be a problem in the USA: any infected bushes should be dug up and burnt.

harvesting and storage All berries rot very quickly once picked. Eat fresh within a few days, freeze, or make jams and jellies.

blackberries & hybrids

cultivation They all like rich, moist conditions but can often fruit well in poor soils and situa-tions, even in moderate shade or on cold walls, though the hybrids need more sun and warmth than blackberries. They flower in late spring, so frost is seldom a problem. Self-fer-tile, with vigorous, rambling growth, they must be trained along wires for support, strongly attached to a wall or stout posts. After plant-ing, cut down each cane to a bud about 30cm (12in) above the ground. Like raspberries, they fruit on one-year-old wood, so it is essential to keep the old and new canes sepa-rate. After fruiting, the old canes are cut down close to the ground and the new canes are tied in. Thornless versions are often less well flavoured and poorer croppers than thorny ones, but are more suitable for small gardens.

varieties A great number of blackberry derivatives are available but these are the best:

Himalayan Giant is the biggest and toughest – it could stop a runaway tank; ideal for keeping out unwanted visitors when planted along boundaries or trained over a fence. Highly pro-ductive from early autumn onwards, but it does need a lot of space – at least 4-4.5m (13½ - 15ft) each way.

Bedford Giant fruits earlier (late summer) and tastes better; the canes are longer than

Himalayan Giant blackberries
ripen in late summer

top The tayberry is a delicious new loganberry variety
above The Japanese wineberry with its bright red jewel-like fruit also makes a welcome addition to an ornamental area

Himalayan but not as thick or prolific, so are more controllable.

Oregon Cutleaf is very decorative and probably the best tasting thornless blackberry but crops rather too late (mid-autumn) for colder regions.

Loch Ness is a new variety that is thornless, compact and early (late summer).

Boysenberries (midsummer) are large, well flavoured blackberries but tend to make a lot of growth with light crops.

Loganberries are a cross between raspberries and blackberries, now redundant as the tayberry is similar but much, much better. However, L654 is productive, with a good flavour, so still worth growing where thornlessness is desirable. They need about 1.8-2.5m (6-8ft) for each bush.

Tayberry is a new loganberry variety with a larger, sweeter fruit and is definitely the best of the whole family. It does better in light shade than full sun and even enjoys a cold wall.

Japanese wineberries are orange-red and tiny, but the flavour is delicious and thirst-quenching; children love them and they are best eaten fresh. The canes are bristly, not thorny, and a lovely russet colour that makes them very attractive trained on a white-washed patio wall. The leaf is a lime-juice colour and so this plant can be effective in an ornamental area. Highly recommended.

problems and solutions These are much the same as for raspberries, i.e. aphids, virus diseases, raspberry beetle, cane spot, spur blight and botrytis. See the section on pests and diseases *pages 45-55*.

harvesting and storage Use quickly, as berries rot fast once picked. They can be frozen, or made into jams and jellies.

blackcurrants

They have very high levels of vitamin C, freeze well and the jam is easiest of all to make.

Blackcurrants are self-fertile but it is worth having several varieties to spread the flowering and miss frosts, this also spreads the cropping from midsummer to early autumn.

cultivation Although related to redcurrants these have different requirements, needing a richer, moister, heavier soil to do really well. None the less they are easy, and will crop even in quite adverse conditions and moderate shade. Blackcurrants are exceptional: they must be planted deep and grown as a stool, as they fruit best on young wood. Plant at least 1.8 m (6ft) apart. Pruning is done in late summer. It consists of cutting out the wood that has fruited and leaving the young shoots. This can be done brutally, with one half of each bush being razed to the ground in alternate years, providing they are being well mulched with compost or well-rotted farmyard manure. I find seaweed meal and seaweed sprays very beneficial, helping to ward off mildew in dry years.

varieties There is little to choose between cultivars in taste or cropping though the new ones, Ben Lomond (midsummer), Ben Sarek (midsummer), and Ben More (midsummer), are excellent and more mildew resistant. Mendip Cross is a good early and Westwick Choice for late. Wellington XXX (midsummer) is reputed to be the best.

Problems and solutions They do not suffer as quickly as many fruits from bird damage but will still disappear if not netted. Aphids can curl the tips in early summer but this can be cured by dipping them into a soft soap solution in a bucket. Big bud is a common problem: about midwinter simply pick off the big buds which are much bigger and rounded, and burn them to reduce re-infection by the microscopic mites. Reversion is a virus infection spread by these. If yields drop without explanation, and do not pick up with feeding, then grub up all the bushes and plant new ones. For treatment of other common diseases such as mildew and leaf spot, see *pages 45-55*.

harvesting and storage Blackcurrants hang well for several weeks if the birds cannot get at them. They are hard to juice unless cooked, but are easy to freeze. I pick the bulk roughly, complete with sprigs, and make jelly to which I add a few berries, carefully picked, for texture.

red & white currants

They are a bit sharp raw but delicious cooked with other fruits and the juice makes other jams and jellies set.

cultivation These prefer a lighter soil than blackcurrants and will also tolerate light shade, even cropping well on a cold wall. They are grown on a 15cm (6in) leg, removing any suckers. Grow as bushes or cordons, bushes 1.5m (5ft) apart and cordons 30cm (12in) apart. Very easy and forgiving to prune and train these just need winter and summer pruning, removing half to three quarters of each young growth. Mulch in the spring with compost and spray with liquid seaweed.

varieties All varieties are very similar with little to choose between them though whitecurrants are sweeter. Earliest of Four Lands is my favourite redcurrant.

problems and solutions Highly productive but the birds love them so must be netted. They often get apparently disastrous attacks of leaf blistering aphids which pucker and colour the leaves but this never affects yields and is cleared away with the summer pruning. They have few other problems. Net over winter to protect fruit buds against birds, and again when the fruit is ripening. For attacks from aphids, sawfly and leaf spot see *pages 45-55*.

harvesting and storage They ripen in early summer, but if protected from pests and wet weather will hang on and remain usable and sweeter until mid autumn. Pick whole clusters to avoid damaging fruit. They can be frozen, or bottled, and make a delicious jelly.

cranberries

cultivation No real pest or disease problems but do not even think about growing them unless you have acid soil and water-logged conditions, say by a pond or stream.

varieties *Oxycoccus palustris* is a native of peat bogs but for fruit grow the American *O. macrocarpus* which has a better flavour.

gooseberrries

These are available in red, green, white and yellow with widely varying flavours and if well grown the berries can be as big and sweet as plums and eaten raw.

cultivation A very forgiving crop that can be trained in any form imaginable but are easiest as bushes on a short leg. Plant 1.5m (5ft) apart and remove any suckers at root level. They need moisture and a rich soil, will tolerate some shade, but detest hot dry spots. After planting, mulch well with a thick layer of manure or compost to help smother weeds and conserve moisture.

Gooseberry fruits on spurs of older wood. Prune after fruiting to achieve an erect, open-centred bush. Prune leaders to upright or upward-facing buds. Keep the centre of the bush open to help picking and improve air circulation, which lessens risk of mildew. If you are short of space, grow as cordons against a wall or fence, 30cm (12in) apart. After harvesting, prune back cordons by cutting back side-shoots to 7cm (3in). If the crop is heavy, thin before fully ripe and use for cooking.

varieties Grow them as cordons and try a dozen different ones. I love London, a large red, Early Sulphur, an early yellow and Langley Gage, a new white, culinary variety Invicta is probably the best where only one can be fitted in, with Jubilee and Greenfinch a close second – all are resistant to mildew.

Jostaberries and Worcesterberries are both very similar to gooseberries but larger bushes, needing 2.5m (8ft) apiece, with fruits that resemble a cross between gooseberries and blackcurrants. They are better resistant to

top Redcurrants have quite a sharp flavour raw but reward well with the minimum of effort **above** Blackcurrants are rich in vitamin C and make excellent jams and jellies

Gooseberries can be deliciously sweet even when raw. Try Keepsake (**top**) and the red variety Crown Bob (**above**)

mildew and currant leaf spot. Jostas have a drooping habit, crop heavily and are thornless, so are a good choice. Worcesterberries are evily thorned plants, excellent for boundaries as they sucker and root from the tips excluding everything bigger than a bird. The fruit makes delicious jams and pies. **problems and solutions** In dry conditions they can get mildew on the tips which may spread to the berries, so keep them well mulched and watered to prevent this. Birds are the main pest: not only do they eat the fruit but they attack the buds in winter. Often pruning is best left until early spring; afterwards, wind the bush with black cotton. The gooseberry sawfly caterpillar will defoliate young bushes but can be killed with a spray of derris. Better still is to put a sheet underneath the bush and shake it – many will fall off to be collected up.

harvesting and storage If you like green gooseberry jam use the thinnings from the young fruits in early summer. Cook at a low temperature or it will turn red. Gooseberries freeze well, and are easier to top and tail when frozen. Most varieties hang on the bushes until late summer if protected from birds and wasps.

grapes

These are wonderful, attractive in leaf especially in autumn, highly productive and tolerant of most soils and positions. Where space is very restricted they can be grown in large pots and wound around a bamboo cane in a spiral, but they do best in the soil, especially against a wall or over a patio. They are also one of the best fruits to grow in the greenhouse, where they are less susceptible to rot, late frosts, and bird damage, though more susceptible to powdery mildew and botrytis. Potted vines can be left outside most of the time, just needing cover in winter and while in fruit. **cultivation** Grapes will grow in most soils, except very wet, and should not be overfed as this produces growth instead of fruit. They can be trained to cover almost any area available or just left to romp over trees or sheds.

A warm wall will always produce better grapes than the open garden but even in the open wine grapes which are smaller and seedier can be grown and these make good juice for drinking even if they are poor eating.

Under cover, grapes do best if planted in an outside border and then trained inside, through a specially made hole with the first year's growth. Make the hole easy to enlarge as the stem grows. Try and keep most of the growth at roughly the same height or the lowest canes will not fruit. For example, three tiers may be fitted to a roof or wall, but if they are spread out equally over both only the top ones will fruit. If a high wall is to be covered, use two vines, one for the highest part, and one for the lower.

Grapes fruit on last year's wood, so usually a framework is formed following horizontal wires. Cover the lowest first and once all are completed, then prune to form fruiting spurs on these. Annual pruning is best done in two stages: in summer, cut off shoots three leaves beyond the fruit bunches and only leave growths to extend or replace the framework. In winter, cut off all but one bud's worth from each new growth except to replace or extend the framework with new canes as required.

Pollination is easy as they are self-fertile. In the greenhouse it can be helped by tapping the canes or brushing the flowers by hand with a cotton, fur or hair ball or paintbrush. Thinning the bunches before they swell is necessary to prevent grapes over-cropping, especially in the early years, but they produce tremendous quantities even so. Limit them to a bunch every half metre or so. Thinning the grapes in the bunches does produce the best quality grapes, though it is very time-consuming and it spoils their bloom if you touch the grapes with your fingers.

varieties Outdoors grow the wine varieties Muller Thurgau, Madeleine Angevine and Madeleine Sylvaner (whites), Seibel 13053/ Cascade and Triomphe d'Alsace (reds). On a wall grow the dual purpose and delicious Siegerrebe (rosé), Strawberry and Schuyler (reds and luscious) or Golden Chasselas (white). Under cover Muscat Hamburg and Black Hamburg (reds), Golden Chasselas and

Buckland Sweetwater (whites). In a heated greenhouse some of the more tender and luscious old varieties can be grown, such as Madresfield Court or Muscat of Alexandria. Seyval Blanc is mildew resistant.

problems and solutions The most common pests are birds and wasps, only defeated by netting, covering the ripening bunches with stockings or net bags. These work well, though in wet years they may cause the fruit to rot. Some varieties are prone to mildew, aggravated by dry conditions at the roots and stagnant air, relieved by more open pruning and seaweed sprays. Other diseases are rare though the fruit is prone to rot in wet years.

Growing under cover with good ventilation produces the best crops in temperate climates, but the vines tend to be very vigorous so need hard summer pruning as indicated above to control them. Under cover, make sure they never run out of water, as if they slow down and restart growth the berries will split. In the greenhouse grapes may be attacked by scale insects and red spider mite (see pages 48, 49). If you are unfortunate mealy bugs may appear, but these can be treated with the bought-in parasitic beetles *Cryptolaemus montrouzieri*.

What is is most important is to get a suitable variety of grape: Black Hamburg is completely unsuitable outside or even in a cold greenhouse most years, but is excellent in a warm greenhouse or conservatory.

harvesting and storage The time of harvesting varies from year to year, but is usually from early autumn outdoors, and from midsummer under cover. In a heated greenhouse the vines can be started in growth earlier and grapes can be picked for midsummer. Grape bunches can be cut when ripe with a stem which inserted in a bottle of water will then keep them fresh in a cool place for weeks.

kiwi
actinidia chinensis

These are delightful fruits but need a warm wall or to be under cover. However, they have lovely leaves and attractive bristly stems, so in a temperate climate you could allow them to ramble over a shed or pergola and if they crop in a hot summer look on it as a bonus. Grown

this way pruning is unnecessary.

cultivation If grown for the fruits, this plant will need a sunny site, or a greenhouse heated enough to be safe from frost. They need a rich, well-drained soil and plants should be 3-4.5m (10-15ft) apart. Plant one male plant as well as several female plants to ensure pollination. Plants in the greenhouse will have to be pollinated by hand. If grown in pots in the greenhouse, feed weekly during the growing season. They are rampant climbers, and can be trained along wires. Stop by pinching out the tips when the space is filled. In the summer, prune back young fruit-bearing shoots to seven leaves beyond the last fruit – this encourages the formation of fruiting spurs.

varieties Try Hayward and Tomari. Self-pollinating cultivars are becoming available, such as Jenny.

problems and solutions They have few pests or diseases.

harvesting and storage The fruit is ripe in mid-autumn, but needs four to six weeks in store to develop the full flavour.

melon

These are treated the same as greenhouse cucumbers (see page 126), but need even more heat to keep them growing well,

top and middle Muscat Hamburg vine grown under cover with its ripening harvest
bottom The Leon Millot vine

163

top I grew this variety of raspberry from self-saved seed
above The pretty and flavourful yellow raspberry

though there are now outdoor varieties (*see below*). When growing take care not to let the neck where the stem leaves the soil get damaged or wet as it will easily rot – they are best planted on a little mound of sterile compost. Nip out the tip after four good leaves to produce sideshoots and later pollinate one flower on each side shoot on the same day with a brush or cottonwool bud to get even-sized fruits. They are even more prone to red spider mite than cucumbers. Keep the air dry when the fruit is ripening and make sure there is enough ventilation. Pick when they give off scent. Watermelons are as difficult as indoor cucumbers and need even more copious watering. However, I have succeeded in growing Green Jade in a heated coldframe in a greenhouse.

varieties Try Blenheim Orange and Ogen. Sweetheart is a variety that is well worth trying without a heated greenhouse or frame. Start it off as for ridge cucumbers in mid spring and plant out under a cloche in late spring, or better still sow under a good cloche in middle to late spring.

problems and solutions They are prone to red spider mite and mildew. Syringe with water frequently and use soft soap sprays. Biological control can be used against whitefly (*see page 53*).

harvesting and storage Cut off with a sharp knife when they reach the right size.

raspberries

Gorgeous fruit that unfortunately rots quickly, especially when picked wet. They are very productive, and the flowers are loved by bees.

cultivation Best planted in a sheltered site, in full sun, though they will tolerate some shade. They are treated in much the same way as blackberries except they produce shorter canes so do not need as many wires to support them and they need more mulching, moisture and a richer soil to do really well. Plant the canes 45cm (18in) apart in a trench one spade deep with a layer of well-rotted manure or compost. It is essential to have good drainage. Mulch well in the spring and water regularly in dry weather. They degenerate rapidly so new stock is best bought-in every ten years or when yields start to drop.

Summer raspberries are pruned after fruiting by cutting out the old canes leaving the new to grow on, it helps to thin these by midsummer to about 15-30cm (6-12in) apart. Autumn raspberries are simpler still, all canes are cut to the ground in mid-winter and again thin the young canes by midsummer to leave the best to fruit later.

varieties New varieties of raspberry are almost the only ones available but many do have good flavour. Try yellow raspberries which are exceptional. As raspberries vary in flavour and texture go to a pick-your-own farm and try several before choosing. Malling Jewel, Malling Admiral and Autumn Bliss are good.

problems and solutions Birds love them so they must be netted or in a cage. The autumn-fruiting varieties come when other soft fruits are getting short and also rarely suffer from maggots, making them a better option. With summer-fruiting raspberries, maggots can be cured by spraying with derris just after most of the flowers have finished but before the fruits start to swell. Spray in the evening when the bees have gone home. Raking over the mulch in winter helps as it allows the birds to eat any overwintering larvae hiding there. Other problems are raspberry beetle, cane spot, cane blight, spur blight, cane midge, wasps and virus diseases (*see pages 45-55*).

harvesting and storage Pick raspberries as they ripen and use immediately before they rot. They freeze well, and make good jam.

strawberries

The favourite fruit of most people. Have you ever had too many?

Cultivation Easy to grow but must have bird protection: use nets, plastic bottles, or even jam jars. Strawberries need soil that is rich in humus so prepare it well beforehand and ensure no weeds are present. Plant in late summer. It is necessary to replace a third of the bed every year with new runners as this ensures consistent cropping – new crowns produce few but big fruits, in the next year more smaller fruits and in the third fewer smaller fruits, the fourth year is rarely productive. Grow from your own runners for say five years and then buy new stock and start again.

varieties The latest varieties all have more resistance to mould and it is a good idea to visit a pick-your-own farm and find which variety you like. Autumn-fruiting strawberries are not as sweet, because of the lack of sun, but are delicious anyway. To make the jam set add redcurrant juice. The best variety for flavour is Aromel which will fruit in the autumn if the first flower trusses are removed. Tyee is also very good as is Silver Jubilee. Royal Sovereign was the standard by which others were judged but it is hard to find good stock nowadays.

Alpine strawberries are different, they do not runner, are easily grown from seed but only live a few years and have tiny fruits. These are very tolerant of soils and sites and will grow almost anywhere, the birds do not eat them as readily and when ripe the flavour is divine. They are also very good at attracting beneficial insects.

problems and solutions If fresh stock is bought every eight years or so and grown on clean ground there is rarely much bother from other pests, except perhaps slugs. The worst problem is wet weather when the fruit is ripening which not only causes mould (botrytis) but lowers their sweetness. By growing several varieties you can spread the cropping time and thus minimize this risk. Cloching once the fruits are green is an alternative. If cloches are in place in late winter they will bring the crop forward by some weeks. Strawing up once the fruits are green helps keep the fruit clean and infection-free as does removing and destroying mouldy fruits that do develop.

harvesting and storage To keep them fresh longer pick carefully with a bit of stem, without touching the fruit. Pick only when dry. They only keep a few days, but they are easy to freeze and make wonderful jam. To make the jam set, add redcurrant juice or mix with blackcurrants. Alpine strawberries give only a few fruits at a time but carry on fruiting from early summer till late autumn. Pick them weekly and freeze until you have enough to make jam which tastes too good to be true.

rhubarb

The first 'fruit' to crop, it is reliable and easy to grow.

cultivation It will grow in between other fruits, in ornamental areas or as ground cover. It is not fussy about shade, site or position, although it prefers a well-drained soil. It is worth buying certified plants initially as these produce much more freely. Dig in well-rotted manure or compost before planting the crowns in winter. Set the crowns 75cm (30in) apart and cover lightly with soil. To force for earlier crops simply cover the crowns with a plastic dustbin. Mulch the crowns with compost or well-rotted manure every year or two to maintain productivity if you pick them hard.

varieties Although hard to find there are a surprising number of varieties. Try Timperley Early and Victoria. Glaskin's Perpetual can be pulled for longer before getting acid.

problems and solutions Rhubarb rarely suffers pests or disease although it can suffer from crown rot and virus disease.

harvesting and storage Pull the stems with a twist rather than cutting them, and never strip the plant. Stop pulling forced rhubarb by early summer to allow the plant to recover. Rhubarb can be eaten in desserts, frozen, or made into jam or wine.

below Cambridge Vigour strawberries in midsummer ready for picking

HERBS
in an organic garden

Herbs are an essential part of any garden, being both decorative and useful. Traditionally they have been cultivated for their culinary and medicinal properties, though there are also herbs that have other uses, providing scents, fibres, dyes, or cosmetics. They are particularly suited to the organic garden as they are virtually invulnerable to pests and diseases, and their scented flowers attract bees and other beneficial insects into your garden.

The aromatic herbs such as rosemary and thyme have traditionally been used in cooking, while raw herbs, freshly chopped, can be added to salads for flavour or sprinkled over cooked dishes. Most herbs are rich in minerals and vitamins, so there is every reason for cooks to have a small herb garden beside the kitchen door,

To take the best advantage of scented herbs, grow them near windows and doors, alongside paths or on patios. Herbs with attractive foliage can be included in ornamental areas – some are good companion plants that benefit others.

Herbs are the best plants to grow if space is limited. With only a tiny area to cultivate it makes sense to grow small, quick-growing herbs for adding to salads and in cooking. You can even grow a few in window-boxes, pots or containers.

I define a herb, whether it is eaten raw or used in cooking, as one that is added to dishes rather than served as a portion on its own. Thus some minor crops are included here rather than in the section on vegetables.

Edible chrysanthemums are popular in the cooking of Japan and China. Here, the bright yellow flowerheads are grown with dill, in flower on the left, and borage behind

167

planning a herb garden

Herbs are often decorative enough to work well with ornamentals in mixed plantings. This mixed bed features flowering angelica with variegated lemon balm and red sage in the foreground

The classic perennial herbs such as rosemary, sage and thyme are native to the Mediterranean and require warm, dry, sheltered spots. The soil for most herbs should be well drained and not too rich, though annuals such as parsley, dill and borage need a moister, richer soil and tolerate less sun. If space is limited it may be necessary to grow them all in the same bed, but ideally the aromatic perennials should be grown separately as many aromatic perennial herbs inhibit the germination of seeds. If there is enough space, grow the annuals with the vegetables or on their own.

Many perennial herbs are useful as companion plants, and in a large garden they can be grown in a variety of places and then picked systematically. Perennial herbs are especially good grown as companions to fruit trees and bushes, and as borders or hedges around other areas, especially vegetable beds. Ornamental areas can be made that consist solely of perennial herbs; they will be productive yet need very little maintenance. The aromatic perennials thrive close to walls, pathways, and ornaments made of brick and stone, which retain the warmth that these plants love. Many attractive herb gardens are designed with brick or stone paths radiating from a central ornament or birdbath.

If shortage of space makes it necessary, most perennial herbs can be grown in pots or containers, but do not expect them to flourish as vigorously as they would in the ground. Of course, in pots they can be stood under cover, in a coldframe or greenhouse, to extend their season. Do not take them into centrally heated rooms. Pot growing is ideal for mints, which are invasive and not easy to control when grown in a bed with other plants.

sowing A good start is essential. Some herbs must be sown directly into their final position, but most are better sown under cover in pots or propapacks, as for vegetables, and planted out once the weather is warmer. Growing them to maturity on the seed bed once the main crops have been planted out makes efficient use of the space, and annual herbs are easy to intercrop amongst vegetables on the main beds. Alternatively, small beds can be made for them surrounding a central perennial herb bed and planted up in auturnn with winter-flowering pansies for later interest.

harvesting

Culinary herbs should ideally be easily and quickly accessible from the kitchen, especially as harvesting herbs is best done at the last minute. If the herb garden is far from the house it might be worth making a duplicate planting of the more important herbs right next to the kitchen door.

drying herbs

Most herbs can be dried and then stored, and while some lose their flavour others have their flavour intensified. Gather herbs in the growing season, but before they flower. Freezing is best for retaining flavour, and is especially good for parsley and basil. All herbs can be frozen and need almost no time to defrost. Freeze individual herbs in small plastic bags and store in a large plastic box in the freezer.

For drying, cut fresh young sprigs once the dew has dried off them, and hang them in bunches upside down in a dry airy place, out of the sun. Once they are completely dry the herbs can be crushed and stored in an air-tight jar. Drying concentrates the flavour of some herbs so use these sparingly.

culinary herbs

Herbs can be used for many culinary purposes but there is only space to suggest a few of the most important. Bay leaves add an aroma to all savoury dishes, while basil can be almost as widely used, especially with tomatoes and in any combination with garlic. Parsley sauce goes well with almost any savoury dish while mint sauce is delicious with most vegetables.

A 'bunch of herbs' for soups and other dishes contains a sprig each of parsley, thyme and bay, though I always add rosemary as well. A bouquet garni is the same combination tied up in a bit of cloth with some peppercorns. *Fines herbes* for French-style egg dishes and sauces are a mixture of finely chopped chervil, chives, parsley and French tarragon. Mixed

herbs are anything you like but usually include parsley, thyme, marjoram and summer savory.

herb salads

Bored with the blandness of many salads, I have experimented with adding fresh herbs to enliven them. Once

flowerdew salad

Small amounts of *rosemary, thyme, sage, marjoram, sweet cicely, summer savory, shungiku, coriander, fennel.*
Very small amounts of: *clary sage, salad burnet, lovage, hyssop, winter savory, rue, lemon verbena, lemon balm, lavender.*
Large amounts of *parsley, chives, chervil, dill, French tarragon and basil.*
Add *pot marigold, rose and daisy petals, borage and rosemary flowers, and a few violet, pansy, bergamot and pelargonium petals.*
Varying quantities to taste of *mint, nasturtium leaves and flowers, purslane, iceplant, good king henry, horseradish, rocket, land cress, citrus leaves, radicchio and alpine strawberries.*
Add as available *shredded carrot, grated red and green cabbage, shredded kohl rabi, chopped red and green pepper, cucumber and gherkin, tender curly kale leaves, corn salad, claytonia and lettuce, chicory, endive and baby peas.*
When ready to serve top with sliced *tomatoes* and sprinkle with *poppy, celery and sunflower seeds.* I rarely use salad dressings, serving it instead with dishes like taramosalata, humous, egg mayonnaise or coleslaw.

Strewn lavender on the floor of my summerhouse creates a tranquil atmosphere which is perfect for relaxation

drying herbs

To dry herbs, hang bunches of stems upside down in a dry, dark, airy place. The stems should be lightly packed together to allow air to circulate.

taste and add texture. During much of the year it is possible to gather many different herbs, though the choice is not as wide in late winter and early spring. It is then that the hardier herbs and vegetables can be valuable, providing salads without requiring expensive, out-of-season produce.

herbs for scent

The medicinal uses for herbs require a book on their own, so I will not deal with them here in detail.

It is worth noting a few more of their uses around the home though. Handfuls of fresh or dried herbs, wrapped in muslin cloth and tied to hang under the hot tap, create a wonderful and relaxing bath to finish off a hard day in the garden. Relaxing herbs include chamomile, jasmine and valerian but for an invigorating bath, use a mixture of the following: lavender, lemon balm, mint, rosemary.

Pot pourris are air fresheners made from dried herbs. Special recipes sometimes require exotic ingredients, but any dried herb in a bowl will eliminate unpleasant scents and give off its own aroma. My favourite is based on lemon verbena leaves with some rose petals, eau de cologne mint leaves and herba-barona thyme. Try whatever you have available and experiment with combinations.

Dried herbs tied in bags keep pests out of drawers and cupboards, and leave a pleasant smell – lavender is the best base for this.

strewing herbs

Scattering a layer of herbs on the floor is better than potpourri for scenting a room and ideal for floor coverings in potting sheds, where they give a pleasant if dusty atmosphere. I prefer mints and cotton lavender for working areas, hyssop by the wellie rack. For the summerhouse and in my car footwells I have thick layers of lavender to create a tranquil atmosphere. In the fruit store I use southernwood for a clean scent and to drive away pests.

The barbecue can be used to scent the air and drive away gnats and flies if small bundles of fresh or soaked dried herbs are added to the coals or left to smoke on top of the grill. They flavour the food while emitting a sweet-smelling aroma at the same time.

started I soon found that the quantity of herbs started to outgrow the lettuce and cucumber component. When some summers were too hot for growing lettuces I discovered that with a mixture of herbs I could make delicious salads without any lettuce or other salad crops. The greater the variety of herbs I mixed, the better the overall taste – so long as very strong or bitter herbs were used in moderation.

The basic principle is to use as many different herbs as possible, without letting any one flavour dominate. Take small quantities of each herb and chop them finely. By varying the proportions the mix can be adjusted to suit most tastes. If the flavour seems too strong, add vegetables to dilute the

PLANT SELECTION

The herbs have been grouped into annuals and perennials, as they benefit from being grown apart. The annuals are mostly used fresh during the summer and are better grown in rows like vegetables, while most perennials are best in their own bed, as companions to fruit, borders to vegetable beds, or as permanent features in ornamental areas. The initial measurements given refer to the average height range.

annual herbs

Most annual herbs are best started off sown in their final position during mid-spring. They resent transplanting, and will not make as much growth if started in small pots or cells. For sowing direct, mark out and station sow as for vegetables; for most annual herbs it is not necessary to sow or thin to one plant per site. Alternatively, sow in small pots, pot up if necessary, then harden off and plant out after the last frost.

It is easy to save seed from herbs; follow the method used for saving vegetable seed (see *page 119*). Sow most annuals just less than 2.5cm (½in) deep, and cover with clean potting compost to mark the site as many are slow to germinate. A label aids later identification. With most, the flavour is ruined by the onset of flowering, so successional small sowings are a good idea, spreading the cropping. The younger shoots and leaves are the most tender and most herbs become more succulent with adequate moisture. They all grow lusher in rich soil, though this may spoil the flavour, so only those with special needs and preferences will be noted.

borage

cultivation 60-90cm (2-3ft) Borage tends to sprawl so is best at the back of borders. Sow in position, thin to 45cm (18in) apart and allow to self-seed thereafter. With occasional trimming, the plants can be in flower most of late spring and summer. The blue flowers are very attractive to bees.

harvesting and storage The flowers add colour to summer drinks and tender young leaves can be added in small amounts to salads. The leaves freeze well.

aniseed

cultivation 60cm (2ft) Station sow 20cm (8in) apart each way in a sunny position in well-drained soil after the last frost.

harvesting and storage The aniseed flavour goes well with sweet and savoury foods. The leaves are used fresh and the seed dried. The aromatic seeds can be used in potpourri, or as a herbal tea.

clary sage

cultivation 60-90cm (2-3ft) This herb is a member of the sage family; its lilac flowers

Iceplant (*Mesembry-anthemum crystallinum*) has thick fleshy leaves which have a unique salty flavour and can be eaten whole or chopped into salads

above I use a small amount of tender young citrus leaves in salads while lemon juice can be used in cosmetics for its mild astringent quality

below Curled parsley adds vitamins and minerals as well as colour to a salad

are attractive to bees. Sow in pots and plant out 30cm (12in) apart.

harvesting and storage Pick the leaves before flowering — they can be used to flavour soups and stews. Used medicinally as an essential oil.

citrus leaves

cultivation See the Fruit chapter (*page 157*) for information on how to grow citrus plants, which can be grown for their leaves, as well as for their fruit. Young plants can be kept indoors for use over winter.

harvesting and storage Young citrus leaves give a wonderful tang to salads.

celery leaves

cultivation 60cm (2ft) Celery is very difficult to grow well, as explained in the vegetable section (*see page 124*). Sow broadcast and leave to self-seed.

harvesting and storage The leaves add flavour to savoury dishes and salads while the seeds are delicious, and especially good on cakes and biscuits.

parsley

cultivation 30cm (12in) The bigger continental plain-leaved variety has more flavour than the common curly-leaved form. It is biennial so flowers in the second year; leave to seed as self-sown plants are always best. Sow soaked seed on the soil surface and barely cover the seed. The seeds can take a long time to germinate. Sow once in spring and again in autumn for two years then use self-sown seedlings. Thin plants to 15cm (6in) apart. It will revel in rich moist conditions and can stand moderate shade.

harvesting and storage Parsley freezes and dries well and plants can be dug up, pot-ted and moved under cover or cloched for fresh leaves throughout the winter.

basil

cultivation 15-60cm (6in-2ft) One of the best-flavoured herbs. There are purple-leaved, tiny-leaved and lemon-flavoured versions as well as the usual sweet basil, and they are all delicious! Start off in pots in the warm and plant them out 20cm (8in) apart each way when all danger of frost is passed. It likes a warm, sheltered position. Grow basil alongside tomatoes or peppers as they like similar conditions. Watch out for aphids and cut the plants back before flowering.

harvesting and storage Use the leaves in salads, with cheese and in quantity with garlic in every tomato dish. The leaves can also be frozen but they do not dry very successfully. Basil oil is used in aromatherapy.

caraway

cultivation 60cm (2ft) Likes a sunny site and a rich soil. This must be sown in position and thinned to 20cm (8in) apart in spring or autumn: if left to flower in the second year it may self-seed.

harvesting and storage The beautiful feathery leaves are gathered young and used with salads and savoury dishes; the tiny pungent seeds are gathered when they turn brown and used likewise. The roots may be boiled as a vegetable.

marigolds (calendula)

cultivation 60cm (2ft) Grow pot marigolds, not French or African ones. Sow in pots or direct in position 30cm (12in) apart from early spring to early autumn, and allow to self-seed. Also a useful companion plant.

harvesting and storage Use the petals and leaves in salads and with seafood to give a tangy flavour. The flowers are used in many medicinal and herbal preparations.

corn salad/lamb's lettuce

cultivation 10cm (4in) This is a very useful winter salad crop so is best grown under cover to keep the weather and dirt off the leaves. Can be sown direct or in pots from

early spring to mid autumn and spaced 10.5cm (4in) apart. Left to flower it resembles small forget-me-nots and self-seeds.
harvesting and storage Pick leaves rather than whole plant.

chervil
cultivation 30cm (12in) This is very like parsley yet easier to grow, and with a milder flavour. Sow from early spring to late summer in partial shade in a light, well-drained soil and thin to 15cm (6in) apart. Chervil will self-seed if left to flower and if plants are cut down before flowering they will produce new crops of fresh foliage.
harvesting and storage Gather the leaves before flowering. A subtle flavour, chervil enhances dishes best when added raw (as a garnish) or only slightly cooked. The root can also be cooked as a vegetable. The leaves can be dried or frozen. Can also be used medicinally as an infusion.

cumin
cultivation 15cm (6in) Likes a warm, sheltered site and a well-drained soil. Station sow in early summer at 5cm (2in) apart. Support the plants with sticks to stop seed-heads falling over and getting dirty.
harvesting and storage The strongly flavoured seeds give an authentic curry taste and need to be well dried indoors to keep. If you acquire the taste they can be used like black pepper with almost every dish. Also used for pickling and chutneys.

land cress
cultivation 12.5cm (5in) This resembles watercress, but grows almost anywhere, even window boxes, if kept moist. Surface sow in position and thin to 7.5cm (3in) apart.
harvesting and storage Gather the leaves when they are young – they give a peppery flavour to salads.

purslane
cultivation 60cm (2ft) This salad crop needs to be grown quickly and kept cut back hard for flushes of shoots. If you let it go, purslane flowers at 60cm (2ft) high. Station

sow successive crops in shallow soil during the summer months.
harvesting and storage Provides excellent crunchy salad leaves, high in vitamin C. Can also be eaten cooked.

claytonia
winter purslane, or miner's lettuce
cultivation 12.5cm (5in) This is a potential weed as it seeds prolifically and comes up everywhere. Surface sow anywhere and thin to 10.5cm (4in) apart. Let it self-seed if you want perpetual supplies.
harvesting and storage This is very tasty in salads – the leaves, stalks and flowers are all edible. The leaves can also be cooked like spinach. Highly recommended.

dill
cultivation 90cm (3ft) Sow direct or in pots and plant out 30cm (12in) apart in full sun in a rich soil. If left to flower, dill attracts hoverflies.
harvesting and storage The fresh leaves are gathered young and can be added chopped to salads, soups, and egg and fish dishes. The flower heads are often added whole to jars of pickled cucumber. The seeds can be used whole or ground in savoury dishes, cakes and bread. They can also be used as a digestive and to sweeten breath. The leaves and seeds can be dried and stored.

coriander
cultivation 30-60cm (1-2ft) Sow in position 26.5cm (10in) apart in late spring. Likes full sun and a rich soil.
harvesting and storage The aromatic leaves can be used in salads and stews. The seeds are dried. When ground they have a

below Dill leaves are delicious added to soups, egg dishes and potato salad
bottom Both the leaves and seeds of coriander are valuable flavourings in cooking

173

above Summer savory is best picked just as the flower buds start to form

below Lavender (*Lavendula stoechas pedunculata*) is decorative and fragrant, making it useful in the ornamental garden as well as for aromatic use around the house

warm spicy flavour that enhances stews, curries, chutneys, pies and cakes.

summer savory

cultivation 45cm (18in) Sow shallowly in pots or direct at 15cm (6in) apart. It can be dug up and potted to put under cover for winter use.

harvesting and storage This is traditionally grown and used with broad beans and the tips are tasty in salads. Do not allow it to flower or the flavour goes.

rocket

cultivation 60cm (2ft). It is very easy to grow but tastes best when grown quickly in moist conditions. Prone to flea beetle. Sow in pots or stations 15cm (6in) apart from early spring to early autumn.

harvesting and storage Italian cress or rocket leaves are spicy and peppery and the flowers add interest to salads.

perennial herbs

Most perennial herbs will tolerate, and indeed often prefer, drier, poorer soils than annual herbs. Many are native to the Mediterranean region and so need sunshine and a light well-drained soil to do well. It is the combination of damp and cold that kills them, and they may need some shelter or a cloche to come through bad winters – growing them against a wall is often sufficient help. In well-sheltered or town gardens most perennial herbs will last for many years. Almost all are good at suppressing weeds, suffer from few pests and diseases and need little maintenance apart from cutting back dead, overgrown and excessive growth. The majority are best bought as young plants rather than grown from seed. Many are very easily grown from cuttings or dividing existing plants, so visit your friends' gardens with something to trade. Do not divide or move herbs during autumn or winter, and if you are planting a new herb bed, do so during spring so that if there is a hard winter the nurseryman loses the plants, not you.

It is the tender young tips and leaves that are used for the most part, so cutting back most herbs each spring removes withered growths and produces a flush of new shoots. Leave pruning till spring so that the old growth protects the new against bad weather. Take care not to cut back too far, or the plant may die – go no further than where live green shoots emerge from the older wood.

lavender

cultivation 30-90cm (1-3ft) A lovely, gorgeously perfumed shrub which will attract bees and butterflies. Good for low hedges and borders. Likes a sunny position. There are large and small varieties in many colours to suit all gardens.

harvesting and storage The dried flowers are often used in pot pourri. The flowers also have many medicinal uses and the essential oil is used in aromatherapy.

chives

cultivation 30cm (12in) Chives can be started from seed or separated from existing clumps – they benefit from being divided every other year. Plant them as border edgings and remove the flowering heads from

alternate plants to get both flowers and foliage. Grow under fruit trees and roses for their companion effects: the flowers attract beneficial insects, especially bees.

harvesting and storage Add to savoury dishes, especially with cheese, and to salads. Does not dry well, but can be frozen.

sweet cicely

cultivation 1m (3ft) Sow in the autumn in light shade and transplant 60cm (2ft) apart in the spring. The plant's fern-like leaves are very decorative.

harvesting and storage The aniseed-tasting leaves are excellent in salads, and the stems, seeds and roots can also be cooked. The seeds can be dried.

fennel

cultivation 1.5m (5ft) An upright, stately plant that can be grown in ornamental areas – the bronze form is particularly attractive. It likes an open, sunny position. Propagate the green form from seed or both by division in the spring. Replant clumps 60cm (2ft) apart. It self-seeds readily. The flowerheads have the benefit of attracting hoverflies.

harvesting and storage The leaves have an aniseed flavour which goes well with savoury fish and cheese dishes as well as in salads. They do not dry well. The seeds are added to breads and biscuits, and also have medicinal uses.

bergamot

cultivation 90cm (3ft) A herbaceous plant with beautiful scarlet flowers, well suited to ornamental areas. Likes a rich, moist soil and partial shade. Divide the clump to propagate and replant every third year

harvesting and storage The aromatic leaves and flowers are dried to make a calming herbal tea.

horseradish

cultivation 60cm (2ft) Usually started from plant cuttings and needs well-cultivated soil. as the roots go very deep. Plant at the bottom of the garden, or in an out-of-the-way spot, as it spreads by the roots and is hard to eradicate once established.

harvesting and storage The root is grated for use in sauces and even in minute amounts in salads. Can also be used in medicinal preparations.

marjoram

cultivation 30cm (12in) There are several varieties, all of which are similar to oregano. Propagate by seed for the best-flavoured ones, which are grown as annuals except in warm climates, and by root division for the tougher perennials. These latter tend to form low mounds that make them useful as informal edging or to go under fruit trees and bushes. There is a particularly attractive golden form that turns a buttercream yellow during summer and reverts to green in winter. In flower, marjorams attract bees and butterflies. All varieties prefer a sunny position.

harvesting and storage The leaves can be added to salads but the flavour goes exceptionally well with savoury dishes. Marjoram has good flavour fresh, dried or frozen and can be grown in a pot under cover for winter use.

lemon balm

cultivation 60cm (2ft). This resembles a mint but does not have the tendency to spread. Compact and dense-growing it excludes weeds when planted 45cm (18in) apart and will flourish almost anywhere. There is a cheerful yellow variegated form (right) especially valuable in ornamental areas.

harvesting and storage Both varieties have a refreshing clean lemon scent that goes well in salads, sauces and soups. Can also be used in fruit drinks and punches. Infuse the leaves in hot water for a refreshing tea.

below Well-established golden marjoram provides a cheering sea of yellow at the foot of the tree
bottom Variegated lemon balm

top There are hundreds of varieties of mint – this one is known as grey mint
above Red sage is a beautiful aromatic plant

mints

cultivation 40cm-1m (18in-3ft) Mints are invasive! Never put mints in with other herbs as the roots penetrate everything. Grow them in pots, containers almost submerged in the soil or in beds surrounded by concrete or regularly cut grass. Cool refreshingly scented forms such as eau de cologne and spearmint suit ornamental areas as do golden and silver variegated, yellow, grey and curly forms which are mostly less vigorous. Mints make cheap, low-maintenance ground cover for large areas, especially under trees, and they are most attractive to bees and beneficial insects. Any bit of root grows almost anywhere any time.

harvesting and storage Mints are famous for making sauces and teas and go well in salads. Best used fresh, they can be potted up for winter under cover. The leaves dry well and retain their flavour.

sage

cultivation 60cm (2ft) Easily grown from cuttings or seed, sage needs replacing every few years as it becomes straggly and resents pruning. The red form has a fine flavour; the more compact, multi-coloured sages are not very hardy.

harvesting and storage The leaves dry well, if picked before flowering. Sage is the traditional stuffing herb but also goes well in moderation in salads and with savoury dishes. Recommended, especially the red.

feverfew

cultivation 45cm (18in) This short-lived perennial self-seeds with a vengeance. It is a good foil for other plants, the golden form being particularly cheerful. It is an excellent companion plant, discouraging pests, making it especially worth growing as a space filler.

harvesting and storage Once grown extensively for its medicinal properties – the leaves are used to make an infusion.

daisies

cultivation 7.5cm (3in) Ordinary *Bellis perennis* or garden daisies have edible petals that enliven salads and they make excellent low edgings and internal dividing margins within herb beds.

good king henry/lincolnshire asparagus

cultivation 60cm (2ft) Sow in spring in a rich soil and thin plants to 30cm (12in) apart. Divide the roots in the autumn. This is a vigorous self-seeder.

harvesting and storage It comes early each year to provide a good standby salad crop. Highly nutritious but a bit drab, the leaves and shoots can also be eaten cooked like spinach.

bay

cultivation 90cm-5.5m (3-18ft) As a small shrub, bay is rather tender, especially suffering from harsh winds, and easily killed by frost. Grow in a warm, sheltered position, or in tubs which can be taken under cover in winter – though it is then more prone to pests. Once established it becomes a tough, medium-sized tree. They can be attractive as specimens if trimmed into shape. Bay is difficult to propagate and expensive to buy – you could have many packets of the leaves for the cost of one plant!

harvesting and storage The leaves dry very well and are highly aromatic. Dry leaves in the sun and store in airtight jars. Bay leaves are one of the traditional components of a bouquet garni and are frequently used in stews and other savoury dishes, especially those with tomatoes and garlic.

lemon verbena

cultivation 90cm (3ft) The shrub has an exquisite lemon sherbet scent which the dried leaves retain for many months. Easily grown from cuttings. It is not very hardy and gets killed above ground by hard frosts. Plant 90cm (3ft) apart against a warm wall and protect the roots from damp and cold – they sprout like fuchsias in the spring. It can be kept in a pot overwintered under cover or as a houseplant, but is then prone to aphids and red spider mite.

harvesting and storage Pick the leaves when the flowers begin to bloom. They give a lovely lemony flavour to salads, fruit salads and sweet dishes. The leaves can also be infused to make herbal teas and cosmetic preparations. The dried leaves are often used in pot pourris.

lovage

cultivation 2m (6ft) Lovage is a tall herbaceous plant which grows best in moist shady spots and is better for large gardens than small. The flowerheads attract hoverflies. Propagate by root division or seed.

harvesting and storage The leaves are used in salads and for giving a rich flavour to savoury dishes in which it is claimed to substitute for salt. The stems can be eaten raw if blanched like celery, the seed used in bread, pastries and in salads. Leaves and seeds can both be dried.

salad burnet

cultivation 30cm (12in) Grow it from seed and plant 20cm (8in) apart each way in blocks and keep regularly cut back.

harvesting and storage This is a herbaceous salad crop that needs boiling and chilling to make it more palatable though some people eat it raw. The leaves must be picked when young and tender.

sorrel

cultivation 30cm (12in) Sorrel is easy to grow. It likes moist, lightly shaded soil and tends to spread. Grow from seed or plant out from root divisions at 45cm (18in) apart and replant every few years. Worth trying if you like sour, lemony flavours.

harvesting and storage Pick fresh leaves in the growing season. Can be cooked like spinach, or used in soups and salads.

rosemary

cultivation 60cm (2ft) Rosemary is not very hardy, but usually survives in colder climates if given a warm spot against a wall and well-drained soil. It makes a good hedging plant if kept well trimmed, otherwise it tends to sprawl. It will also grow in a pot under cover. Easily propagated from cuttings in the spring. The flowers are loved by bees.

harvesting and storage As an evergreen rosemary can be picked all year round, so there is no need to dry and store the leaves. Delicious for adding its distinctive flavour to almost all savoury dishes in moderation; the leaves and flowers also go well in salads.

thyme

cultivation 20cm (8in) Thyme smells wonderful, and the bees love it. It is low-growing so goes well under fruit trees and bushes if it's sunny enough. Thyme

below Rosemary is useful because it can be picked all the year round
bottom Mounds of thyme

comes in varied scents, colours and forms so can be extremely attractive in ornamental beds, and will thrive in poor, dry, situations. Try the caraway-flavoured herba-barona and, for colour, Anderson's Gold. Thymes can be grown from seeds, or propagated from cuttings.

harvesting and storage Can be used fresh or dried. Pick the growing tips regularly. For drying, cut sprigs before flowering.

angelica

cultivation 2.5m (8ft) Because of its size it is only worth growing in larger gardens. This is a tough herbaceous plant which likes rich, moist soil and partial shade. It looks attractive planted at the back of ornamental borders and the flowerheads will attract hoverflies.

harvesting and storage Difficult to dry but the stems can be preserved by candying in sugar syrup for use in cake-making. Adding angelica and sweet cicely stems to stewed rhubarb removes the tartness and makes it sweeter.

rue

cultivation 60cm (2ft) Rue is a beautiful, blue-green plant, easily grown from cuttings or seed, and is mostly of ornamental value. Plant 45cm (18in) apart.

harvesting and storage Rue is poisonous and an irritant, especially in hot weather, but has long been used as a medicinal herb. The bitter leaves can be used sparingly to flavour egg and fish dishes.

hyssop.

cultivation 45cm (18in) A rather tender and small shrub, hyssop needs a very warm dry spot to do well. It's rich blue and purple flowers are very popular with bees and butterflies. Propagate from cuttings, root division or seed.

harvesting and storage Used to be widely cultivated for medicinal uses. The young leaves are delicious added to salads or with any rich savoury food.

winter savory

cultivation 30cm (12in) Summer savory tastes better but this is shrubbier and survives most winters. Grows easily from seed which should be surface sown and not buried. Plant out in a sunny position and well-drained soil at 23cm (9in) apart each way. In flower it attracts bees.

harvesting and storage It will crop most of the year, longer in a pot under cover. Small amounts improve the taste of salads, the flavour of beans and the smell of cooking brassicas.

tarragon

cultivation 60cm (2ft) Do not confuse the French variety with the Russian. Taste the leaves: the French is sweet and piquant, while the Russian tastes rank and sour. Unfortunately the Russian variety, which is hardier, comes from seed and root division and is common. The French variety needs a warm spot and protection from cold and damp. Cover with straw to protect from frost. It is only propagated by root division. Replant every few years.

harvesting and storage Pick fresh leaves during the growing season. Can be dried, but loses much of the flavour. Tastes wonderful with eggs and fish, salads, savoury dishes and flavours vinegar.

dandelion

cultivation 30cm (12in) This maligned plant is surprisingly good in salads. As the leaves are bitter they are best blanched first by covering the heads with a flower pot for a week or so.

harvesting and storage Use young leaves in salads. The root is used in some medicinal preparations.

opposite from top Angelica, rue, and dwarf hyssop
left Borage is grown as an annual for its pretty blue flowers which can be added to refreshing summer drinks
below Pak choi, an oriental green which adapts well to the the climate of temperate zones

oriental greens

I sometimes treat these fast-growing greens as herbs, adding them to other dishes. They are pest and disease resistant.

chop suey/shungiku

cultivation An edible chrysanthemum which is also a good companion plant, keeping pests away from other plants. It can be sown direct or in pots and planted out 12.5cm (5in) apart from late winter to autumn.

harvesting and storage Use like Pak choi – it has a very strong flavour and becomes bitter after flowering.

pak choi & leaf mustards

cultivation 30cm (1ft) Sow in pots or direct and plant out 26.5cm (10in) apart from early summer to autumn. They benefit from a moist, rich soil. Slugs may cause problems (see page 43). These fast-growing plants grow best in the relative cool of spring and autumn.

harvesting and storage Highly productive, they can be cut and come again all summer. Use raw in salads or in stir-fries.

10 A YEAR
in the organic garden

The changing seasons are such a delight. Flowers and leaves make their entrances and exits so the garden constantly changes, and no view ever remains the same for long.

After the depths of winter have passed, buds swell and excitement increases with the arrival of the first early flowers. The first of the seasonal jobs include chitting potatoes, planting out shallots, clearing green manures and weed infestations and sowing seeds under cover.

During late spring leaves appear, flowers bloom and weeds come up everywhere. It is a time of frantic activity when the weeding, potting up, transplanting and grass-cutting all need doing at once. It is also the time when the first new potatoes can be dug up, salads selected and flowers picked.

The height of the summer brings a wonderful variety of fruit, vegetables and colour to the garden. For a moment time seems to slow, the flowers release their fragrance, evenings are longer and work lets up for a moment.

Next comes the harvest and the produce needs picking, anything from herbs and berries, peaches and plums, peas and beans to sweetcorn and courgettes. Food arrives in abundance to be frozen, dried, pickled and made into jam.

The chilly autumn air, musty dampness and fading leaves warn us that it is time to store the last of the crops, to gather nuts and to make wine. Bright crisp days are perfect for pruning, tidying and changing the garden round while potential improvements are still fresh in mind.

Autumn harvest of pumpkins and marrows marks the end of another rewarding year in the garden

mid winter

prune Remove damaged or diseased growths only.

plant Chit potato seed on trays in light, frost-free place.

feed Spread lime or calcified seaweed on soil every few years.

jobs Check and use stored fruits and vegetables.

Make bird boxes, slug pubs, insect traps and bottle cloches.

Put out food, hang up fat and provide water for birds.

Plan and make changes and new beds. Plan and order seeds.

late winter

spray Outdoor peaches and almonds with Bordeaux mixture.

prune Remove damaged or diseased growths only.

plant Garlic, onion sets, shallots, shrubs, trees and soft fruit.

feed Spread seaweed on grass, bare soil and mulches and rake in.

sow *under cover in warm*: indoor tomatoes, early peas, broad beans, cabbages, cauliflowers, lettuce, spinach, turnips, carrots, radishes, potatoes *under cover in pots*: onions, spring onions, sweet peas.

turf Cut grass on high setting in mild conditions and return clippings.

jobs Check and use stored fruits and vegetables.

Sieve and mix home-made potting composts and top up indoor beds.

Put out cloches, sheet mulches and low tunnels to warm soil.

Inspect woody plants, check staking, ties and labels.

Pick off big buds on blackcurrants.

Empty insect traps and nests; retouch sticky bands.

Firm in roots of autumn plantings after hard frosts finish.

early spring

spray Everything with a diluted seaweed solution; outdoor peaches and almonds with Bordeaux mixture.

prune Less hardy and hollow-stemmed shrubs such as buddleias. Remove old canes of autumn-fruiting raspberries. Cut back evergreens and conifer hedges.

plant Garlic, onion sets, shallots, artichokes, asparagus, potatoes, evergreens, shrubs, trees, grapevines, soft fruit, rhubarb.

feed Spring greens with comfrey liquid or seaweed solution; grassed areas with sieved compost, seaweed or diluted urine.

mulch Spread mulches under and around everything possible.

sow *under cover in warm*: tomatoes, cucumbers, aubergines, peppers; *outside in warm soil or under cover*: peas, broad beans, leeks, beetroot, kohl rabi, cabbages, cauliflowers, lettuce, spinach, turnips, carrots, chards, salsify, scorzonera, parsnips, herbs, radishes, spring onions, sweet peas.

turf Cut grass weekly once it is growing fast, returning clippings.

jobs Check and use stored fruits and vegetables.
Put down carpet or sheet mulches on new ground or green manures.
Compost, dig in or invert green manures and any weed flushes.
Move, lay and repair turf this month in non-frosty weather.
Weed everything in sight regularly.
Retouch sticky bands.
Protect early flowers and budding plants against frosts.

mid spring

spray Everything with a diluted seaweed solution.

prune Cut back most early flowering shrubs once flowers die. Remove seed heads from bulbs as they die back.

plant Potato sets, onion seedlings, perennial herbs, evergreens.

feed Top dress all permanent container plants with compost.

mulch Spread mulches under and around everything possible.

sow *under cover in warm*: tomatoes, ridge cucumbers, gherkins, melons, courgettes, marrows, pumpkins, sweetcorn, half-hardy flowers; *outside and under cover*: peas, broad beans, French beans, runner beans, most brassicas, lettuces and salad plants, herbs, spinach, turnips, carrots, swedes, salsify, scorzonera, radishes, kohl rabi, fennel, leeks, parsnips, sweet peas.

turf Cut the grass weekly, use clippings for mulching. Use slug pubs.

jobs Use stored fruits and vegetables, clean out stores once empty.
Take cuttings of herbs and less hardy plants; repot houseplants.
Weed everything in sight regularly.
Retouch sticky bands.
Inspect regularly for early signs of pests and diseases.
Protect tender flowers, fruitlets and plants against frosts.

late spring

spray Everything with a diluted seaweed solution.

prune Remove crowded and ill-placed shoots on apricots and peaches. Cut back most flowering shrubs once flowers die. Tie in and support growing climbers and tall herbaceous plants.

plant out Sweetcorn, ridge cucumbers, courgettes and marrows under cover or in open once last frost is well past.

feed Incorporate compost with all transplants this month. Tomatoes and pot plants with comfrey liquid or seaweed solution.

mulch Spread mulches under and around potatoes.

sow *under cover outside*: tomatoes, ridge cucumbers, gherkins, melons, courgettes, marrows, pumpkins, sweetcorn, half-hardy flowers; *outside without cover*: peas, broad beans, French beans, runner beans, most brassicas, lettuces and salad plants, herbs, spinach, turnips, carrots, swedes, salsify, scorzonera, radishes, kohl rabi, fennel, leeks, parsnips, sweet peas, wallflowers.

turf Cut the grass weekly, use clippings for mulching. Use slug pubs.

jobs Weed everything in sight regularly. Retouch sticky bands. Inspect regularly for signs of pests and diseases, especially aphids, cabbage caterpillars and red spider mite indoors.
Protect tender flowers, fruitlets and plants against frosts.
Pay special attention to watering autumn and spring plantings.

early summer

spray Everything with a diluted seaweed solution.

prune Deadhead and cut back most flowering shrubs once flowers die. Summer prune grapes and redirect new growths.

plant Transplant brassica and leek plants.

feed Incorporate compost with all transplants this month. Feed tomatoes and pot plants with comfrey liquid or seaweed solution.

mulch Spread mulches under and around potatoes.

sow Lettuces and salad plants, beetroot, kohl rabi, swedes, turnips, spinach, chicory, endive, biennial and perennial flowers.

turf Cut the grass weekly; use clippings for mulching.

jobs Weed everything in sight regularly. Water as required.
Inspect regularly for pest and disease infestations, especially aphids, caterpillars, gooseberry sawfly and red spider mite.
Protect fruit from birds.
Retouch sticky bands.
Thin, harvest and use or preserve ripening fruits.

mid summer

spray Everything with a diluted seaweed solution. Spray maincrop potatoes with Bordeaux mixture if warm and humid.

prune Plums and flowering and fruiting cherries. Summer prune apples, pears, red and white currants and grapes. Keep on deadheading. Cut back evergreens and conifer hedges.

plant Potato sets for late crop.

feed Incorporate compost with potato sets.

sow Lettuces and salad plants, carrots, swedes, turnips, Chinese cabbage, winter spinach, kohl rabi, chards.

turf Cut the grass as needed, use clippings for mulching.

jobs
Weed everything as needed.
Retouch sticky bands.
Inspect regularly for escalating pests and diseases.
Protect fruit and provide water for birds instead.
Thin, harvest and use or preserve ripening fruits.
Dry peas and beans for use as seed and in kitchen.
Dry and freeze herbs.
Dry onions and garlic in sun.
Use or store early potatoes to free ground for sowing.
Pause to enjoy the result of your labours at least once.

late summer

spray Everything with a diluted seaweed solution.

prune Cut oldest blackcurrant stems back hard after fruit harvested.

plant Daffodil bulbs; transplant rooted strawberry runners.

sow Winter lettuces and salad plants, Japanese and spring onions, winter spinach, green manures as soil becomes vacant.

turf Cut the grass if needed; use clippings for mulching.

jobs
Weed everything if needed.
Retouch sticky bands.
Inspect regularly for pests and diseases.
Protect fruit and provide water for birds instead.
Thin, harvest, and use, store or preserve ripening fruits.
Harvest and store potatoes and onions.
Order hardy trees and shrubs for autumn planting.
Clean, paint and repair timber, gutters and brickwork.

early autumn

spray Everything with a diluted seaweed solution.

prune Cut back herbaceous plants to 15cm (6in) as the stems wither. Remove old canes and tie in new for raspberries and blackberries.

plant Garlic and other bulbs. Transplant biennial flowering plants.

feed Incorporate compost with all transplants this month.

sow *under cover*: winter lettuces and salad plants, early carrots, turnips, Chinese greens. *outside*: green manures.

turf Cut the grass if needed; use clippings for mulching.

jobs Weed everything if needed.
Retouch sticky bands.
Protect flowers, fruits and tender plants from early frosts.
Harvest and use, store or preserve fruits and nuts.
Make fruit juices, cider and wine with surplus fruit.
Collect and dry seeds.
Lift gladioli and dahlias as they wither.
Go on a pest hunt to thin them out for winter; rake over old mulch.
Take cuttings of most woody plants just before leaves drop.

mid autumn

prune Late-flowering shrubs, soft fruit and grapes as leaves fall. Cut back herbaceous plants to 15cm (6in) as the stems wither. Remove old canes and tie in new for raspberries and blackberries.

plant Garlic and other bulbs. Deciduous shrubs, trees and soft fruit.

feed Incorporate compost with all plantings this month. Spread sieved compost around trees, shrubs and soft fruit.

mulch Spread mulches under and around everything possible.

sow *under cover*: winter lettuces and salad plants, summer cauliflower, sweet peas, green manures in greenhouse and polytunnel.

turf Cut the grass weekly, raising height and returning clippings with shredded leaves or collect them together for mulching.

jobs Weed everything if needed.
Retouch sticky bands.
Protect all less hardy plants against frost, move pots indoors.
Put cloches over salad plants and autumn strawberries.
Turn compost heaps and sieve for use or cover and store.
Make new beds and borders, move turf or stack and rot down.
Lift and divide tougher herbaceous perennials and rhubarb.
Harvest and use, store or preserve fruits and nuts.
Collect and dry seeds and berries for seed and to feed birds.

late autumn

prune Late-flowering shrubs, soft fruit and grapes as leaves fall. Cut back herbaceous plants to 15cm (6in) as the stems wither.
Rework and winter prune apples, pears and non-stone fruits.

plant Deciduous shrubs, trees and soft fruit.

feed Incorporate compost with all plantings this month. Spread compost on top of asparagus and globe artichokes.

mulch Spread mulches under and around everything possible.

sow Hardy peas and broad beans for extra early crop.

turf Cut the grass if needed; collect with leaves for mulching.

jobs Weed everything if needed.
Retouch sticky bands.
Order seed catalogues, potatoes and herbaceous plants for spring.
Harvest and store last fruits and root vegetables in hard areas.
Collect up all wastes for composting or shred for mulching.

early winter

prune Late-flowering shrubs, soft fruit and grapes as leaves fall.
Rework and winter prune apples, pears and non-stone fruits.

plant Deciduous shrubs, trees and soft fruit.

feed Incorporate compost with all plantings this month. Spread compost on top of crowns of herbaceous plants.

turf Lime the grass, aerate and spike if needed, adding sharp sand.

jobs Weed everything if needed.
Retouch sticky bands.
Clean greenhouse, coldframe and cloche glass and plastic.
Clean out gutters and drains once last leaves have settled.
Harvest and store root vegetables in milder areas.
Check fruits in store. Plan for next year.
Celebrate this one.

index